# On This Day in Baseball History

Cover photograph credit: The Rucker Archive / Transcendental Graphics
Interior design: Ljiljana Pavkov

ISBN (print): 978-1-7349325-0-8

ISBN (e-book): 978-1-7349325-1-5

To connect with the staff at Baseball Time Machine, visit BaseballTimeMachine.com.

# Table of Contents

# On This Day in
# Baseball History

# JANUARY

## 1

**1894** In one of the most one-sided deals in baseball history, the Baltimore Orioles trade Billy Shindle and George Treadway to the Brooklyn Grooms for future Hall of Famers Dan Brouthers and Willie Keeler.

> ⓘ Brouthers posted his last great season in 1894, batting .347 and driving in a team-high 128 runs, while the 22-year-old Keeler had a breakout campaign, batting .371 and scoring 165 runs.

**1923** Future Hall of Famer William Henry "Wee Willie" Keeler dies at age 50 in Brooklyn, New York. The diminutive outfielder, known to have advised hitters to "keep your eye clear, and hit 'em where they ain't," posted a then-record 44-game hitting streak in 1897 and finished his 19-year big league career with two batting titles, eight 200-hit seasons and a .341 lifetime batting average.

**1943** Negro League superstar Josh Gibson collapses and is hospitalized. Despite learning that he has a brain tumor, Gibson will soon join the Homestead Grays in time for spring training and will not inform them of his condition.

**2009** Major League Baseball launches the MLB Network in approximately 50 million homes, making it the largest network debut in cable history to date.

## 2

**1912** Charles Ebbets holds a dinner to announce his plans to build a new 18,000-seat concrete and steel ballpark in an area dubbed "Pigtown" in Brooklyn. Cost overruns will force Ebbets to sell half his team ownership to the McKeever Brothers, but the land that formerly included a garbage dump will be successfully transformed into Ebbets Field, the intimate home of the Dodgers until 1957.

1977   Less than one year into his tenure as Atlanta Braves owner, Ted Turner is suspended by Commissioner Bowie Kuhn for tampering with the signing of Gary Matthews.

1986   William Louis "Bill" Veeck Jr. dies at age 71 in Chicago, Illinois. As maverick owner of the Cleveland Indians, St. Louis Browns and Chicago White Sox, Veeck became well known for his creative promotions and zany stunts. As a trailblazer and visionary, he left an indelible imprint on baseball history when he signed Larry Doby - the American League's first black player - in 1947 and 42-year-old Negro League legend Satchel Paige one year later.

> (i)   In recognition of his many contributions to the game, Veeck was inducted into the Baseball Hall of Fame in 1991.

## 3

1888   Second baseman Fred Dunlap receives the largest known player contract to date when he signs a two-year pact with the Pittsburgh Alleghenys that reportedly pays him $5,000 per season plus $2,000 of the $5,000 paid to the Detroit Wolverines for his release.

1973   George Steinbrenner, heading a limited partnership that includes Lester Crown, John DeLorean and Nelson Bunker Hunt, purchases the New York Yankees from CBS for approximately $10 million. Steinbrenner's Yankees will go on to win seven World Series titles during his tumultuous 37-year reign.

## 4

1942   Rogers Hornsby, one of the greatest hitters in baseball history, becomes the 14th player elected to the Baseball Hall of Fame after receiving 78.1% of the vote.

1977   Mary Shane is hired by Bill Veeck's Chicago White Sox to join Harry Caray, Jimmy Piersall and Lorn Brown in the broadcast booth for the 1977 season, thus becoming the first female announcer to do play-by-play for a major league team on a regular basis.

2005   Wade Boggs and Ryne Sandberg are elected to the Baseball Hall of Fame. Boggs, a five-time batting champion with 3,010 career hits, receives 91.8% of the vote while Sandberg, a nine-time Gold Glove winner and 1984 National League MVP, receives six votes more than necessary, garnering 76.1% of the ballots cast.

# 5

1916 Charles H. Weeghman, heading a syndicate that includes chewing gum manufacturer William Wrigley Jr., purchases the Chicago Cubs from Charles P. Taft for a reported $500,000. The Cubs will soon relocate to the newly built Weeghman Park, more commonly known today as Wrigley Field.

1963 Hall of Famer Rogers Hornsby dies of a heart attack at age 66 in Chicago, Illinois. One of the greatest hitters in baseball history, "The Rajah" dominated the National League in the 1920s, claiming seven batting titles, three .400 seasons, two MVP awards and two Triple Crowns. Hornsby finished his remarkable 23-year major league career with a .358 lifetime average, ranking him second only to Ty Cobb on the all-time list.

1993 Reggie Jackson, a 5-time World Series champion and 14-time All-Star, is elected to the Baseball Hall of Fame by the Baseball Writers Association of America, receiving 93.6% of the ballots cast. He becomes the first position player honoree with more career strikeouts than hits.

 Reggie Jackson became the first player in history to hit at least 100 home runs for three different major league clubs when he did so for the Oakland Athletics (269), New York Yankees (144) and California Angels (123).

1999 George Brett (98.2%), Nolan Ryan (98.8%) and Robin Yount (77.5%) are elected to the Baseball Hall of Fame, marking the first time since the Hall's initial vote in 1936 that three players are elected simultaneously on their first try.

2005 After denying it for nearly 15 years, Pete Rose admits on ABC's *Good Morning America* that he bet on baseball and on his own team while managing the Cincinnati Reds.

# 6

1920 Eleven days after the deal was completed, the New York Yankees announce their purchase of Babe Ruth from the Boston Red Sox. *The New York Times'* prescient response: "The short right field wall at the Polo Grounds should prove an easy target for Ruth next season and, playing seventy-seven games at home, it would not be surprising if Ruth surpassed his home run record of twenty-nine circuit clouts next summer."

**1940** New York Yankees team president Ed Barrow announces that longtime star Lou Gehrig's No. 4 will be permanently retired from use.

 Lou Gehrig was the first player in major league history to have his uniform number retired.

**1942** Cleveland Indians ace Bob Feller, the American League leader in wins and strikeouts the previous three seasons, reports to Norfolk, Virginia to begin a three-and-a-half-year stint in the Navy.

ⓘ At the end of the 1941 season, "Rapid Robert," then just 22 years old, had already amassed 107 wins and 1,233 strikeouts.

**2000** Major league officials order Atlanta Braves reliever John Rocker to undergo psychological testing after he spewed derogatory racial and ethnic remarks in an interview with *Sports Illustrated*. Commissioner Bud Selig will ultimately fine and suspend Rocker and order him to undergo sensitivity training, saying his remarks "offended practically every element of society."

**2016** Two former greats gain entrance to Cooperstown as Ken Griffey Jr. (99.3%), a smooth and powerful centerfielder who tallied 630 home runs, 13 All-Star selections and 10 Gold Glove Awards during his brilliant 22-year career, and Mike Piazza (83.0%), the greatest offensive catcher in major league history, are elected to the Baseball Hall of Fame. Griffey Jr. is named on 437 of 440 ballots, breaking the voting percentage record previously held by Tom Seaver (98.8%).

 In 2016, Ken Griffey Jr. became the first former No. 1 Draft Pick to be inducted into the Baseball Hall of Fame.

# 7

**1924** The New York Yankees acquire future Hall of Fame centerfielder Earle Combs from Louisville of the American Association for two players and $50,000.

ⓘ Combs, considered the best American League leadoff man of his day, went on to score 100 or more runs in his first eight full seasons in the majors.

**1933** Commissioner Kenesaw Mountain Landis voluntarily cuts his own pay by forty percent in response to the Great Depression's continued adverse economic impact on baseball.

**1991**  Pete Rose is released from a minimum security federal prison in Marion, Illinois after serving a five-month sentence for tax evasion. Later in the day he reports to a halfway house, where he will spend the next three months and begin serving 1,000 hours of community service at Cincinnati inner-city schools.

**1992**  Pitchers Rollie Fingers and Tom Seaver are elected to the Baseball Hall of Fame by the Baseball Writers Association of America, with Seaver garnering a then-record 98.8% of the votes cast.

> (i) Pete Rose, ineligible for election because of his ban from baseball, received 41 write-in votes in what would have been his first year of eligibility.

**2003**  Gary Carter (78%), an 11-time All-Star and key member of the 1986 New York Mets World Championship team, and Eddie Murray (85.3%), the only switch-hitter with at least 3,000 hits and 500 home runs, are elected to the Baseball Hall of Fame.

# 8

**1991**  Eighteen-time All-Star Rod Carew (90.5%) and standout pitchers Ferguson Jenkins (75.4%) and Gaylord Perry (77.2%) are elected to the Baseball Hall of Fame by the BBWAA, with Carew earning enshrinement in his first year of eligibility.

**1995**  Mike Schmidt, an eight-time home run champ and three-time MVP during his 18-year career with the Philadelphia Phillies, is easily elected to the Baseball Hall of Fame, garnering 96.5% of the vote.

**2001**  Hank Aaron is presented with the Presidential Citizens Medal by President Bill Clinton. Aaron becomes only the second major leaguer to be so honored, joining Roberto Clemente, who in 1973 was the initial recipient of the prestigious award.

**2002**  Ozzie Smith, a 15-time All-Star shortstop and 13-time Gold Glove Award winner, is elected to the Baseball Hall of Fame in his first year of eligibility, receiving 91.7% of the vote.

# 9

**1894**  Boston Beaneaters catcher Charlie Bennett sees his major league career come to an abrupt end when, while trying to reboard a train, he slips under the wheels and loses both of his legs. Bennett will eventually move back to Detroit where he had previously starred for the hometown Wolverines, and when the Detroit club builds a new ballpark in 1896 they'll name it Bennett Park in his honor.

> (i) It became a tradition for Bennett to catch the Opening Day first pitch in Detroit, an honorary event that continued from 1896 until 1926.

> DID YOU KNOW? Charlie Bennett is credited with inventing the catcher's chest protector in 1883.

1903 The American League gets a critical presence in New York City when Bill Devery and Frank Farrell purchase the league's defunct Baltimore franchise for $18,000 and move the club to Manhattan. Initially known as the Highlanders, the team will officially be renamed the Yankees in 1913.

1915 University of Michigan star George Sisler is granted free agency by the National Commission upon his entry into the major leagues. Pittsburgh Pirates owner Barney Dreyfuss had claimed rights to Sisler after he purchased a minor league contract that Sisler had signed several years before, but the commission ruled that the contract was void since Sisler was just 17 when he signed it. This declaration frees Sisler to sign with the St. Louis Browns, who are managed by his former Michigan coach Branch Rickey.

> (i) In his rookie season of 1915, George Sisler experienced what he claimed was his greatest thrill in baseball when he outdueled the great Walter Johnson in a complete game 2-1 victory over the Senators.

1952 The Marines announce their plan to recall Boston Red Sox star Ted Williams to active duty. Williams, who earlier served for three years as a bomber pilot during World War II, will fly 39 missions in the Korean War and earn an Air Medal and two Gold Stars for his efforts.

1989 Johnny Bench (96.4%), considered by many to be the greatest catcher of all time, and Carl Yastrzemski (94.6%), owner of 3,419 career hits, are elected to the Baseball Hall of Fame. Bench's total is the third-highest figure to date behind Ty Cobb (98.2%) and Hank Aaron (97.8%).

> DID YOU KNOW? Carl Yastrzemski was the first former Little Leaguer to be elected to the Baseball Hall of Fame.

2007 Tony Gwynn (97.6%), eight-time batting champion and a .338 career hitter, and legendary ironman Cal Ripken Jr. (98.5%) are elected to the Baseball Hall of Fame. Slugger Mark McGwire (23.5%), however, falls well short in his first try thanks in large part to unanswered questions regarding his involvement in ongoing steroids investigations.

# 10

**1984** Luis Aparicio (84.6%), Don Drysdale (78.4%) and Harmon Killebrew (83.1%) are elected to the Baseball Hall of Fame by the Baseball Writers Association of America.

**1991** In what would later be viewed as a disastrous trade for the Orioles, Baltimore acquires slugging first baseman Glenn Davis from the Houston Astros in exchange for pitchers Curt Schilling and Pete Harnisch and outfielder Steve Finley. Davis, who hit over 30 home runs three times with the Astros, will hit a total of 24 homers in three injury-filled seasons with the Orioles, while Harnisch and Finley will become All-Stars and Schilling will develop into one of the game's top pitchers.

> (i) Curt Schilling, who went on to win 215 games after this trade, was involved in an even more lopsided trade the following year when the Astros moved him to the Philadelphia Phillies for journeyman Jason Grimsley.

# 11

**1971** Detroit Tigers 27-year-old lefty John Hiller suffers a heart attack that will sideline him for most of the next two seasons. In 1973, following a full recovery, Hiller will set a new saves mark with 38, earning him the AL Fireman of the Year Award and the AL Comeback Player of the Year Award.

**1973** In one of baseball's most controversial moves, major league owners vote in favor of the Designated Hitter rule. Initially approved as a three-year experiment, the American League will continue to use the DH going forward while the National League never adopts it.

> (i) One week after the Designated Hitter rule was approved, Hall of Famer Orlando Cepeda became the first player signed exclusively as a DH when he agreed to a deal with the Boston Red Sox.

**2000** Carlton Fisk (79.6%), an 11-time All-Star catcher, and Cuban-born slugger Tony Pérez (77.2%), a key member of the 1970s Big Red Machine, are elected to the Baseball Hall of Fame. This is Perez's ninth try, while Fisk is chosen in his second year on the ballot.

2007 The *New York Daily News* reports that Barry Bonds had tested positive for amphetamines at some point during the 2006 season. According to the report, Bonds had initially cited a supplement he had received from San Francisco Giants teammate Mark Sweeney as a possible reason for the positive test.

2010 In an afternoon statement to news outlets, Mark McGwire admits that he used performance-enhancing substances during much of his major league career, including in 1998 when he hit 70 home runs and broke Roger Maris' single-season home run record. In the evening, he addresses the situation further in an interview with Bob Costas on MLB Network: "I wish it never came into my life, but we're sitting here talking about it. I'm so sorry that I have to. I apologize to everybody at Major League Baseball, my family, the Marises, Bud Selig... Today was the hardest day of my life."

# 12

1946 Ted Williams receives his discharge from the Marines after a three-year stint serving in World War II. In spite of his long absence from competitive baseball, the star Red Sox outfielder will quickly return to dominance, batting .342 with 38 home runs and 123 RBIs during the 1946 season.

1999 Mark McGwire's 70th home run ball, thought to be the crown jewel of sports memorabilia, is sold at Guernsey's Auction House in New York for a record-shattering price of $3,000,000. Todd McFarlane, creator of the comic book *Spawn*, is later revealed to be the buyer.

2009 Rickey Henderson (94.8%), Major League Baseball's career leader in runs scored and stolen bases, and Jim Rice (76.4%), 1978 AL MVP and eight-time All-Star, are elected to the Baseball Hall of Fame. Henderson is chosen in his first year of eligibility while Rice makes the cut on his 15th try, becoming the first player elected in his final year of BBWAA ballot eligibility since Ralph Kiner in 1975.

# 13

1939 New York Yankees owner Colonel Jacob Ruppert dies from phlebitis at the age of 71. Ruppert's will names current Yankees GM Ed Barrow team president.

DID YOU KNOW? Col. Ruppert served four terms in the United States Congress from 1899 to 1907.

1972  A lower court ruling of Bernice Gera's discrimination suit against Organized Baseball is affirmed by the New York State Court of Appeals, opening the door for Gera to become the first female umpire in professional baseball.

> (i)  Gera later gained national attention when she umpired the first game of a Class A minor league double header on June 24, 1972. Sensing that she was not receiving full cooperation from her fellow umpires, Gera decided to resign between games, ending her umpiring career.

1978  Joseph Vincent "Joe" McCarthy dies at age 90 in Buffalo, New York. Best known for his leadership of the New York Yankees dynasty in the 1930s and '40s, "Marse Joe" won seven World Series titles during his 24-year managerial career and set all-time records with his .615 regular season winning percentage and .698 postseason winning percentage. McCarthy's exceptional accomplishments as a field pilot earned him induction into the Baseball Hall of Fame in 1957.

1982  Hank Aaron (97.8%) and Frank Robinson (89.2%) become just the 12th and 13th players elected to the Baseball Hall of Fame in their first year of eligibility since 1936. To date, Aaron's election percentage is second only to Ty Cobb's 98.2%.

# 14

1954  Joe DiMaggio and actress Marilyn Monroe marry at San Francisco City Hall. The couple, who had captivated the nation with what seemed to be the All-American romance, will see their volatile marriage end in divorce within 274 days.

1963  Two future Hall of Famers - shortstop Luis Aparicio and pitcher Hoyt Wilhelm - are involved in the same trade as the Chicago White Sox send Aparicio and outfielder Al Smith to the Baltimore Orioles for Wilhelm, shortstop Ron Hanson, outfielder Dave Nicholson and third baseman Pete Ward.

1976  National League owners approve the sale of the Atlanta Braves to WTCG-TV owner Ted Turner for a reported $12 million. When the FCC allows Turner's station to use a satellite later this season to transmit content to local cable TV providers around the nation, the Braves will quickly become known as "America's Team."

1981  Frank Robinson is hired to pilot the San Francisco Giants, becoming the first black manager in the history of the National League. Six years earlier

Robinson had the distinction of being the first black manager in major league history when he was named skipper of the Cleveland Indians.

# 15

1942   President Franklin D. Roosevelt sends the famed "Green Light" letter to Commissioner Kenesaw Mountain Landis, encouraging Major League Baseball to continue playing during World War II. All sixteen teams will continue to play regular schedules for the duration of WWII despite the loss of many star players, including Joe DiMaggio, Bob Feller and Ted Williams, to military service.

1964   Willie Mays signs a one-year contract with San Francisco Giants for a reported $105,000, making him the highest paid player in baseball. The 33-year-old superstar will have another outstanding season in 1964, leading the National League with 47 home runs and a .990 OPS.

1981   St. Louis Cardinals pitcher Bob Gibson (84%), 1968 NL MVP and five-time 20-game winner, is elected to the Baseball Hall of Fame by the BBWAA in his first year of eligibility.

1990   Returning to Major League Baseball after hitting 38 home runs in his one season with the Hanshin Tigers of Japan's Central League, Cecil Fielder signs a one-year deal with the Detroit Tigers for a reported $1.25 million. Fielder will proceed to lead both leagues in home runs (51) and RBIs (132) in 1990 and finish second to Rickey Henderson in AL MVP voting.

 In 1990, Cecil Fielder became the first player since George Foster in 1977 to hit 50 or more homers in a season.

# 16

1970   Veteran outfielder Curt Flood refuses to report to the moribund Philadelphia Phillies following his recent trade from the St. Louis Cardinals and instead files a $1 million lawsuit against Major League Baseball, alleging violation of federal antitrust laws. The U.S. Supreme Court will ultimately side with Baseball, but Flood's legal action will be viewed historically as a vital first step in the fight for player free agency.

1974   New York Yankees teammates Whitey Ford (77.8%) and Mickey Mantle (88.2%) are elected to the Baseball Hall of Fame. Mantle becomes only the seventh player since the inaugural HOF class of 1936 to be elected in his first year of eligibility.

**1996** A concept that had been considered as far back as the 1930s is finally approved as Major League Baseball's executive board agrees to adopt interleague play for the 1997 season. The Players' Association will follow suit, enabling official regular season games to be played between teams in different leagues for the first time in major league history.

> ⓘ Interleague play was implemented at least in part as an effort to renew the public's interest in Major League Baseball following the 1994 players' strike.

>  In 1956, Cleveland Indians General Manager Hank Greenberg proposed an interleague play format that was very similar to the current version.

**2001** Do-everything outfielders Kirby Puckett (82.1%) and Dave Winfield (84.5%) are elected to the Baseball Hall of Fame, each in their first year on the ballot.

**2003** MLB owners approve Commissioner Bud Selig's plan to annually give World Series home-field advantage to the team from the league that wins the All-Star Game.

# 17

**1915** The Cleveland major league club changes its name from Naps to Indians following Nap Lajoie's sale to the Philadelphia Athletics. The new name is said to be intentionally similar to "Braves," the team from Boston which captured an improbable title a season before.

**1970** Willie Mays is named Player of the Decade for the 1960s by *The Sporting News*. Mays averaged 35 home runs, 105 runs scored and 100 RBIs during the decade while being selected an All-Star every season.

**2003** Despite being permanently ineligible for Cooperstown in the United States, Pete Rose is nominated for induction into the Canadian Baseball Hall of Fame. Rose, a former member of the 1984 Montreal Expos, will ultimately fail to get elected.

# 18

**1938** Grover Cleveland Alexander (80.9%), owner of 373 victories and a career 2.56 ERA, becomes the tenth player elected to the Baseball Hall of Fame.

Grover Cleveland Alexander was the first pitcher in major league history to win three Pitching Triple Crowns (1915, 1916 and 1920). Only Sandy Koufax (1963, 1965 and 1966) has matched the feat since.

**1947**   Following a lengthy salary dispute, the Detroit Tigers sell aging star Hank Greenberg to the Pittsburgh Pirates for $75,000. Greenberg will hit 25 home runs for the Pirates in 1947, becoming the first player to hit 25 or more homers in a season in each league.

**2012**   After acquiring Yu Darvish from Japan's Nippon-Ham Fighters for a record $51.7 million, the Texas Rangers sign the Japanese pitching sensation to a six-year, $60 million deal.

> ⓘ Darvish won 16 games and made the All-Star team in his first season with the Rangers.

# 19

**1937**   The BBWAA announces the second group of inductees to the Baseball Hall of Fame. Nap Lajoie (83.6%), Tris Speaker (82.1%) and Cy Young (76.1%) are chosen for enshrinement, joining last year's class of Ty Cobb, Walter Johnson, Christy Mathewson, Babe Ruth and Honus Wagner.

**1938**   The Brooklyn Dodgers hire the innovative Larry MacPhail to take over as general manager of their struggling franchise. Within two years Brooklyn's record will improve by 22 games and attendance at Ebbets Field will almost double, and in 1941 the club will win 100 games and capture their first National League pennant since 1920.

**1972**   Yogi Berra (85.6%), Sandy Koufax (86.9%) and Early Wynn (76%) are elected to the Baseball Hall of Fame. Koufax gains entrance in his first year on the ballot and, at age 36, becomes the youngest honoree in history.

**2004**   Roger Clemens, a six-time Cy Young Award winner with 310 victories to date, retracts his retirement vows and signs a one-year contract with the Houston Astros. The 41-year-old Clemens won't disappoint, going 18-4 and winning his unprecedented seventh Cy Young Award.

**2013**   Hall of Famer Stanley Frank "Stan" Musial dies at age 92 in Ladue, Missouri. Beloved for his modesty and friendly demeanor, Musial also proved to be one of the greatest hitters in baseball history. During his brilliant 22-year career, "Stan the Man" won seven batting titles and three MVP awards, and helped lead his St. Louis Cardinals to three World Series titles. At the time of his retirement in 1963, he held or shared 17 major league records, including most extra-base hits (1,377) and total bases (6,134).

# 20

**1871** The Boston Base Ball Club, known as the Red Stockings, is founded by businessman Iver Whitney Adams with the help of future Hall of Fame manager Harry Wright. Under Wright's guidance the Red Stockings will soon dominate professional baseball, winning six of the first eight pennants in history.

 The baseball franchise that began in 1871 as the Boston Red Stockings and is currently the Atlanta Braves is the oldest continuously running professional sports franchise in the United States.

**1947** Future Hall of Famer Joshua "Josh" Gibson dies at age 35 in Pittsburgh, Pennsylvania. Considered the greatest power hitter in the history of the Negro Leagues, Gibson was one of the finest catchers and most feared sluggers in baseball history. Called "the black Babe Ruth," he used a compact swing and tremendous upper body strength to drive the ball, often resulting in legendary, tape-measure blasts. It was reported that Gibson won four batting titles and at least nine home run titles during his remarkable 16-year career with the Pittsburgh Crawfords and Homestead Grays.

**1966** Boston Red Sox iconic outfielder Ted Williams (93.4%) is elected to the Hall of Fame by the Baseball Writers Association of America. The "Splendid Splinter" becomes just the third player since 1936 to be selected in his first year of eligibility.

# 21

**1921** Major League Baseball installs its first commissioner as Kenesaw Mountain Landis, a United States federal judge, officially takes office after signing a seven-year, $350,000 contract.

**1947** Dodgers manager Leo Durocher and actress Laraine Day marry in El Paso, Texas shortly after Day obtains a divorce in Juarez, Mexico. Durocher had been criticized by Brooklyn's Catholic Youth Organization for having an affair with the actress while she was still married. The couple will stay together for 14 years, and Day will become known as "The First Lady of Baseball."

1953   Two all-time greats, pitcher Dizzy Dean (79.2%) and outfielder Al Simmons (75.4%), are elected to the Baseball Hall of Fame. One player who isn't selected for induction is Joe DiMaggio, who receives only 44.3% of the vote in his first year of eligibility.

1960   Stan Musial is granted a salary reduction from $100,000 to $80,000 after he opines that, in view of his recent subpar performance, he had been overpaid by the Cardinals.

1993   Hall of Famer Charles Leonard "Charlie" Gehringer dies at age 89 in Bloomfield Hills, Michigan. Nicknamed "The Mechanical Man," Gehringer methodically tore apart American League pitching during much of his 19-year major league career. The former Detroit Tigers star second baseman compiled seven 200-hit seasons, scored 100-plus runs 12 times, made six straight All-Star Game starts and captured the AL MVP in 1937.

2005   Star right-hander Roger Clemens and the Houston Astros avoid arbitration and agree to a one-year, $18 million contract. The deal sets a new record for the highest annual salary earned by a pitcher.

> (i) The 42-year-old Clemens dominated once again in 2005, leading the majors with a career-low 1.87 ERA.

# 22

1857   The New York Knickerbockers and fifteen other New York area clubs form the National Association of Base Ball Players - the first organization to govern the sport and establish a championship.

1929   The New York Yankees announce that they will put numbers on the backs of their uniforms, beginning a trend that will become mandatory league-wide within two seasons.

> (i) Originally, uniform numbers were assigned based on the players' position in the batting order; hence, Babe Ruth #3, Lou Gehrig #4, etc.

1969   A pair of three-time National League MVPs, Roy Campanella (79.4%) and Stan Musial (93.2%), are voted into the Baseball Hall of Fame. Musial becomes just the fourth player since 1936 to be elected in his first year of eligibility, joining Bob Feller (1962), Jackie Robinson (1962) and Ted Williams (1966).

1982   Free agent Reggie Jackson signs a four-year, $4 million contract with the California Angels, thus ending a tumultuous five-year stint with the New

York Yankees. During his time in the Bronx, the Yankees made the postseason four times, winning the World Series in 1977 and 1978.

(i) The 35-year-old Jackson belted a league-leading 39 homers in 1982, powering the Angels to a division title. His presence also helped the franchise lead the American League in attendance.

1988   Arbitrator Thomas Roberts announces the damages in the 1986 collusion suit won by the MLB Players Association against the owners. Roberts determines that $10.5 million should be paid by the owners to the players, and awards Juan Beníquez, Tom Brookens, Carlton Fisk, Kirk Gibson, Donnie Moore, Joe Niekro and Butch Wynegar second chances as "no-risk" free agents.

2003   After having been released by the Minnesota Twins following the 2002 season, David Ortiz signs a one-year, $1.25 million contract with the Boston Red Sox. "Big Papi," who battled various injuries and hit only .266 during his six years with the Twins, will quickly become a star in Boston and will help lead the Red Sox to World Championships in 2004, 2007 and 2013.

2003   Looking to add a seasoned veteran to their young and talented roster, the Florida Marlins sign 10-time All-Star catcher Ivan Rodriguez to a one-year, $10 million deal. The move will soon prove to be one of the best in franchise history when Rodriguez's leadership and all-around excellence helps propel the Marlins to a surprising 2003 World Championship.

2017   Baseball mourns the loss of two of its own as 25-year-old Kansas City Royals pitcher Yordano Ventura and former major leaguer Andy Marte, 33, die within a few hours of each other in separate car crashes in their native Dominican Republic.

(i) On October 28, 2014, Ventura dedicated his World Series Game 6 start to his friend and countryman Oscar Tavares, the St. Louis Cardinals young phenom outfielder who had recently lost his life in a car accident in the Dominican Republic.

2019   Mariano Rivera, the greatest closer in baseball history, becomes the first player unanimously voted into the Baseball Hall of Fame. The New York Yankees icon is joined by former ace right-handers Roy Halladay (85.4%) and Mike Mussina (76.7%) as well as two-time batting champ Edgar Martinez (85.4%).

# 23

1927   American League owners prepare to fire Ban Johnson, president of the league since its inception in 1900, because of his continued public criticism of

Commissioner Landis, but delay their action because of Johnson's poor health. The situation will prove to be untenable, though, and Johnson will be forced to resign later this year.

1950  The Associated Press selects the "Miracle Braves" of 1914 as the greatest sports upset of the 20th century.

1962  Bob Feller (93.8%) and Jackie Robinson (77.5%) are selected for the Hall of Fame by the Baseball Writers Association of America, becoming the first two players since 1936 to be elected in their first year of eligibility.

1979  Willie Mays easily earns enshrinement in the Baseball Hall of Fame in his first year of eligibility, receiving 409 of 432 votes (94.7%) from the BBWAA.

2015  Ernie Banks, baseball's beloved "Mr. Cub," dies from a heart attack at age 83 in Chicago, Illinois. Known for his exceptional baseball talent, grace and "let's play two" enthusiasm, Banks became one of the most iconic figures in Chicago sports history during his 19 seasons with the Cubs. The 14-time All-Star won back-to-back MVP awards in 1958 and 1959 and slugged 512 big league homers, making him an easy choice for induction into the Baseball Hall of Fame in 1977.

# 24

1939  In the Baseball Hall of Fame's fourth election, Eddie Collins (77.7%), Willie Keeler (75.5%) and George Sisler (85.8%) are chosen for enshrinement by the Baseball Writers Association of America.

1950  Following his stellar MVP season of 1949, Jackie Robinson signs a one-year contract for $35,000, reportedly making him the highest paid player in Brooklyn Dodgers history.

1973  Warren Spahn (83.2%), the winningest left-handed pitcher in major league history with 363 victories, is elected to the Baseball Hall of Fame in his first year of eligibility.

1980  The New York Mets are sold to a group headed by Nelson Doubleday Jr. for an estimated $21.1 million, the highest amount ever paid for a baseball franchise to date.

# 25

1945  The estate of the late Jacob Ruppert sells the New York Yankees for $2.8 million to Larry MacPhail, Dan Topping and Del Webb. MacPhail replaces Ed Barrow as president and general manager.

(i) Topping and Webb bought out MacPhail in 1947 and 17 years later sold their controlling interest to CBS for $11.2 million.

**1974** McDonald's mogul Ray Kroc buys the Padres for $12 million, saving the franchise from a potential move to Washington, D.C.

**1978** The San Diego Padres acquire Gaylord Perry from the Texas Rangers in exchange for middle reliever Dave Tomlin and $125,000. The 39-year-old Perry will go on to capture the National League Cy Young Award this season after posting a 21-6 record with a 2.73 ERA.

# 26

**1951** Two of baseball's greatest sluggers - Jimmie Foxx (79.2%) and Mel Ott (87.2%) - are selected for induction into the Baseball Hall of Fame.

(i) At the time of their election, Foxx (534) and Ott (511) trailed only Babe Ruth (714) on the all-time home run list.

**1962** Following their thrilling home run chase in 1961, New York Yankees sluggers Mickey Mantle and Roger Maris sign contracts with Columbia Pictures to star as themselves in *Safe at Home!*, a sports comedy movie. Fellow Yankees Whitey Ford and manager Ralph Houk are scheduled to make cameo appearances in the film as well.

**2012** One week after losing DH Victor Martinez to a season-ending knee injury, the Detroit Tigers respond quickly by signing All-Star first baseman Prince Fielder to a nine-year, $214 million contract, the most lucrative deal in franchise history. Fielder, joining the team his father Cecil once starred for, will help lead the Tigers to the World Series this season after batting a career-high .313 with 30 homers and 108 RBIs.

(i) To make room for Fielder at first base, Tigers star Miguel Cabrera volunteered to move across the diamond to third base. With many wondering how the position change would affect his offensive production, Cabrera responded with baseball's first Triple Crown in 45 years.

# 27

**1927** Ty Cobb and Tris Speaker, both accused by pitcher Dutch Leonard of conspiring to throw a game in 1919, are fully exonerated by Commissioner Landis. The pair will continue their playing careers, but neither will manage in the majors again.

1944  A group headed by construction magnate Lou Perini buys the struggling Boston Braves franchise. The team will fare better on the field in the coming years, but dwindling attendance will persuade Perini to move his team to Milwaukee in 1953.

1982  Former Philadelphia Phillies manager Dallas Green, now the GM of the Chicago Cubs, pulls off one of the most one-sided trades in baseball history when he acquires shortstop Larry Bowa and prospect Ryne Sandberg from Philadelphia in exchange for shortstop Ivan DeJesus. The steal of the deal is Sandberg, who will go on to win the 1984 National League MVP award and fashion a Hall of Fame career with the Cubs.

# 28

1901  The American League, a descendant of the minor Western League, formally organizes as a rival major league. Ban Johnson is the driving force behind it, and will serve as its first president. The charter franchises, after the contraction of the Buffalo Bisons, Indianapolis Hoosiers and Minnesota Millers, are the Baltimore Orioles, Boston Americans, Chicago White Stockings, Cleveland Bluebirds, Detroit Tigers, Milwaukee Brewers, Philadelphia Athletics and Washington Senators.

1958  Dodgers catcher Roy Campanella suffers a broken neck in an early morning car accident near his home in Glen Cove, New York. Campanella's spinal column is nearly severed in the crash, leaving him permanently paralyzed from the waist down.

1980  Hank Aaron refuses to accept a *Baseball Magazine* award honoring his record-breaking 715th home run from Commissioner Bowie Kuhn, charging that baseball has neglected black players.

1982  The Baltimore Orioles trade veteran third baseman Doug DeCinces to the California Angels, opening up a spot for top prospect Cal Ripken Jr. Ripken will go on to win the American League Rookie of the Year Award this season, while DeCinces will have a career year for the Angels and finish third in AL MVP voting.

> (i) DeCinces was one of Cal Ripken Jr.'s most influential baseball mentors and, in 1972 while playing for Ashville in the Southern League, DeCinces may have saved young Cal's life. Cal Ripken Jr. spent time with the Ashville team during the summer, tagging along with his father, the club's manager. While Cal Jr. and DeCinces played catch before one game, a bullet struck the ground between

them after a teenage boy opened fire on the players from his home just beyond the right field fence. DeCinces, a member of the Air National Guard Reserve at the time, grabbed the 12-year-old Ripken and rushed him safely to the dugout. The shooter was arrested soon after, and no one was harmed.

# 29

**1898**  With 45-year-old Cap Anson's contract soon to expire, Albert Spalding announces that Chicago will not re-sign him, thus unceremoniously ending Anson's 19-year tenure as player-manager of the Colts. Anson will retire as baseball's all-time leader in hits, doubles, runs batted in, runs scored and games played as well as wins by a manager.

> ⓘ The Chicago club soon became known as the Orphans in reference to the loss of "Pop" Anson.

**1915**  Jacob Ruppert and Tillinghast L. Huston buy the struggling New York Yankees franchise from Bill Devery and Frank Farrell for a reported $480,000. After eventually buying out Huston, Col. Ruppert will build his Yankees into a powerhouse that will win seven World Series titles before his death in 1939.

**1958**  Stan Musial becomes the highest paid player in National League history to date when he agrees to a one-year, $100,000 contract with the St. Louis Cardinals. The 37-year-old Musial is coming off another stellar season, having won his seventh National League batting title (.351) and finishing a close second to Hank Aaron in the 1957 NL MVP voting.

**1988**  Free agent outfielder Kirk Gibson signs a three-year, $4.5 million contract with the Los Angeles Dodgers. Thanks in large part to Gibson's fiery leadership and excellence on the field, the Dodgers will win the World Series in his first season in Los Angeles, and Gibson will be named National League MVP.

 Since the inception of the All-Star Game in 1933, Kirk Gibson remains the lone player in major league history who won an MVP award but never made an All-Star team.

**1995**  Deion Sanders' appearance with the San Francisco 49ers in Super Bowl XXVIX makes the cornerback the first athlete to have played in both a Super Bowl and a World Series. In 1992, Sanders played outfield for the Atlanta Braves in the Fall Classic.

# 30

1919   With former manager Christy Mathewson serving overseas in World War I, the Cincinnati Reds hire Pat Moran to take his place. Under Moran the Reds will proceed to win their first World Series later this season, defeating the Chicago "Black Sox" five games to three.

1923   The New York Yankees acquire future Hall of Famer Herb Pennock from the Boston Red Sox for three prospects and $50,000. Pennock, another in a long line of ex-Red Sox now on the New York roster, will go 19-6 in 1923 and help lead the Yankees to their first World Series title.

1954   The New York Giants trade playoff hero Bobby Thomson and Sam Calderone to the Milwaukee Braves for Johnny Antonelli, Don Liddle and Ebba St. Claire. Antonelli will pay immediate dividends, helping the Giants become World Champions in 1954 after going 21-7 and leading the National League with a 2.30 ERA.

1958   Upset by the Redlegs fan's ballot box stuffing prior to the 1957 All-Star Game, Commissioner Ford Frick announces that players and managers, rather than the fans, will select the All-Star rosters going forward. The vote will not return to the fans until 1970, when Commissioner Bowie Kuhn reverses Frick's action.

1959   The Pittsburgh Pirates strengthen their roster when they acquire Smoky Burgess, Harvey Haddix and Don Hoak from the Cincinnati Reds in exchange for Whammy Douglas, Jim Pendleton, John Powers and Frank Thomas. Haddix will famously bring a perfect game into the 13th inning later this season, and in 1960 all three players will help the Pirates win the World Series.

# 31

1919   Baseball star and revered trailblazer Jackie Robinson is born in Cairo, Georgia.

1950   The Pittsburgh Pirates sign high school star pitcher Paul Pettit, making him baseball's first $100,000 "Bonus Baby." Pettit will post a 1-2 record with a 7.34 ERA in his 12-game major league career.

1959   Joe Cronin, former big league shortstop, manager and general manager, succeeds Will Harridge as American League president, becoming the first former player to be so elected. Cronin will remain in the post until 1973, when he'll be succeeded by Lee MacPhail.

1961   Harris County, Texas voters approve a bond issue of $22 million for a domed stadium for their new major league franchise. The Astrodome, dubbed "the Eighth Wonder of the World," will be the result of today's approval and will serve as the Astros home from 1965-1999.

1996   All-Star centerfielder Ken Griffey Jr. becomes the highest-paid player in major league history to date when he signs a four-year, $34 million contract extension with the Seattle Mariners.

> ⓘ  Griffey's record average salary of $8.5 million surpassed Barry Bonds' $7.29 million per season.

# FEBRUARY

## 1

1913   Jim Thorpe, the 1912 Olympic champion in both the pentathlon and decathlon, signs the largest rookie contract in baseball history to date when he agrees to a three-year, $18,000 deal with the New York Giants. Thorpe will compile a .252 batting average during his six-year major league career, which will also include stints with the Cincinnati Reds and Boston Braves.

1985   The St. Louis Cardinals acquire slugging first baseman Jack Clark from the San Francisco Giants for David Green, Dave LaPoint, Gary Rajsich and Jose Uribe. Clark will be a key contributor on the Cards' pennant-winning teams of 1985 and 1987, finishing in the top 10 in MVP voting both seasons.

1999   After signing incumbent third baseman and reigning World Series MVP Scott Brosius to a three-year deal, the New York Yankees ship third base prospect Mike Lowell to the Florida Marlins for three minor league pitchers. The move will prove to be regrettable for the Yankees when Lowell, after recovering from testicular cancer, launches an excellent career which will include four All-Star selections and the 2007 World Series MVP award.

## 2

1876   After recruiting several top teams from the National Association of Professional Base Ball Players, Chicago White Stockings principal owner William Hulbert forms the National League. Hulbert's vision for the new league includes stronger central authority and exclusive territories in larger cities only. Charter clubs include the Boston Red Stockings, Chicago White Stockings, Cincinnati Red Stockings, Hartford Dark Blues, Louisville Grays, Mutual of New York, Philadelphia Athletics and St. Louis Brown Stockings. Dark Blues owner Morgan Bulkeley is selected as the league's first president.

1936   Ty Cobb, Walter Johnson, Christy Mathewson, Babe Ruth and Honus Wagner comprise the first class elected to baseball's new Hall Fame, which is scheduled to open in the summer of 1939 as part of the game's celebration of its presumed centennial.

**1976**   The Veteran's Committee selects Roger Connor, Freddie Lindstrom and Cal Hubbard for induction into Cooperstown, making Hubbard, who starred as an offensive tackle in the NFL before becoming an outstanding major league umpire, the first man elected to both the Pro Football Hall of Fame and Baseball Hall of Fame.

**1977**   The Special Committee on the Negro Leagues elects Martin Dihigo, the first Cuban-born Hall of Famer, and shortstop John Henry "Pop" Lloyd, who was dubbed the "Black Honus Wagner," to the Baseball Hall of Fame.

**1989**   Former eight-time All-Star first baseman and long-time Yankee broadcaster Bill White is elected National League president, making him the highest ranking black official in United States professional sports.

**1991**   Roger Clemens, considered the top pitcher in baseball, becomes the highest-paid player in the sport when he signs a four-year, $21.5 million deal with the Boston Red Sox. The Rocket, who previously won the AL Cy Young Award in 1986 and 1987, will win his third this season after going 18-10 with a league-leading 2.62 ERA.

**2008**   Two-time Cy Young Award winner Johan Santana signs the richest contract given to a pitcher to date when he agrees to a six-year, $137.5 million deal with the New York Mets after being traded by the Twins for speedy outfielder Carlos Gomez and pitching prospects Deolis Guerra, Philip Humber and Kevin Mulvey.

# 3

**1979**   The California Angels acquire seven-time batting champ Rod Carew from the Minnesota Twins in exchange for outfielders Dave Engle and Ken Landreaux and pitchers Paul Hartzell and Brad Havens. Carew will hit .314 and garner six All-Star selections in seven seasons with the Angels, and will help lead his new club to their first two postseason appearances.

**2009**   Joe Torre's book "The Yankee Years," written by Tom Verducci, hits bookstores. Torre, who managed the Yankees to four World Series titles during his 12-year tenure in the Bronx, offered critical statements about Alex Rodriguez, including ARod's propensity to shrink in big moments and his need for attention. The book also states that teammates and clubhouse attendants referred to Rodriguez as "A-Fraud."

2009 According to a *New York Times* report, a urine sample submitted by Barry Bonds in 2003 as part of Major League Baseball's anonymous testing program that did not show the presence of performance-enhancing drugs under that program is re-examined by federal authorities and comes back positive for anabolic steroids.

# 4

1956 As a tribute to the legendary pitcher who died three months earlier, Major League Baseball establishes the Cy Young Award to annually honor the outstanding pitcher of the year. Don Newcombe of the Brooklyn Dodgers will be the inaugural recipient this season.

1969 Bowie Kuhn, long-time legal counsel for the National League, is unanimously selected by the major league owners to become baseball's fifth commissioner, replacing the ousted William Eckert. Kuhn, who will be elected to the Baseball Hall of Fame posthumously in 2008, will oversee an especially turbulent time in baseball during his 15-year tenure.

1991 The twelve members of the Baseball Hall of Fame board of directors vote unanimously to bar Pete Rose from the ballot. Rose, baseball's all-time hit king, will still receive 41 write-in votes in 1992.

# 5

1932 Bernhard "Barney" Dreyfuss, vice president of the National League and owner of the Pittsburgh Pirates, dies at age 66 in New York City, New York. Dreyfuss is credited with the creation of the modern World Series and also built one of the first steel and concrete baseball parks. His beloved Pirates won six National League pennants and two World Series titles during his 32-year tenure.

1934 Hank Aaron, one of baseball's greatest and most cherished superstars, is born in Mobile, Alabama.

1999 Hank Aaron learns at his 65th birthday celebration that Major League Baseball has introduced a new award in his honor. The Hank Aaron Award is created to annually recognize the best overall offensive performer in each major league. It is the first major award to be introduced by baseball in more than thirty years, and has the distinction of being the first award named after a living player.

2002 Major League Baseball ends its effort to disband the Minnesota Twins and Montreal Expos this upcoming season, but Commissioner Bud Selig remains determined to eliminate two teams in 2003. Contraction efforts stalled due to a series of legal decisions and opposition from the MLB Players Association.

# 6

1895 George Herman "Babe" Ruth, baseball's most prodigious and celebrated icon, is born in Baltimore, Maryland.

1921 After being forced out of the Polo Grounds, New York Yankees owners Jacob Ruppert and Tillinghast L. Huston announce the purchase of a ten-acre plot of land in west Bronx directly across the Harlem River from their former baseball home. The land, purchased from the estate of William Waldorf Astor for $675,000, will soon become the site of Yankee Stadium, baseball's first triple-decked structure.

1956 Supporting the bill proposed by New York mayor Robert Wagner and Brooklyn borough president Frank Cashmere to build a $30 million sports center in downtown Brooklyn that will include a new 50,000-seat domed stadium to house his team, Brooklyn Dodgers owner Walter O'Malley pledges to stand for more than half the $8.5 million bond issue.

1958 Following a remarkable season in which he led the majors in batting (.388), on-base percentage (.526) and slugging percentage (.731), 39-year-old Ted Williams signs for a reported $135,000 with the Boston Red Sox, making him the highest paid player in major league history to date.

1968 Voters in King County, Washington approve the issue of $40 million in municipal bonds to construct a domed multi-purpose stadium, soon to be dubbed "The Kingdome." After four years of construction the stadium will open in 1976 and become the home of the Seattle Mariners from 1977 until its demolition in 2000.

# 7

1908 Southpaw ace Rube Waddell, known for both his considerable talent and eccentricity, is sold by the Philadelphia Athletics to the St. Louis Browns for $5,000. Despite averaging 22 wins per year and leading the league in strikeouts in each of his six seasons with the Athletics (including a then-record 349 Ks in 1904), Waddell is jettisoned after wearing out his welcome with both his fellow teammates and Connie Mack.

1949  Joe DiMaggio becomes the first baseball player to receive a six-figure salary, signing with the New York Yankees for a reported $100,000.

1959  Napolean "Nap" Lajoie dies at age 84 in Daytona Beach, Florida. A graceful fielder and powerful hitter, Lajoie was the American League's first superstar and one of the greatest second baseman of all time. He won five batting titles and three RBI crowns during his 21 major league seasons, and finished his extraordinary Hall of Fame career with 3,242 hits and a .338 batting average.

1959  Bill Veeck heads a group that purchases Dorothy Comiskey Rigney's stake in the Chicago White Sox, thus gaining a controlling interest in the team.

> (i) The "Go-Go Sox" broke a franchise home attendance record (1.4 million) in 1959 on their way to winning their first pennant in 40 years.

1994  Four months after the first of his three retirements from the NBA, basketball superstar Michael Jordan shocks the sporting world by signing a minor league contract with the Chicago White Sox. Jordan will later be assigned to the organization's Double A Birmingham Barons, where he'll hit .202 and steal 30 bases in his one and only professional baseball season.

2009  *Sports Illustrated* reports that Alex Rodriguez had tested positive for anabolic steroids, testosterone and Primobolan in 2003, the year he led the American League with 47 home runs and won his first MVP award. Days later ARod also admits to using performance-enhancing drugs in 2001 and 2002. In a 2007 *60 Minutes* interview with Katie Couric, Rodriguez had flatly denied ever taking steroids.

2019  Former star outfielder and distinguished trailblazer Frank Robinson dies at age 83 in Los Angeles, California. A powerful hitter and fiery competitor, Robinson fashioned a 21-year, Hall of Fame career that included a Triple Crown in 1966, two MVP awards, 14 All-Star selections and 586 lifetime home runs. Toward the end of his playing days, Robinson earned special distinction as the first African American manager in major league history when he took on that role with the Cleveland Indians in 1975.

# 8

1901  The newly-formed American League adds its first superstar when Nap Lajoie jumps from the Philadelphia Phillies to the crosstown Athletics for financial reasons. Lajoie will dominate the fledgling league this year, leading it in almost every significant offensive category, including an AL-record .426 batting average.

1927 After recently being cleared by Judge Landis of a game-fixing charge and subsequently freed by the Detroit Tigers, Ty Cobb signs a lucrative contract with the Philadelphia Athletics. The 40-year-old Cobb will perform well in 1927, batting .357 and scoring 104 runs in 133 games.

1956 Hall of Famer Cornelius Alexander McGillicuddy, better known as Connie Mack, dies at age 93 in Philadelphia, Pennsylvania. The gentlemanly Mack, nicknamed "The Tall Tactician," earned acclaim as the longest-serving and winningest manager in major league history. He guided the Philadelphia Athletics during the club's first 50 seasons, capturing nine pennants and five World Series titles over that span.

1972 Homestead Grays stars Josh Gibson and Buck Leonard are elected to the Baseball Hall of Fame, becoming the first position players from the Negro Leagues to be so honored.

1982 The Los Angeles Dodgers' starting infield since 1974 – first baseman Steve Garvey, second baseman Davey Lopes, shortstop Bill Russell and third baseman Ron Cey - is broken up when Lopes is traded to the Oakland Athletics. The group had been together longer than any other infield foursome in MLB history.

1995 Nippon Professional Baseball pitching star Hideo Nomo leaves his native Japan and signs with the Los Angeles Dodgers, ultimately becoming the first Japanese-born player to shift permanently to the American major leagues.

> [i] Nomo was an immediate hit, winning the 1995 National League Rookie of the Year Award after leading the league in strikeouts. His success helped pave the way to the majors for the many other Japanese players that followed.

# 9

1943 After years of sustaining operating losses caused by struggles on the field and at the gate, Philadelphia Phillies majority owner Gerry Nugent sells his club to the National League for a meager $250,000.

1971 Legendary pitcher Satchel Paige becomes the first Negro League star to be elected to the Baseball Hall of Fame.

2001   After 13 months of negotiations, reigning World Series MVP Derek Jeter and the New York Yankees agree to a 10-year, $189 million contract. The deal for the 26-year-old shortstop is the second largest in baseball history to date, trailing only the 10-year, $252 million contract given to Alex Rodriguez by the Texas Rangers.

# 10

1920   At the annual winter meetings in Chicago, Major League Baseball's Joint Rules Committee announces that it has barred all trick pitches, including the spitball. The committee will clarify the ruling the following season when they announce that certain pitchers will be "grandfathered" in and allowed to keep throwing doctored pitches until they retire.

1924   The Washington Senators name 27-year-old second baseman Bucky Harris as their new player-manager. Later this season, Harris will become the youngest manager to win a World Series when his Senators defeat the New York Giants in the 1924 Fall Classic.

(i)   The World Championship earned Harris the nickname "Boy Wonder."

1971   The New York Yankees announce that former All-Star first baseman Bill White will join Phil Rizzuto and Frank Messer on the WPIX-TV broadcast team, making White the first African American to do play-by-play regularly for a major league team.

1984   Keith Hernandez forgoes free agency and signs a five-year, $8 million deal with the New York Mets. The All-Star first baseman will prove his worth, finishing in the top 10 in MVP voting three times and leading the Mets to a World Series title in 1986.

2000   After months of stalled trade talks, the Seattle Mariners accommodate superstar centerfielder Ken Griffey Jr., trading him to his hometown Cincinnati Reds for Mike Cameron, Jake Meyer, Antonio Perez and Brett Tomko.

(i)   The deal was finalized when Griffey signed a nine-year, $112.5 million contract with the Reds, then the richest contract in baseball history.

2011   Following a season in which he helped lead the Texas Rangers to the World Series, reigning American League MVP Josh Hamilton and the Rangers avoid arbitration by agreeing to a two-year, $24 million contract. With Hamilton in the fold, Texas will win 96 games this season and come within one out of capturing their first World Championship.

# 11

1914   After being replaced as the manager of the Chicago Cubs, second baseman Johnny Evers is traded to the Boston Braves for infielder Bill Sweeney and cash. In what will be his last full season in the majors, the 32-year-old Evers will capture the Chalmers Award as the National League MVP in 1914 and will help lead the "Miracle Braves" to an improbable World Series title.

1923   Judge Emil Fuchs, Christy Mathewson and banker James McDonough purchase the Boston Braves from George W. Grant for $300,000. Despite his ongoing battle with tuberculosis, Mathewson will take on the role of club president.

1974   One year after Major League Baseball's new collective bargaining agreement allows for salary arbitration as a means for resolving salary disputes, pitcher Dick Woodson of the Minnesota Twins wins the first arbitration ruling in baseball history.

1982   In a memorable swap of talented young shortstops, the St. Louis Cardinals acquire Gold Glover Ozzie Smith along with pitcher Steve Mura from the San Diego Padres in exchange for two-time All-Star Garry Templeton and outfielder Sixto Lezcano. The trade will prove to be one of the best in major league history for the Cardinals when Smith blossoms into a first-ballot Hall of Famer in St. Louis while Templeton, who was a 25-year-old star with a .305 lifetime average at the time of the trade, hits just .252 in 10 lackluster seasons with the Padres.

( i )   During his 15-year stint with the Cardinals, Ozzie Smith earned 14 All-Star selections and 11 straight Gold Glove Awards.

2005   Details of Jose Canseco's controversial book *Juiced* surface in a *New York Times* article two days before Canseco's appearance on CBS's *Sixty Minutes* is scheduled to air. The former slugger and admitted steroid user alleges in his tell-all that the vast majority of major leaguers - including Juan Gonzalez, Mark McGwire, Rafael Palmeiro and Ivan Rodriguez - took performance-enhancing drugs.

# 12

1876   After jumping to the White Stockings, pitcher/manager Albert Spalding launches his career as a sporting goods magnate as he and his brother open A. G. Spalding & Bros. in Chicago.

1878   Harvard University player-manager Fred Thayer receives a patent for the catching mask, a piece of equipment he invented to help protect Harvard's star catcher.

> (i) Initially met with derision, the Thayer mask soon caught on with professionals and amateurs alike and was widely used by the 1880s.

1955   Willie Mays hits a game-winning home run in the 11th inning to lead the Santurce Crabbers of Puerto Rico to a 4-2 victory over Magallanes of Venezuela in the Caribbean World Series. A crucial homer was also hit earlier in the game by Mays' teammate Roberto Clemente. The two stars are the cornerstones of a Santurce team that will go on to capture the 1955 Caribbean World Series and be considered by many the greatest Winter League baseball team of all time.

1980   Charlie Finley's potential sale of his Oakland A's to oil tycoon Marvin Davis falls apart when the city of Oakland rejects Finley's attempt to buy out the lease that binds the A's to the Coliseum. Davis had hoped to move the franchise to Denver.

> (i) Finley later sold the team to San Francisco-based Walter J. Haas, president of Levi Strauss and Co., who kept the A's in Oakland.

2002   In an orchestrated series of moves, Major League Baseball buys the Montreal Expos from Jeffrey Loria for $120 million and then helps subsidize Loria's $158.5 million purchase of the Florida Marlins from John Henry. With the Marlins sale finalized, Henry formally takes control of the Boston Red Sox, the team he purchased the previous December. The Expos then make Omar Minaya the majors' first Hispanic general manager.

# 13

1920   At a meeting in a Kansas City YMCA, Rube Foster, owner and manager of the Chicago American Giants, spearheads the formation of the Negro National League. The eight charter franchises include the Chicago Giants, Cuban Stars, Dayton Marcos, Detroit Stars, Indianapolis ABCs, Kansas City Monarchs, St. Louis Giants and Foster's American Giants. The new circuit will be the first African American baseball league to achieve real stability and last more than one season.

1953   The Philadelphia Athletics change the name of their ballpark from Shibe Park to Connie Mack Stadium in honor of their legendary owner and former manager. The 90-year-old Mack had guided the Athletics to nine American League pennants and five World Series titles during his 50-year managerial tenure.

1974 The Baseball Hall of Fame opens its doors to another fantastic Negro League star as Cool Papa Bell is selected for induction by the Special Committee on the Negro Leagues.

2008 In a highly anticipated congressional hearing, Roger Clemens and his former personal trainer, Brian McNamee, testify before the House Oversight Committee concerning allegations of Clemens' use of performance-enhancing drugs. McNamee claims he injected Clemens with steroids and HGH numerous times while Clemens denies it.

# 14

1887 Albert Spalding and the Chicago White Stockings sell popular star Mike "King" Kelly to the Boston Beaneaters for a reported $10,000. The amount is more than double the price ever paid for any other player to date.

(i) As a result of the sale, Kelly became known as the "$10,000 Beauty."

1911 The American League introduces a new, livelier cork-centered baseball that will have a profound impact on the upcoming season. Batting averages will increase by an average of 30 points and the number of .300 hitters will rise from eight in 1910 to 27 this year, with Ty Cobb batting .420 and Joe Jackson hitting a rookie-record .408.

1948 Future Hall of Famer Mordecai Peter Centennial "Three Finger" Brown dies at age 71 in Terre Haute, Indiana. As one of the elite pitchers of the Dead Ball Era, Brown won 20-plus games from 1906 through 1911, helping the Chicago Cubs win four National League pennants and two World Championships over that span.

2001 In an effort to dissuade "head hunting," Major League Baseball directs umpires to immediately eject a pitcher for deliberately throwing at a batter's head.

# 15

1893 The Brooklyn Grooms sell player/manager/union organizer John Montgomery Ward to the New York Giants for $6,000.

1910 Ground is broken on St. Patrick's Day in Chicago for a modern concrete-and-steel ballpark to replace the obsolete wooden South Side Park. The new home of the White Sox, originally known as White Sox Park, will soon be renamed Comiskey Park after the club's founder and owner Charles Comiskey.

> (i) Boasting a record seating capacity of 28,000, the $750,000 structure was impressive for its time and was briefly nicknamed "The Baseball Palace of the World."

**1916**   Under pressure from American League President Ban Johnson, Philadelphia Athletics owner Connie Mack sells Home Run Baker's contract to the New York Yankees for $37,500, ending the slugger's year-long holdout.

**1964**   Chicago Cubs second baseman Ken Hubbs, the 1962 National League Rookie of the Year and Gold Glove Award winner, dies at the age of 22 when the plane he is piloting crashes in Provo, Utah during a winter storm. Hubbs had taken flying lessons to overcome his intense fear of flying and had just recently received his pilot's license. Fellow Cubs Ernie Banks and Ron Santo will serve as pallbearers at his funeral.

**1990**   Without a new Basic Agreement in place due to long-standing disagreements over free agency and arbitration, Major League Baseball owners refuse to open spring training camps, beginning a lockout that will last 32 days.

**1994**   Ila Borders becomes the first woman to pitch in an NCAA or NAIA game when she appears for Southern California College. Borders throws a five-hitter against Claremont-Mudd-Scripps and earns a 12-1 victory.

**2011**   A year after the St. Louis Cardinals launched a campaign to build support on his behalf, Stan Musial is awarded the Presidential Medal of Freedom - America's highest civilian honor - by President Barack Obama.

# 16

**1909**   The Boston Red Sox trade Cy Young to the Cleveland Naps for Charlie Chech, Jack Ryan and $12,500. The 42-year-old Young will go 19-15 for the Naps in 1909, upping his career win total to 497.

**1915**   Twenty-eight years old and at the peak of his Hall of Fame career, Frank "Home Run" Baker announces his retirement from baseball following a contract dispute with Connie Mack. Baker will return to the majors a year later when Mack sells him to the New York Yankees.

**1989**   Following a historic season in which he won the National League Cy Young Award and World Series MVP honors, pitcher Orel Hershiser becomes the highest paid player in baseball history to date when he agrees to a three-year, $7.9 million contract with the Los Angeles Dodgers.

(i) Hershiser finished the 1988 regular season with a major league-record streak of 59 consecutive scoreless innings.

2004 Reigning American League MVP Alex Rodriguez is traded by the Texas Rangers to the New York Yankees for All-Star second baseman Alfonso Soriano and a player to be named later. The Rangers had initially agreed to trade ARod to the Boston Red Sox for Manny Ramirez two months earlier, but the MLB Players Association vetoed the move because it called for a voluntary reduction in salary by Rodriguez.

2012 Hall of Fame catcher Gary Edmund Carter, nicknamed "Kid" for his youthful exuberance, dies of brain cancer at age 57 in Palm Beach Gardens, Florida. A great competitor and leader behind the plate, Carter also excelled as both an offensive and defensive force, winning five Silver Slugger Awards and three Gold Glove Awards while starring primarily for the Montreal Expos and New York Mets during his 19-year career.

# 17

1943 Joe DiMaggio trades his New York Yankees salary for a payment of $50 per month when he enlists in the United States Army. Despite not asking for special treatment, DiMaggio will spend most of his service time entertaining the troops by playing baseball.

1953 Less than two weeks into his tour in Korea, United States Marine fighter pilot Ted Williams is hit with small arms ground fire during a combat mission aimed at Kyomipo, North Korea and crash lands his F9 Panther jet. Despite the fiery landing, Williams suffers only minor scrapes and will return to the sky the following day.

1971 Carl Yastrzemski signs the largest deal in baseball history to date, agreeing to a three-year, $500,000 contract with the Boston Red Sox.

1987 Just four days after Detroit Tigers ace Jack Morris receives a record $1.85 million through the salary arbitration process, first baseman Don Mattingly of the New York Yankees tops it when he wins his arbitration case and is awarded $1.975 million.

(i) Mattingly's record deal followed a 1986 season in which he set new Yankees single-season records for both hits (238) and doubles (53).

2003 Greg Maddux receives the largest one-year contract in major league history to date when he and the Atlanta Braves avoid arbitration and agree to a $14.75 million deal.

# 18

1943 At 33 years of age, New York lumber broker William Cox becomes the youngest owner in the major leagues when he buys the Philadelphia Phillies from the National League. Cox's ownership won't last long, though, as Commissioner Kenesaw Mountain Landis will ban him from baseball for life later this year for betting on the Phillies.

1944 After waiting until his high school basketball season was completed, 15-year-old Joe Nuxhall signs a major league contract with the Cincinnati Reds. Later this year Nuxhall will become the youngest player ever to appear in a major league game when he pitches two-thirds of an inning at the age of 15 years, 316 days.

1960 Dodgers owner Walter O'Malley secures the site for his new ballpark when he completes the purchase of Chavez Ravine land just north of downtown Los Angeles. O'Malley reportedly pays $494,000 for the property.

1998 Iconic broadcaster Harry Caray dies at age 83 in Rancho Mirage, California. Caray, who called games primarily for the St. Louis Cardinals, Chicago White Sox and Chicago Cubs during his 53-year career, possessed an unforgettable voice and great passion for the game. In 1989, he was presented with the Ford C. Frick Award by the Baseball Hall of Fame for his "major contributions to baseball."

1999 The New York Yankees acquire five-time Cy Young Award winner Roger Clemens from the Toronto Blue Jays in exchange for David Wells, Homer Bush and Graeme Lloyd. The deal was struck when the Blue Jays dropped their demand for the inclusion of prospect Alfonso Soriano in the trade.

> (i) Clemens won 14 games for the Yankees during the 1999 regular season and two more in the postseason, including the World Series Game 4 clincher against the Atlanta Braves.

2001 Edwin Lee "Eddie" Mathews, one of the greatest third basemen in baseball history, dies at age 69 in La Jolla, California. The powerful slugger hit 30 or more home runs in nine consecutive seasons, finishing his career with 512, and helped lead the Milwaukee Braves to their first World Series title in 1957. A twelve-time All-Star, Mathews was inducted into the Baseball Hall of Fame in 1978.

2005 Thirty Venezuelan police officers raid a mountain camp and rescue the mother of Detroit Tigers pitcher Ugueth Urbina from kidnappers who were holding her for $6 million in ransom. Urbina's mother, Maura Villarreal, had been held captive in a Venezuelan jungle for over five months before the successful rescue.

# 19

1957 The New York Yankees strengthen their club by acquiring third baseman Clete Boyer and pitchers Art Ditmar and Bobby Shantz, among others, from the Kansas City Athletics in a thirteen-player trade. Shantz will provide instant value for New York, going 11-5 this season with a league-leading 2.45 ERA, while Ditmar will post an 8-3 record with a 3.25 ERA and 6 saves. Boyer will shine as a defensive standout for the Yankees from 1959-1966.

 Upon retirement from pro baseball, Clete Boyer operated a souvenir shop near the Baseball Hall of Fame in Cooperstown, New York.

1970 Baseball commissioner Bowie Kuhn suspends Detroit Tigers ace Denny McLain for his involvement in a bookmaking operation. The two-time Cy Young Award winner will be suspended twice more this season, and will be out of baseball within three years.

1983 Star pitcher Fernando Valenzuela of the Los Angeles Dodgers becomes the first player granted a $1 million salary through the arbitration process.

# 20

1943 Chicago Cubs owner Philip K. Wrigley announces the formation of the All-American Girls Softball League, a venture he hopes will help maintain public interest in baseball during a time when many of the major leaguers are in military service.

[i] The circuit, later renamed the All-American Girls Professional Baseball League, employed over 600 female athletes during its 12-year existence.

1949 The first ever Caribbean World Series is inaugurated with a doubleheader at Havana, Cuba. The host country will win the best-of-six-days series with a perfect 6-0 record, outclassing Venezuela (3-3), Panama (2-4) and Puerto Rico (1-5).

1953  St. Louis Cardinals owner Fred Saigh, who was recently convicted of income tax evasion, sells his team to local brewery Anheuser-Busch for $3.75 million. August "Gussie" Busch is named team president.

1963  Following another dominant season in which he narrowly missed winning his second MVP award and led his San Francisco Giants to a National League pennant, Willie Mays gets a raise to $105,000, making him the highest paid player in baseball. Mickey Mantle, the 1962 American League MVP, is second with a $100,000 salary.

2004  Although still under team control as an arbitration-eligible player, 24-year-old Albert Pujols signs a lucrative seven-year, $100 million contract with the St. Louis Cardinals, the richest deal in team history to date.

> (i) The investment proved to be a wise one as Pujols captured three National League MVP awards in the next six seasons and led the Cardinals to World Championships in 2006 and 2011.

2006  Ford C. Frick Award recipient Curtis Edward "Curt" Gowdy dies of leukemia at age 86 in Palm Beach, Florida. Known for his warm, gravelly voice and unforced commentating style, Gowdy earned acclaim in baseball circles as the longtime voice of the Boston Red Sox and for his coverage of many nationally televised baseball games.

# 21

1931  The Chicago White Sox and New York Giants become the first major league teams to play a game under artificial lighting when they compete in a night exhibition game at Buffs Stadium in Houston, Texas.

1945  The 1945 All-Star Game, scheduled to be played at Boston's Fenway Park, is cancelled due to wartime travel restrictions.

> (i) New baseball commissioner Happy Chandler reportedly considered holding the game in newly liberated Berlin, but ultimately dismissed the idea as impractical.

1968  Union leader Marvin Miller negotiates the first-ever collective bargaining agreement in professional sports. The agreement raises the minimum salary in baseball from $6,000 to $10,000 and sets the stage for future advances.

1969  In a celebrated return to baseball, Hall of Famer Ted Williams signs a five-year contract to manage the Washington Senators. Williams will claim the AL Manager of the Year Award later this season after leading the Senators to a franchise-record 86 wins.

1974 Reigning Cy Young Award winner Tom Seaver, who won 19 games and led the National League in ERA and strikeouts in 1973, becomes the highest paid pitcher in MLB history to date when he re-signs with the New York Mets for $172,000.

# 22

1936 As part of the celebration commemorating the 200th anniversary of George Washington's birth, pitching legend Walter Johnson matches Washington's fabled feat by throwing a silver dollar across the Rappahannock River.

# 23

1960 Wrecking crews begin the job of demolishing Ebbets Field, the former home of the Brooklyn Dodgers. As part of the ceremony, pop singer Lucy Monroe sings the National Anthem. In attendance are a group of former Dodgers including Otto Miller, who caught the first game played at Ebbets in 1913, and star catcher Roy Campanella, who is given an urn of dirt from behind home plate.

1964 The San Francisco Giants sign three Japanese players sent to the United States by the Nankai Hawks to gain experience. One of these players is left-handed pitcher Masanori Murakami, who will become the first Japanese-born player to appear in a Major League Baseball game when he debuts for the Giants later this season.

1988 Chicago lawmakers pass legislation that will allow the Cubs to install lights at Wrigley Field. The Cubs, the last team to play all of its home games during the day, will now be allowed to play up to 18 night games per year.

(i) In 1942, then-owner P.K. Wrigley had planned to install lights at Wrigley Field, but instead the lights and stands were used for the war effort.

 The first night game at Wrigley was actually played on July 1, 1943 when the All-American Girls Professional Baseball League's first All-Star Game was played under temporary lights.

# 24

**1874**  Slugging shortstop Honus Wagner, a supreme star of Major League Baseball's Deadball Era, is born in Chartiers, Pennsylvania.

**1948**  The New York Yankees acquire pitcher Eddie Lopat from the Chicago White Sox in exchange for All-Star catcher Aaron Robinson and pitchers Fred Bradley and Bill Wright. Lopat, who will join aces Allie Reynolds and Vic Raschi to form the Yankees' "Big Three," will post a 113-59 record during his eight seasons in New York and will help lead the Yankees to an unprecedented five straight World Series titles by going 4-1 with a 2.60 ERA in seven postseason starts.

> (i)  The White Sox recovered from the loss of Lopat by trading Robinson to the Detroit Tigers later that year for $10,000 and a young pitching prospect named Billy Pierce, who developed into a seven-time All-Star and 186-game winner in thirteen seasons with Chicago.

**1966**  University of Southern California star pitcher Tom Seaver signs a $40,000 contract with the Atlanta Braves. Six days later the deal will be voided by Commissioner William "Spike" Eckert because USC's baseball season is still in progress. In response to Seaver's dilemma, Eckert will hold a special lottery later this year for all big league teams interested in matching the Braves' offer, and the New York Mets will beat out the Cleveland Indians and Philadelphia Phillies for the right to sign Seaver.

# 25

**1882**  In an effort to increase home attendance, the Providence Grays, led by manager Harry Wright, proclaim that they will require their players and the opposing team to parade through the streets of Providence in full uniform while accompanied by a brass band on game days.

**1917**  The Chicago White Sox reacquire first baseman Chick Gandil from the Cleveland Indians for $3,500. Gandil will play a key role in Chicago's World Championship run later this year, but in 1919 he'll allegedly help the White Sox throw the World Series as the ringleader of the players involved in the infamous Black Sox scandal.

  Chick Gandil reportedly pocketed $35,000 for his role in throwing the World Series, an amount nearly nine times his 1919 salary.

1933  Four days after inheriting a $40 million fortune from his stepfather/ uncle, 30-year-old Tom Yawkey purchases the Boston Red Sox from Bob Quinn for $1.2 million on the advice of his longtime friend and former classmate Eddie Collins, the former big league star. Yawkey will remain the sole owner of the Red Sox for the next 44 seasons, the longest such tenure in Major League Baseball history.

1934  Future Hall of Famer John Joseph McGraw, nicknamed "Little Napoleon" and "Muggsy," dies from prostate cancer at age 60 in New Rochelle, New York. One of the most influential figures in baseball's Deadball Era, the pugnacious McGraw gained fame for his great success as manager of the New York Giants, a team he led to ten pennants and three World Championships during his 31-year reign.

1972  Following a salary dispute, future Hall of Famer Steve Carlton of the St. Louis Cardinals is shipped to the Philadelphia Phillies for another All-Star pitcher, Rick Wise. The trade will prove to be a boon for Philadelphia, as Carlton will proceed to win 241 games and collect four Cy Young Awards during his 15 seasons with the Phillies.

1973  A new collective bargaining agreement is signed between the baseball owners and the players union which provides for salary arbitration as a means for resolving salary disputes. Union leader Marvin Miller had pressed for the abolishment of the reserve clause, but management resisted and offered the salary arbitration process instead. This allowance by the owners will give the players unprecedented leverage, and it will be viewed as a vital early step in the movement towards free agency.

# 26

1952  Brooklyn Dodgers ace Don Newcombe is sworn into the Army. The 25-year-old Newcombe, a 20-game winner in 1951 and 56-28 in three major league seasons, will miss two years of baseball while serving in the Korean War.

2004  At Harry Caray's restaurant in Chicago, the foul ball made famous by Steve Bartman in the 2003 NLCS playoffs is blown up by an Oscar-winning special effects expert on live television.

2006  Kansas City Royals pitcher Zack Greinke leaves spring training for unspecified personal reasons. He is later diagnosed with social anxiety disorder and will undergo extensive treatment before returning to action later this season. His remarkable comeback will reach an apex in 2009, when Greinke will earn the American League Cy Young Award after winning 16 games and leading the league with a 2.16 ERA.

# 27

1901 The National League Rules Committee decrees that foul balls with less than two strikes will now be counted as strikes. The American League will not adopt this rule until 1903, accounting for greater offense in the Junior Circuit's first two seasons.

1973 Chicago White Sox slugger Dick Allen signs a three-year deal worth a reported $250,000 per season, making him the highest-paid player in major league history to date.

> (i) The landmark deal followed an MVP season for Allen in which he led the American League in home runs, RBIs and slugging percentage.

1989 Washington State University first baseman John Olerud undergoes successful brain surgery for the removal of an aneurysm. Olerud will be drafted by the Toronto Blue Jays later this year and go on to enjoy a successful 17-year major league career. As a precaution, he will wear a helmet at all times while on the playing field.

2011 Hall of Famer Edwin Donald "Duke" Snider, nicknamed "The Duke of Flatbush," dies at age 84 in Escondido, California. While sharing the spotlight with fellow New York centerfielders Mickey Mantle and Willie Mays for much of his career, Snider excelled in his own right, posting five consecutive 40-homer seasons from 1953 through 1957 and leading all batters in home runs and RBIs during the 1950s.

# 28

1959 New York Yankees superstar Mickey Mantle ends his holdout after one day, agreeing to a $72,000 salary plus a $2,000 bonus. After batting .304 with a league-leading 42 home runs and 127 runs scored for the Yankees in 1958, Mantle had asked for a salary of $85,000.

1966 Los Angeles Dodgers All-Star pitchers Sandy Koufax and Don Drysdale begin a joint holdout, seeking an unheard-of sum of $1.05 million over three years to be divided equally among the two aces.

1986 Baseball Commissioner Peter Ueberroth reacts to the Pittsburgh drug trials of 1985 and the cocaine cloud that hangs over baseball by handing out the most severe disciplinary penalties since the 1919 Black Sox scandal. Ueberroth gives seven admitted drug users - Joaquín Andújar, Dale Berra, Enos Cabell, Keith Hernandez, Jeffrey Leonard, Dave Parker and Lonnie Smith - year-long suspensions without pay, but allows them to play under the condition that they donate 10 percent of one year's base salary to a drug rehabilitation facility in their area, devote 100 hours of community service in each of the next two years and submit to drug testing for the remainder of their careers. The commissioner also doles out lesser penalties to fourteen other players.

# 29

1972  Hank Aaron becomes the first player in major league history to earn $200,000 in average annual salary after signing a three-year deal with the Atlanta Braves. The 38-year-old slugger is coming off one of his most productive seasons, having posted a .327 batting average, 47 home runs and 118 RBIs in 1971.

# MARCH

## 1

**1909** Ground is broken on a new home for the Pirates near Schenley Park in the Oakland section of Pittsburgh on land purchased by owner Barney Dreyfuss with the help of his friend, industrialist Andrew Carnegie. The new three-tiered structure, named Forbes Field in honor of John Forbes, the 16th century British general who named Pittsburgh, will be the first ballpark in the country to be built out of steel and concrete.

> (i) Construction was completed in only 122 days, and the park opened to rave reviews when the Pirates hosted the Chicago Cubs on June 30.

**1954** Boston Red Sox star Ted Williams fractures his collarbone on the first day of spring training while diving for a ball in the outfield. As a result, Williams' season won't begin until May 15. Despite the injury and the missed time, the "Splendid Splinter" will still lead the American League in walks (136) and finish seventh in league MVP voting.

**1965** After contracting malaria in the offseason, reigning National League batting champ Roberto Clemente is absent when the Pittsburgh Pirates spring training camp opens. Despite missing most of March and struggling until mid-May, Clemente will finish the 1965 season with a .329 batting average, good enough for his second straight batting title.

**1969** After several years of decline, 36-year-old New York Yankees legend Mickey Mantle announces his retirement. Despite battling persistent knee injuries throughout his 18 major league seasons, Mantle fashioned a remarkable career that included 536 home runs, three MVP awards, the 1956 AL Triple Crown, 20 All-Star appearances and seven World Championships.

**1993** George Steinbrenner returns to his role as general partner of the New York Yankees after a 30-month exile. "The Boss" had been banned from day-to-day operation of the Yankees for life on July 30, 1990 by MLB Commissioner Fay Vincent after it became known that Steinbrenner had hired confessed gambler Howard Spira to dig up dirt on Dave Winfield and the Winfield Foundation, but Vincent later allowed for his reinstatement.

2002 San Francisco Giants All-Star second baseman Jeff Kent breaks his left thumb and is expected to be out four to six weeks. Kent, the 2000 National League MVP, claims he incurred the injury while washing his truck, but evidence will eventually surface that indicates he was actually injured while doing stunts on his motorcycle.

# 2

1949 New York Yankees superstar Joe DiMaggio leaves spring training camp to have his right heel examined at Johns Hopkins Hospital. DiMaggio is assured that surgery is unnecessary, but the discomfort in his heel, which will later be diagnosed as a bone spur, will continue to bother him.

> (i) Despite the lingering pain, DiMaggio returned to the Yankees lineup on June 28 and led his club to another World Series title this year after batting .346 with 67 RBIs over the season's final three months.

1992 All-Star second baseman Ryne Sandberg becomes the highest-paid player in baseball history to date when he signs a four-year, $28.4 million contract extension with the Chicago Cubs.

2005 Former Brooklyn Dodgers great Jackie Robinson is posthumously awarded the Congressional Gold Medal, the highest civilian award bestowed by Congress. Rachel Robinson accepts the award from President George W. Bush on behalf of her late husband.

> (i) Jackie Robinson joined Roberto Clemente, Joe Louis and Jesse Owens as the only athletes among the 300 Gold Medal recipients.

2012 Major League Baseball announces that starting this season an extra wild card team will be added to each league, increasing the total number of playoff teams from eight to ten. The new postseason format calls for the two wild card teams in each league to play a one-game playoff against each other to determine which team advances to the Division Series.

# 3

1959 The new San Francisco ballpark, originally called Bay View Stadium, is renamed after the winning entry in the Giants' Name-the-Park contest is announced. The stadium will now be called Candlestick Park, named after the rock formations in the area known as Candlestick Point.

2006 South Korea wins the first-ever World Baseball Classic game, beating Taiwan 2-0 as starter Jae-Weong Seo pitches two-hit ball and Chan Ho Park works three effective innings for the save. Japan will go on to win the inaugural tournament, defeating Cuba in the championship game.

> (i) Japanese pitcher Daisuke Matsuzaka was named tournament MVP after going 3-0 with a 2.54 ERA. Soon after this performance, Matsuzaka received a multi-million dollar contract offer from the Boston Red Sox.

# 4

1927 The New York Yankees announce that superstar Babe Ruth will earn $70,000 per season for the next three years, making the Bambino the highest-paid player in major league history to date.

> (i) Ruth proceeded to have one of his finest seasons in 1927, hammering a record-setting 60 home runs and leading his 110-win Yankees team to a sweep of the Pittsburgh Pirates in the World Series.

1948 Stan Musial ends his holdout and signs a one-year, $31,000 contract with the St. Louis Cardinals. The deal will prove to be a bargain as Musial will go on to fashion one of the greatest seasons in baseball history, leading the National League in batting average (.376), hits (230), runs (135), RBIs (131), total bases (429), doubles (46), triples (18), on-base percentage (.450) and slugging percentage (.702) while earning his third MVP award.

1976 The Stoneham family chooses to sell the San Francisco Giants to businessmen Bob Lurie and Bud Herseth for a reported $8 million with the promise that the team will stay in San Francisco. It had been rumored that the Labatt Brewing Company was interested in buying the Giants and moving the franchise to Canada.

2004 Commissioner Bud Selig announces that Major League Baseball will celebrate "Jackie Robinson Day" in every ballpark on April 15, the anniversary of Robinson's historic big league debut.

# 5

1922 Following one of the greatest offensive campaigns in baseball history, Babe Ruth signs a three-year deal with the Yankees for a record $52,000 per season.

1936  The "Gashouse Gang" St. Louis Cardinals are defeated by the Cuban All-Stars in an exhibition game in Havana. Left-handed screwball artist Luis Tiant, whose son Luis Jr. will win 229 major league games, is the starting pitcher for the home team.

1966  In what will prove to be an exceptionally significant event, the Major League Baseball Players Association elects former United Steelworkers union official Marvin Miller as their new executive director. Under Miller's leadership, the players' union will see considerable increases in pay and benefits, as well as the advent of salary arbitration and free agency.

1973  New York Yankees pitchers Mike Kekich and Fritz Peterson announce they have swapped wives and families. The scandal, which started in 1972 as a joke between the good friends, eventually evolved into reality as Kekich traded his wife Susan, his two kids and a Bedlington terrier for Marilyn Peterson, the two Peterson children and a poodle.

# 6

1938  The cash-strapped Philadelphia Phillies trade first baseman Dolph Camilli to the Brooklyn Dodgers for Eddie Morgan and $45,000. The deal will work out well for Larry MacPhail and the Dodgers, as Camilli will drive in 100 or more runs in four of the next five seasons, including 1941 when he'll be named the National League's MVP and help lead Brooklyn to their first pennant since 1920.

 Camilli's brother Francesco, who boxed under the name Frankie Campbell, died of cerebral hemorrhaging following a 1930 match with eventual heavyweight champion Max Baer.

1987  Facing a depressed free agent market due to collusion, star outfielder Andre Dawson presents a signed blank contract to the Chicago Cubs and eventually agrees to a below-market rate of $500,000 plus incentives. Dawson will pay immediate dividends this season for an otherwise woeful Cubs team as he'll lead the league with 49 home runs and 137 RBIs and earn the National League MVP award.

 In 1987, Andre Dawson became the first player to earn league MVP honors while on a last place team.

2005  Suzyn Waldman becomes the first female full-time color commentator in major league history, making her debut with John Sterling on the New York Yankees' radio flagship station WCBS-AM 880.

2006 Kirby Puckett dies at age 45 in Phoenix, Arizona. An excellent all-around centerfielder during his 12-year career with the Minnesota Twins, Puckett led the American League in batting once and in hits four times, won six Gold Glove Awards, was named an All-Star ten times and led the Twins to two World Series titles. He finished with a .318 career batting average, the highest by any right-handed American League hitter since Joe DiMaggio, and was inducted into the Baseball Hall of Fame in 2001.

# 7

1893 Arguably the most significant rule change in major league history occurs as the National League establishes the modern pitching distance of 60 feet, 6 inches.

> ⓘ The new pitching distance wasn't universally embraced initially. Within two years of the change, baseball officials discussed the possibility of reinstating the old pitching distance of 50 feet after there was dismay over the explosion of offense. Despite this concern, the new pitching distance was here to stay.

1991 Hall of Famer James Thomas "Cool Papa" Bell dies at age 87 in St. Louis, Missouri. A star in the Negro Leagues for over two decades, Bell put his legendary speed to great use as a fantastic leadoff hitter, baserunner and outfielder. He later served as a coach with the Kansas City Monarchs, grooming such young stars as Jackie Robinson for the major leagues.

# 8

1930 Babe Ruth agrees to a two-year, $160,000 contract with the New York Yankees, becoming the highest-paid player in baseball history to date. When informed that he will be earning more than President Hoover, Ruth famously quipped "I had a better year than he did."

1966 The Baseball Hall of Fame Special Veterans Committee waives one of its election rules and selects recently retired manager Casey Stengel for induction. The 75-year-old Stengel was given special consideration by the committee because of his age.

> ⓘ When baseball celebrated its centennial in 1969, Stengel was named the game's greatest living manager.

1999 Hall of Famer Joseph Paul "Joe" DiMaggio, nicknamed "Joltin' Joe" and "The Yankee Clipper," dies of lung cancer at age 84 in Hollywood, Florida.

One of baseball's greatest and most iconic players, DiMaggio helped the New York Yankees win nine World Championships during his 13-year career while capturing three MVP awards and earning All-Star selections every year he played. His 56 consecutive-game hitting streak in 1941 is considered one of the greatest baseball feats of all time.

2011  Los Angeles Dodgers Assistant General Manager Kim Ng, the highest-ranking woman in the major leagues, is named MLB's Vice President of Baseball Operations. Ng will report to Joe Torre, who was recently named Executive Vice President.

# 9

1995  Major League Baseball owners unanimously approve the Arizona Diamondbacks and the Tampa Bay Devil Rays as expansion teams. The Diamondbacks will join the National League and the Devil Rays will join the American League, with both clubs scheduled to begin play in 1998. In order to keep an even number of teams in both leagues, the Milwaukee Brewers will switch to the National League prior to the 1998 season.

# 10

1963  Cincinnati's Pete Rose, a relative unknown, goes 2-for-2 against the Chicago White Sox in his first spring training game. The 22-year-old Rose will make the Reds' Opening Day roster this season as the starting second baseman, and will go on to win the 1963 National League Rookie of the Year Award.

1993  Sherry Davis becomes the first full-time female stadium announcer in major league history when she is hired by the San Francisco Giants.

> ⓘ Davis, a legal secretary by trade, won the job by beating out 500 other candidates at an open audition.

1995  After batting .202 at the AA level, Michael Jordan announces that he is leaving the Chicago White Sox organization and will return to the NBA's Chicago Bulls.

# 11

1958  American League officials announce that starting this season all of the league's batters will be required to wear either a batting helmet or a protective liner inside their cap.

**1974**  With Hank Aaron entering the season one homer short of Babe Ruth's all-time home run record total of 714, the Atlanta Braves plan to sit their slugging outfielder on the road in order to increase his chances of tying and breaking the iconic mark at home, but Commissioner Bowie Kuhn orders the Braves to play Aaron in at least two of the team's season-opening three-game series with the Cincinnati Reds.

> ⓘ  On Opening Day in Cincinnati, Hank Aaron hit a three-run homer off Reds starter Jack Billingham to tie Babe Ruth's career home run record. The record-breaker came in Atlanta in the fourth game of the season when Aaron belted a two-run home run off Al Downing of the Dodgers.

**2002**  Former top prospect Ruben Rivera, cousin of star closer Mariano Rivera, is released by the New York Yankees when it's discovered that he stole Derek Jeter's glove and sold it for $2,500.

# 12

**1902**  Baltimore Orioles star Mike Donlin is arrested for accosting two women. Donlin will plead guilty and miss most of this season while serving a six-month jail sentence.

**1921**  In a swift response to what has become known as the "Black Sox Scandal," newly appointed baseball commissioner Kenesaw Mountain Landis suspends eight members of the Chicago White Sox for their alleged involvement in the fixing of the 1919 World Series. The group includes star outfielder Shoeless Joe Jackson as well as Eddie Cicotte, Happy Felsch, Chick Gandil, Fred McMullin, Swede Risberg, Buck Weaver and Lefty Williams. None of the eight will ever play in Organized Baseball again.

**1951**  MLB owners vote 9-7 to oust Happy Chandler as Commissioner of Baseball. Chandler, who served for six years as baseball's second commissioner, will be succeeded by Ford Frick.

> ⓘ  Chandler's approval of Jackie Robinson's first contract with the Brooklyn Dodgers in 1945 helped pave the way for the integration of Major League Baseball.

> ⓘ  Happy Chandler eventually returned to politics and, in 1955, secured a second stint as governor of Kentucky.

**1980**  Star outfielder Chuck Klein and former Boston Red Sox owner Tom Yawkey are selected for induction by the Baseball Hall of Fame's Special

Veterans Committee. Yawkey's election is unique as he becomes the first club owner inducted who never served as a player, manager or general manager.

## 13

1960   The Chicago White Sox unveil new road uniforms that include player names above the number on the back, marking the first time player names appear on major league uniforms. The idea was conceived by creative White Sox owner Bill Veeck, who hoped the innovation would make it easier for fans watching games on television to identify the Chicago players.

1969   Major League Baseball reacts to the game's dearth of offense by shrinking the strike zone and lowering the pitcher's mound from 15 to 10 inches.

## 14

1932   The Cincinnati Reds acquire 23-year-old catcher Ernie Lombardi along with outfielder Babe Herman and infielder Wally Gilbert from the Brooklyn Dodgers for infielders Tony Cuccinello and Joe Stripp and catcher Clyde Suckforth. The deal will prove to be lopsided in favor of the Reds when Lombardi develops into a five-time All-Star and hits .311 in ten seasons in Cincinnati, including a league-leading .342 in 1938 when he captures the National League MVP award.

1954   Taking advantage of a recent injury suffered by starting outfielder Bobby Thomson, 20-year-old Hank Aaron shows well in his first spring training start for the Milwaukee Braves, pounding a home run and two other hits in an exhibition game against the Boston Red Sox. Aaron will earn a starting spot with the Braves by Opening Day and will perform well enough to finish fourth in NL Rookie of the Year voting.

 Hank Aaron did not wear his iconic #44 until his second season; in his rookie season of 1954 he wore #5.

## 15

1869   The Cincinnati Base Ball Club (soon to be known as the Cincinnati Red Stockings) forms, becoming the first openly all-professional baseball team.

(i) Led by Hall of Famer Harry Wright, the Red Stockings barnstormed the nation and defeated every team it played in 1869, finishing with a 57-0 record.

1884   Baseball pioneer Henry Chadwick writes in a newspaper column that a St. Louis groundskeeper had started using tarpaulins to protect his park's bases from rain. The idea will catch on, and soon clubs will cover the batting area and pitching mound as well.

1978   One of the last remaining players from the Oakland Athletics' championship teams of 1972-1974 departs as Vida Blue is dealt to the San Francisco Giants for seven players and $300,000. Blue, the 1971 American League MVP and three-time 20-game winner, will post an 18-10 record this season and finish third in NL Cy Young Award voting.

> (i)   Athletics owner Charlie Finley had previously attempted to sell Vida Blue twice, first to the New York Yankees for $1.5 million in 1976 and then to the Cincinnati Reds a year later for $1.75 million. Both transactions were voided by Commissioner Bowie Kuhn, who deemed them bad for baseball.

> DID YOU KNOW?   In 1978, Vida Blue became the first pitcher to start an All-Star Game for each league. He had previously started for the American League in 1971 and 1975 while with the Athletics.

# 16

1908   Pittsburgh Pirates 34-year-old superstar Honus Wagner announces his retirement from baseball. His "retirement" won't last long, though, once owner Barney Dreyfuss quickly doubles his annual salary to $10,000.

> (i)   Wagner fashioned his greatest season ever in 1908, leading the National League in every significant offensive category other than runs scored (second) and home runs (second).

1961   Faced with the need to build a new stadium for their recently-granted New York Mets franchise, the state of New York approves a bond issue for the construction of a multi-purpose stadium in the Flushing Meadows area of Queens. Originally named Flushing Meadow Park Municipal Stadium, the new park will become known as Shea Stadium in honor of William A. Shea, the man who brought National League baseball back to New York.

1978   Newly-acquired starter Andy Messersmith of the New York Yankees separates his shoulder while running into first baseman Cliff Johnson during a spring training game. A former 20-game winner for both the Angels and the Dodgers, Messersmith won't win a game in his one injury-shortened season in the Bronx.

1985  Denny McLain, the last major league pitcher to reach 30 wins in a season, is convicted of racketeering and sentenced to 23 years in prison.

> (i) McLain ultimately served 29 months as his conviction was later reversed due to prosecutorial misconduct.

# 17

1871  In New York, ten clubs establish the National Association of Professional Base Ball Players, laying the groundwork for the future National League.

1886  *The Sporting News*, founded by Alfred H. Spink, publishes its first issue. Soon to be nicknamed "The Bible of Baseball," it will be considered the dominant American publication covering the sport.

1946  City Island Park in Daytona Beach is the site of modern Organized Baseball's first integrated game when Jackie Robinson and the Montreal Royals take the field against their parent club, the Brooklyn Dodgers.

> (i) Daytona Beach was the first Florida city to allow for an integrated baseball game; both Jacksonville and Sanford had previously refused to allow the game due to segregation laws. Jacksonville's refusal forced the Dodgers to move their spring training home from there to Daytona Beach in 1947 and then more permanently to Vero Beach in 1948.

1965  Jackie Robinson becomes the first black network broadcaster when he's hired by ABC as an analyst for their *Major League Baseball Game of the Week* telecasts.

1969  The St. Louis Cardinals trade 1967 National League MVP Orlando Cepeda to the Atlanta Braves for five-time All-Star Joe Torre. The deal will benefit both teams as Cepeda will help the Braves make the playoffs this season and Torre will go on to win the 1971 National League MVP award and have six productive seasons in St. Louis.

1990  The Chinese Professional Baseball League plays its first game, with the Uni-President Lions defeating the Brother Elephants 4-3 in Taipei.

2005  Jose Canseco, Mark McGwire, Rafael Palmeiro, Curt Schilling and Sammy Sosa appear before the House Committee on Government Reform to discuss the topic of performance enhancing drugs in Major League Baseball.

McGwire's image will be instantly tarnished when he refuses to discuss his past or deny taking PEDs.

> (i) Rafael Palmeiro, who while under oath adamantly denied ever using performance-enhancing drugs, tested positive for PEDs soon after the hearing.

2010   Texas Rangers manager Ron Washington publicly acknowledges that he tested positive for cocaine in 2009 and apologizes for his behavior. He also admits that he smoked marijuana and took amphetamines during his playing career. Washington submits his resignation, but Rangers management rejects it.

> (i) Washington guided the Texas Rangers to American League pennants in 2010 and 2011.

# 18

1942   Despite the current state of segregation in Major League Baseball, two black players - Jackie Robinson and Nate Moreland - request a tryout with the White Sox. Chicago manager Jimmie Dykes allows the two to work out during spring training, but fails to make either an offer.

> (i) Jackie Robinson had to wait five more years before making his major league debut.

1953   After a period of unprecedented stability in Major League Baseball, the Braves, who had been in Boston for 77 years, become the first major league franchise to move since 1903 when they relocate to Milwaukee.

> (i) During their first season in Milwaukee the Braves broke the National League attendance record with a figure of 1,826,397.

1957   Cleveland Indians GM Hank Greenberg turns down a staggering $1 million offer from the Boston Red Sox for 23-year-old pitching star Herb Score. Greenberg states that the Indians are serious about building for the future and are not interested in selling premier players like Score, who earned Rookie of the Year honors in 1955 and went 20-9 with 263 strikeouts in 1956. Unfortunately, Score will be hit in the eye by a Gil McDougald liner just six weeks later and will never be the same, winning only 19 more games over the rest of his career.

 In 1955, Herb Score became the first starting pitcher in major league history to average more than one strikeout per inning, and his total of 245 strikeouts was a rookie record that stood until Dwight Gooden surpassed it in 1984.

1985  Commissioner Peter Ueberroth reinstates Hall of Famers Mickey Mantle and Willie Mays, who had been banned from Organized Baseball by Ueberroth's predecessor Bowie Kuhn due to their employment by Atlantic City casinos.

2008  As part of their response to the April 2007 Virginia Tech shootings that left 32 people dead, the New York Yankees visit a campus memorial at Virginia Tech and play an exhibition game at the university's English Field to help support those affected by the tragedy. George Steinbrenner and the Yankees had previously donated $1 million to the Hokie Spirit Memorial Fund, created to cover grief counseling, memorials and other costs for the victims and their families.

# 19

1961  The Boston Red Sox announce that 21-year-old rookie Carl Yastrzemski will start the season in left field, succeeding the legendary Ted Williams.

> (i) Yastrzemski became a legend in his own right as a fixture in Boston's lineup for the next 23 seasons, and joined Ted Williams in the Baseball Hall of Fame in 1989.

1964  Future Hall of Famer John Henry "Pop" Lloyd dies at age 79 in Atlantic City, New Jersey. A tremendous line drive hitter and gifted fielder, Lloyd drew favorable comparisons to Honus Wagner and is generally considered to be the greatest shortstop in Negro League history.

1998  Media mogul Rupert Murdoch's Fox Entertainment Group acquires the Los Angeles Dodgers from Peter O'Malley for $311 million, the highest price ever paid for a United States sports franchise to date.

2019  Amidst an unprecedented flurry of big dollar extensions, superstar outfielder Mike Trout nets the largest contract in sports history when he signs a 10-year, $426.5 million deal to stay with the Los Angeles Angels.

# 20

1937  In what is considered the largest transaction in the history of the Negro Leagues, the Homestead Grays acquire future Hall of Famers Josh Gibson and Judy Johnson from the Pittsburgh Crawfords for $2,500 and a pair of lesser players.

**1973**   Eleven weeks after his tragic death, Roberto Clemente is easily elected to the Baseball Hall of Fame after the Hall's Board of Directors agrees to wave the mandatory five-year waiting period.

> [i] It's also announced that the Commissioner's Award, given annually to honor a major league player for performance on the field as well as in the community, will be renamed the Roberto Clemente Award.

> DID YOU KNOW? Roberto Clemente was the first Latin American elected to the Baseball Hall of Fame.

**2006**  In the inaugural World Baseball Classic, Japan defeats Cuba 10-6 in the championship game before a sellout crowd at San Diego's PETCO Park. Japanese starting pitcher Daisuke Matsuzaka, who also defeated Cuba in the 2004 Olympics, earns his third victory of the tournament and is named the WBC Most Valuable Player.

> [i] Despite the fact that the 2006 World Baseball Classic was open to players from Major League Baseball, the two championship game participants fielded a total of only two major leaguers - Japanese players Ichiro Suzuki (Seattle Mariners) and Akinori Otsuka (Texas Rangers).

# 21

**1975**   Hall of Famer Joe Medwick, a 10-time All-Star and the last National League player to win the Triple Crown, dies at age 63 in St. Petersburg, Florida.

**1977**   Detroit Tigers sensation Mark "The Bird" Fidrych, who gained national attention last season for his pitching brilliance and unusual mannerisms on the mound, tears cartilage in his left knee. The injury will force him to miss the first two months of the season.

**2010**   Three-time batting champ and reigning American League MVP Joe Mauer signs an eight-year, $184 million contract extension with the Minnesota Twins. The deal for Mauer, a hometown hero who grew up in St. Paul, is the fourth-largest to date in Major League Baseball history.

**2019**   Seattle Mariners 45-year-old icon Ichiro Suzuki ends his storied 27-year professional playing career when he announces his retirement following the Mariners' 5-4 win over the Oakland Athletics in Tokyo, Japan.

# 22

**1936**  New York Yankees spring sensation Joe DiMaggio suffers serious burns on his foot while receiving treatment in a diathermy machine. The injury will delay the young outfielder's highly anticipated major league debut until May.

> (i) After making a full recovery, DiMaggio scored 132 runs in 138 games while leading the American League in triples (15), and his stellar all-around play helped the Yankees capture the 1936 World Championship.

**1962**  An Associated Press article reports that a sign-stealing spy stationed in the centerfield clubhouse at the Polo Grounds aided the New York Giants in their legendary playoff run in 1951. Outfielder Bobby Thomson, the man who hit the famous pennant-winning home run, and manager Leo Durocher both vehemently deny the claim. The article, which relied on an anonymous source and offered only vague details, gains little traction.

> (i) Decades later considerable evidence surfaced which substantiated earlier reports of the Giants' elaborate sign-stealing operation.

**1972**  In a lopsided trade between two American League rivals, the New York Yankees acquire relief ace Sparky Lyle from the Boston Red Sox in exchange for first baseman Danny Cater and shortstop Mario Guerrero. Lyle will be voted *The Sporting News* Fireman of the Year this season after establishing a new single-season record for saves by a left-hander with 35, and he'll go on to post 141 saves and a 2.41 ERA in seven seasons in the Bronx while winning the 1977 AL Cy Young Award and helping the Yankees claim World Series titles in 1977 and 1978.

**1991**  At Sotherby's in New York, a mint condition T206 Honus Wagner baseball card sells for $451,000 to hockey legend Wayne Gretzky and Los Angeles Kings owner Bruce McNall.

> (i) Other significant baseball items sold that day included a 1952 Topps Mickey Mantle rookie for $49,500 and a baseball signed by 12 players at the 1939 Baseball Hall of Fame induction ceremony for $20,900.

**1993**  During a spring training off-day, Cleveland Indians pitchers Steve Olin and Tim Crews are killed and pitcher Bob Ojeda is seriously injured in Clermont, Florida when Crews' 18-foot bass boat strikes a dock at high speed.

> (i) Crews and Olin were the first active major leaguers to die since Thurman Munson in 1979.

# 23

1936  Star pitcher Dizzy Dean ends his well-publicized holdout and signs a one-year, $24,000 contract with the St. Louis Cardinals.

> (i) After winning the National League MVP in 1934 and finishing second in the voting in 1935, the 26-year-old Dean finished second again in 1936 after going 24-13 and leading the league with 28 complete games.

1938  In another attempt to clean up baseball's growing player development program, Commissioner Kenesaw Mountain Landis makes free agents of 74 St. Louis Cardinals minor leaguers when he finds the Cardinals in violation of working agreements with several minor league clubs. Among these minor leaguers is 19-year-old outfielder Pete Reiser, a player destined for brief stardom with the Brooklyn Dodgers.

2000  The St. Louis Cardinals get the best of a heavily one-sided deal with the Anaheim Angels when they acquire All-Star centerfielder Jim Edmonds in exchange for 18-game winner Kent Bottenfield and second baseman Adam Kennedy. Edmonds will capture six Gold Glove Awards while averaging 30 home runs, 98 RBIs and 100 runs scored during his first six seasons in St. Louis, while Bottenfield will win just 10 more games before retiring in 2001.

2009  Japan defeats South Korea to claim their second World Baseball Classic championship. Japanese star Daisuke Matsuzaka wins his second World Baseball Classic MVP award.

> (i) Japan's Ichiro Suzuki went 4-for-6 and drove in the winning run in the 10th inning, while Yu Darvish was credited with the win in relief.

# 24

1933  New York Yankees superstar Babe Ruth, like countless others, is impacted by the Great Depression as his salary is slashed by 30% despite batting .341 and slugging 41 home runs in 1932.

1982  Pitcher Fernando Valenzuela, last year's National League Cy Young Award winner and Rookie of the Year, ends his holdout after receiving a $350,000 salary from the Los Angeles Dodgers. Valenzuela, who was paid only $42,500 in his rookie campaign, had asked for $1 million following his sensational 1981 season.

1984  In a critical move that will help propel the Detroit Tigers to a World Series title this season, the Philadelphia Phillies agree to trade relief pitcher

Willie Hernandez and first baseman Dave Bergman to the Tigers in exchange for outfielder Glen Wilson and catcher John Wockenfuss. The gem of the deal is Hernandez, who will capture both the American League MVP award and Cy Young Award this season after posting a 1.92 ERA and saving 32 games in 80 appearances.

# 25

1910    The Chalmers Automobile Company of Detroit announces a promotion in which a car will be given to the league batting champions.

1917    Manager John McGraw signs a five-year, $200,000 contract extension with the New York Giants, making him the highest-paid figure in Major League Baseball.

> (i) At the time of his contract extension, McGraw owned a 1,321-867 record and had guided the Giants to five National League pennants and one World Series title in his 15 seasons in New York.

1951    Hall of Famer Edward Trowbridge "Eddie" Collins dies at age 63 in Boston, Massachusetts. A confident, fiery competitor and fantastic all-around second baseman, Collins generated 3,315 hits, a .333 lifetime average, 1,821 runs scored and 741 stolen bases during his 25-year career. He won the American League Chalmers Award in 1914, and was a key player on four World Series winners. After his playing days Collins served as general manager of the Boston Red Sox from 1933-1947.

1959    The St. Louis Cardinals take advantage of the San Francisco Giants' historic embarrassment of riches when they acquire 25-year-old first baseman Bill White in exchange for strikeout artist Sam Jones and prospect Don Choate. White, who became available when the Giants sought to clear space for future Hall of Famers Orlando Cepeda and Willie McCovey, will go on to win six Gold Glove Awards and garner five All-Star Game selections during his seven full seasons in St. Louis.

>  San Francisco Giants stars Orlando Cepeda and Willie McCovey each won Rookie of the Year honors unanimously (in 1958 and 1959, respectively), becoming the first teammates to do so.

2001    In a spring training game in Tucson, fans witness a startling explosion of feathers when reigning Cy Young Award winner Randy Johnson of the Arizona Diamondbacks hits and kills a dove with a pitch.

# 26

1951   In an exhibition game at the University of Southern California, 19-year-old Mickey Mantle of the New York Yankees launches a home run estimated at 660 feet. Mantle further blisters Trojans pitching with a second home run and a bases-loaded triple.

1973   George Harold Sisler, nicknamed "Gorgeous George," dies at age 80 in Richmond Heights, Missouri. A gifted fielder at first base and a superb baserunner, Sisler's main weapon was his graceful left-handed swing, which he used to bat over .300 fourteen times, finishing with a lifetime .340 batting average. Considered the greatest player in St. Louis Browns history, Sisler was inducted into the Baseball Hall of Fame in 1939.

1976   The American League approves the sale of the Toronto expansion franchise to a group consisting of the Labatt Brewing Company, Imperial Trust Ltd., and the Canadian Imperial Bank of Commerce for a reported $7 million.

> (i) The Blue Jays drew 1,701,052 fans in their inaugural season, a figure which shattered the previous attendance high for an expansion franchise.

1984   President Ronald Reagan posthumously awards Jackie Robinson the Presidential Medal of Freedom, the highest civilian award in the United States.

2000   Thousands of spectators watch as Seattle's Kingdome, home of the Mariners since 1977, is demolished.

# 27

1902   In a *Chicago Daily News* article, the nickname "Cubs" is used for the first time in reference to the young players that manager Frank Selee will have to work with on the Chicago National League ball club. Within five years the new nickname will stick permanently.

1982   The Korea Baseball Organization begins its inaugural season as the MBC Dragons defeat the Samsung Lions in 10 innings. Samsung's Man-soo Lee hits the league's first home run.

1987   The New York Mets get the best of a one-sided trade with the Kansas City Royals when they acquire 24-year-old David Cone in exchange for catcher Ed Hearn and two pitching prospects. Cone will soon blossom into a dominant starting pitcher, posting a 20-3 record and finishing third in the National League Cy Young Award race in only his second season in New York.

1989   Cincinnati Reds manager Pete Rose's gambling activities are revealed in a *Sports Illustrated* article. Rose, baseball's all-time hits leader, will accept a lifetime ban from Major League Baseball later this year.

1992   The San Diego Padres acquire 23-year-old infielder Gary Sheffield and a minor leaguer from the Milwaukee Brewers in exchange for pitcher Ricky Bones, outfielder Matt Mieske and shortstop Jose Valentin. Sheffield, who batted just .259 with 21 home runs in four stormy seasons in Milwaukee, will lead the National League in batting and challenge for the Triple Crown in his first season in San Diego.

 In 1986, Gary Sheffield won the inaugural baseball Gatorade National Player of the Year award after batting .500 with 15 home runs during his senior year at Hillsborough High School in Tampa, Florida.

## 28

1907   The baseball world is stunned when popular outfielder Chick Stahl, who had just replaced his friend Jimmy Collins as player-manager of the Boston Americans at the end of the 1906 season, commits suicide by drinking carbolic acid while traveling with the club in West Baden Springs, Indiana.

ⓘ The reasoning behind Chick Stahl's suicide has remained a mystery. His final words to some of his teammates were "Boys, I just couldn't help it. It drove me to it," with many left to wonder what "it" was that drove Stahl to take his own life.

1931   Byron Bancroft "Ban" Johnson, founder and first president of the American League, dies at age 66 in St. Louis, Missouri.

1977   While in Orlando for an exhibition game with the Minnesota Twins, Texas Rangers utility man Lenny Randle confronts his manager Frank Lucchesi during batting practice and, after a heated argument, punches him in the face. The 49-year-old Lucchesi will be hospitalized for a week, needing plastic surgery to repair his shattered cheekbone. The Rangers will suspend Randle for 30 days without pay and fine him $10,000 before trading him to the New York Mets on April 26. Lucchesi will recover in time for Opening Day, but will be fired by June.

1986   The Boston Red Sox swap veteran designated hitters with the New York Yankees, obtaining slugger Don Baylor in exchange for Mike Easler. Baylor will hit 31 home runs and drive in 94 runs this season, helping the Red Sox capture the American League pennant and come within one out of a World Series title.

 Don Baylor was the first player to reach the World Series in three consecutive years with three different teams (1986: Red Sox, 1987: Twins, 1988: Athletics).

**1996** Kirby Puckett of the Minnesota Twins is taken to a Fort Myers, Florida hospital after he awakes with blurred vision in his right eye. The 36-year-old star will soon be diagnosed with glaucoma. After three surgeries over the next few months fail to restore his vision, Puckett will retire from baseball.

> At the time of his retirement, Kirby Puckett was the Twins' all-time leader in hits (2,304), doubles (414), total bases (3,453), at bats (7,244) and runs scored (1,071).

**1999** In a historic event in which baseball and politics intersect, the Baltimore Orioles become the first major league team to visit Cuba since 1959 when they play an exhibition game in Havana against a team of Cuban All-Stars. The Orioles, playing in front of a raucous crowd of 50,000 spectators that includes Cuban President Fidel Castro and MLB Commissioner Bud Selig, defeat the Cuban team 3-2 in 11 innings.

# 29

**1867** Renowned pitching star Denton True "Cy" Young is born in Gilmore, Ohio.

**1973** The "Alert Orange Baseball," an invention of Oakland Athletics owner Charlie Finley, is used for the first time in an exhibition game between the Athletics and the Cleveland Indians. Finley contends that the orange baseball will be easier for both players and fans to see, but batters are unable to pick up the spin of the ball without seeing the seams and pitchers complain that the ball is difficult to grip. Although Finley pushes for the use of colored baseballs during the regular season, the idea will never come to fruition.

**2000** In the first major league game ever played outside of North America, the Chicago Cubs defeat the New York Mets 5-3 at the Tokyo Dome in Japan.

**2008** A crowd of 115,300, the largest ever assembled at a baseball game, watch the Los Angeles Dodgers and the Boston Red Sox play an exhibition game at the Los Angeles Memorial Coliseum, the Dodgers' original Los Angeles home. The game is held to commemorate the 50th anniversary of the Dodgers' move to Los Angeles.

ⓘ The previous attendance record had also been set at an exhibition game held at the Los Angeles Memorial Coliseum. On May 7, 1959, a crowd of 93,103 witnessed a game between the Los Angeles Dodgers and the New York Yankees that was held in honor of paralyzed Dodger great Roy Campanella.

# 30

**1966** Los Angeles Dodgers stars Sandy Koufax and Don Drysdale end their landmark 32-day joint holdout, signing for a reported $125,000 and $110,000, respectively. The pair of aces had threatened retirement and signed movie contracts before receiving their pay raises.

ⓘ This holdout was the impetus for what eventually became collective bargaining.

**1978** The Boston Red Sox obtain All-Star pitcher Dennis Eckersley and catcher Fred Kendall from the Cleveland Indians in exchange for pitchers Rick Wise and Mike Paxton, catcher Bo Diaz and infielder Ted Cox. The 23-year-old Eckersley will go 20-8 with a 2.99 ERA this season, helping the Red Sox notch a 99-win campaign and get within one game of the postseason.

**1992** The Chicago Cubs make one of their best trades ever when they acquire 23-year-old outfielder Sammy Sosa and Ken Patterson from the crosstown White Sox for outfielder George Bell. While Bell's career will last only two more seasons, Sosa will blossom into a star and hit a Cubs-record 545 home runs in his 13 seasons with the club.

**2006** Commissioner Bud Selig appoints former U.S. Senate Majority Leader and current Red Sox director George J. Mitchell to head a formal probe into the use of performance-enhancing drugs in Major League Baseball.

# 31

**1995** Major League Baseball's 232-day work stoppage, the longest strike in sports history, effectively ends when U.S. District Court Judge Sonia Sotomayor issues a preliminary injunction preventing Major League Baseball from unilaterally implementing a new collective bargaining agreement and using replacement players. A condensed 144-game schedule will commence on April 26.

 In 1994, Major League Baseball became the first professional sport to lose its entire postseason due to a labor dispute.

2010  During a Grapefruit League game against the New York Yankees in his hometown of Tampa, Minnesota Twins outfielder Denard Span lines a foul ball into the third base stands which hits his mother, Wanda Wilson, in the chest. Span rushes to check on his mother, who proves to be alright after being evaluated by paramedics. Span leaves the game two innings later and stays by his mother's side for the remainder of the contest.

2011  An Opening Day game in Los Angeles between the Dodgers and the San Francisco Giants is marred by an ugly incident when Giants fan Bryan Stow, a 42-year-old paramedic and father of two, is brutally beaten in the Dodger Stadium parking lot by two men in Dodgers gear. Stow suffers a severely fractured skull which leaves him in a coma. After an exhaustive investigation, two suspects will be arrested within four months and charged with the crime.

(i) After participating in an intensive therapy program at the Santa Clara Valley Medical Center, Stow's condition slowly improved, and on October 25, 2012 he was well enough to cheer on his Giants while attending Game 2 of the 2012 World Series at AT&T Park.

# APRIL

## 1

**1914**   Future Hall of Famer George Edward "Rube" Waddell dies from tuberculosis at age 37 in San Antonio, Texas. Known for his eccentricities on and off the field, Waddell was also one of the most dominant pitchers in baseball history. The imposing lefty led the American League in strikeouts six consecutive years (1902-1907), including the 1905 season when he also paced the league with 27 wins and a 1.48 ERA while leading the Philadelphia Athletics to the pennant.

**1972**   For the first time in Major League Baseball history, a regular season fails to begin on time as the MLB Players Association goes on strike. Baseball will resume on April 13 after the owners agree to add salary arbitration to the collective bargaining agreement and increase pension fund payments. A total of 86 games will be lost due to the strike, and an uneven shortened schedule will result.

> (i)   The Detroit Tigers (86-70) won the American League East by 1/2 game over the Boston Red Sox (85-70) in 1972 thanks in part to the uneven schedule which allowed them to play one more game than the Red Sox.

**1996**   During an Opening Day game between the host Reds and the Montreal Expos at Cincinnati's Riverfront Stadium, veteran umpire John McSherry, age 51, collapses on the field during the first inning and dies of a massive heart attack.

> (i)   Reds owner Marge Schott soon came under fire for her insensitive response to the tragedy after she publicly blamed the umpire's death for spoiling her team's Opening Day events.

**2013**   In the Los Angeles Dodgers' season-opening 4-0 win over the San Francisco Giants, ace Clayton Kershaw becomes the first pitcher since Bob Lemon in 1953 to homer and throw a shutout in an Opening Day game.

# 2

**1931**  Seventeen-year-old female pitcher Jackie Mitchell, a member of the Southern Association's Chattanooga Lookouts, strikes out Babe Ruth and Lou Gehrig in succession during an exhibition game with the New York Yankees at Engel Stadium in Chattanooga, Tennessee.

> (i) Soon after, Baseball Commissioner Kenesaw Mountain Landis voided Jackie Mitchell's contract with the Lookouts, declaring that baseball is "too strenuous" for women. Mitchell continued her professional baseball career by barnstorming with the House of David team.

**1992**  In a swap of young pitchers, the Philadelphia Phillies acquire future ace Curt Schilling from the Houston Astros in exchange for right-hander Jason Grimsley. Schilling will go 14-11 with a 2.35 ERA this season, and in 1993 will help lead the Phillies to a National League pennant. Grimsley will be released within a year without ever pitching for the Astros.

> DID YOU KNOW? In 1993, Curt Schilling became the first pitcher to claim an NLCS Most Valuable Player award without recording either a win or save in the series. Schilling was dominant (1.69 ERA in 16 innings), especially in the closeout Game 5, but it was reliever Mitch Williams who was credited with the win in both of Schilling's starts.

**2001**  Ichiro Suzuki debuts with the Seattle Mariners, becoming the first Japanese-born position player to participate in a Major League Baseball game. Suzuki will go on to lead the American League with a .350 batting average and 56 stolen bases in his historic rookie campaign.

> (i) Thought by many to be too frail to succeed in the majors, Ichiro quickly silenced his doubters by becoming the first player since Fred Lynn in 1975 to capture both the Rookie of the Year Award and MVP award in the same season.

> (i) In 2001, Ichiro also became the first player to lead his league in both batting average and steals since Jackie Robinson in 1949.

**2017**  San Francisco Giants ace Madison Bumgarner becomes the first pitcher in major league history to hit two home runs on Opening Day when he goes deep twice against the Arizona Diamondbacks at Chase Field.

**2019**  On the heels of his sensational rookie season, 21-year-old outfielder Ronald Acuña Jr. becomes the youngest player in big league history to sign a nine-figure deal when he agrees to an eight-year, $100 million contract extension with the Atlanta Braves.

# 3

**1966**   After having one professional contract voided and subsequently being ruled ineligible by the NCAA, University of Southern California pitching star Tom Seaver signs with the New York Mets. The right-handed prospect had previously agreed to a contract with the Atlanta Braves after they selected him in the January draft, but MLB Commissioner Spike Eckert voided the deal because the Braves had signed Seaver while USC's season was in progress. A lottery was then proposed, offering any other organization that was willing to match Atlanta's offer a chance to obtain Seaver's rights, and the Mets won out over the Cleveland Indians and Philadelphia Phillies.

**1987**   The Chicago Cubs trade fading starting pitcher Dennis Eckersley to the Oakland Athletics for three minor leaguers. Eckersley will resurrect his career in Oakland and emerge as the game's dominant closer, saving 320 games over the next nine seasons with the Athletics while making four All-Star teams and winning the 1992 American League Cy Young and MVP awards.

**1989**   At Oakland-Alameda County Coliseum, 19-year-old phenom Ken Griffey Jr. of the Seattle Mariners doubles in his first major league plate appearance off Oakland Athletics starter Dave Stewart.

**2003**   At 27 years, 249 days of age, Texas Rangers shortstop Alex Rodriguez becomes the youngest player in major league history to reach 300 career home runs. Rodriguez's fifth inning three-run blast allows him to surpass the mark of Hall of Famer Jimmie Foxx by 79 days.

**2005**   Tampa Bay Devil Rays Alex Sanchez becomes the first Major League Baseball player to violate the league's newly adopted drug policy and is suspended for 10 days without pay for testing positive for performance-enhancing substances.

# 4

**1911**   Automobile maker Hugh Chalmers introduces the concept of a Most Valuable Player award upon announcing that he will give a new Chalmers Model 30 roadster to the player in each league who is considered the most important and useful by a vote of baseball writers.

> (i)   In 1911, the winners of the inaugural Chalmers Award were Ty Cobb in the American League and Frank "Wildfire" Schulte in the National League.

**1974**   On his first swing of the 1974 season, Atlanta Braves slugger Hank Aaron ties Babe Ruth's all-time home run record when he slams No. 714 off Cincinnati Reds pitcher Jack Billingham at Riverfront Stadium.

**1988**   At Kansas City's Kauffman Stadium, George Bell of the Toronto Blue Jays becomes the first major leaguer to hit three home runs on Opening Day. Bell's homers, all coming against Royals ace Bret Saberhagen, power the Jays to a 5-3 victory.

**1994**   On Opening Day at Wrigley Field, Chicago Cubs outfielder Tuffy Rhodes becomes the first player in major league history to homer in his first three at-bats of a season, victimizing pitcher Dwight Gooden in the Cubs' 12-8 loss to the New York Mets.

> (i) Tuffy Rhodes homered only 13 times in six seasons as a part-time major leaguer, but hit 464 homers during his stellar 13-year stint in Japan's Nippon Professional Baseball.

**2001**   In his first start since joining the Boston Red Sox as a free agent, Hideo Nomo throws his second career no-hitter, defeating the Baltimore Orioles 3-0 at Camden Yards. The performance allows Nomo to join Jim Bunning, Nolan Ryan and Cy Young as the only pitchers to date to register no-hitters in both major leagues. The Japanese right-hander's gem is also the earliest no-hitter in major league history to date, occurring three days earlier than the no-hitters thrown by Houston's Ken Forsch in 1979 and Detroit's Jack Morris in 1984.

> (i) Nomo's first no-hitter came while pitching for the Los Angeles Dodgers against the Colorado Rockies at Denver's Coors Field on September 17, 1996.

**2003**   Chicago Cubs slugger Sammy Sosa belts his 500th career home run off Cincinnati Reds pitcher Scott Sullivan at Great American Ball Park, becoming only the 18th major leaguer to hit 500 or more home runs, as well as the first Hispanic player to do so.

# 5

**1913**   The first game is played at Brooklyn's Ebbets Field, with the Superbas defeating the crosstown Yankees 3-2 in a preseason exhibition before 25,000 fans.

> (i) Brooklyn outfielder and future Hall of Fame manager Casey Stengel hit the park's first home run on this day.

**1925** Following a New York Yankees spring training trip north to Ashville, North Carolina, star slugger Babe Ruth collapses at the railroad station. His condition is serious enough for him to be sent to St. Vincent's hospital in New York City, where he eventually undergoes surgery for what is believed to be an intestinal abscess. The Babe will remain hospitalized for seven weeks, keeping him out of the Yankee lineup until June 1.

> (i) The incident garnered international concern and became famously known as "The Bellyache Heard 'Round The World" as local sportswriters speculated that Ruth's illness was due to binging on hot dogs and soda pop.

**1983** On Opening Day at Shea Stadium, pitcher Tom Seaver makes his first start for the New York Mets since his trade to Cincinnati in 1977 and combines with Doug Sisk to shut out Steve Carlton and the Phillies 2-0. For "Tom Terrific," it's his 14th Opening Day assignment, tying the record set by Walter Johnson.

**1989** One of the most impressive streaks in baseball history comes to an end when Los Angeles Dodgers ace Orel Hershiser allows a run in the first inning of a game against the Cincinnati Reds. Hershiser's record scoreless innings streak ends at 59, one full inning better than Hall of Famer Don Drysdale's run of consecutive scoreless innings in 1968.

# 6

**1973** The late Roberto Clemente's uniform number 21 is retired by the Pittsburgh Pirates in a moving pregame ceremony before 51,695 fans at Three Rivers Stadium. Clemente, a four-time batting champion and 12-time All-Star during his eighteen seasons with the Pirates, died just months before in a New Year's Eve crash of a cargo plane carrying relief supplies to earthquake victims in Nicaragua.

>  The Pittsburgh Pirates wore a "21" patch for Roberto Clemente during the 1973 season, marking the first time a memorial patch ever appeared on a Major League Baseball uniform.

**1973** On Opening Day at Fenway Park, 24-year-old Ron Blomberg of the New York Yankees becomes the first designated hitter in major league history. In his first plate appearance, Blomberg walks with the bases loaded against Boston Red Sox ace Luis Tiant.

(i) Blomberg, the No. 1 overall pick in 1967 MLB Amateur Draft, adapted well to the new role and had his finest season in 1973, leading the Yankees in batting with a .329 average.

 As a prep star at Atlanta's Druid Hills High School, Ron Blomberg became the first athlete to earn Parade All-America honors in baseball, basketball and football.

**1987** A media firestorm erupts when Los Angeles Dodgers General Manager Al Campanis makes racially insensitive remarks during an appearance on the ABC news program *Nightline*. When asked why more African Americans had not become managers or executives, Campanis, a former teammate of Jackie Robinson, states that Blacks may lack certain "necessities" for those jobs, drawing the ire of host Ted Koppel.

(i) In response to the ensuing onslaught of harsh criticism, the Dodgers forced Campanis to resign within two days and Major League Baseball hired sociologist and civil rights activist Harry Edwards soon after to head an initiative to increase diversity among its leadership.

**2006** At Citizens Bank Park, Philadelphia Phillies shortstop Jimmy Rollins' hitting streak ends at 38 games after he goes 0-for-4 against the visiting St. Louis Cardinals.

(i) At the time, Rollins' streak ranked as the eighth-longest in major league history.

**2014** Texas Rangers ace Yu Darvish becomes the fastest starter in major league history to amass 500 career strikeouts after fanning David DeJesus and Wil Myers in the first inning of a game against the Tampa Bay Rays. Darvish reaches the milestone in only 401 2/3 innings, surpassing the mark of 404 2/3 innings set by Kerry Wood.

# 7

**1969** Bill Singer of the Los Angeles Dodgers earns the first official save in major league history when he tosses three scoreless innings in relief of Don Drysdale to close out the Dodgers' 3–2 Opening Day win over the Cincinnati Reds.

(i) The save, invented by sportswriter Jerome Holtzman, became an official statistic prior to the 1969 season.

**1979** Ken Forsch of the Houston Astros throws the earliest no-hitter in major league history to date, shutting down the Atlanta Braves 6-0 at the

Astrodome. Forsch's gem tops the previous mark set by Bob Feller, who threw a no-no on the 16th of April for the Cleveland Indians against the Chicago White Sox in 1940. Ken also became half of the first brother tandem to each throw major league no-hitters, joining younger brother Bob, who no-hit the Philadelphia Phillies in 1978 as a member of the St. Louis Cardinals.

1984   In front of a national television audience, Detroit Tigers ace Jack Morris no-hits the Chicago White Sox at Comiskey Park, earning a 4-0 victory and tying Ken Forsch's mark for the earliest no-hitter in a major league season. The no-hitter is the first by a Tiger since Jim Bunning accomplished the feat in 1958.

(i) Jack Morris was magnificent in his first 11 starts of the 1984 season, posting a 9-1 record with a 1.97 ERA during that stretch. Morris' sustained excellence was a big reason why the Detroit Tigers rocketed to a major league-record 35-5 start to the season.

# 8

1963   At Crosley Field in Cincinnati, hometown kid Pete Rose of the Reds draws a walk against Earl Francis of the Pittsburgh Pirates in his first major league plate appearance. Over the course of his remarkable 24-year career, Rose will shatter the record for major league plate appearances, finishing with 15,890.

(i) Rose also scored his first major league run in this game when Frank Robinson plated him with a first inning two-run homer.

1974   In front of a national television audience and a record crowd at Atlanta Stadium, Braves outfielder Hank Aaron hits home run No. 715, breaking Babe Ruth's legendary career home run record. The historic blast, served up by Los Angeles Dodgers pitcher Al Downing, comes on Aaron's first swing of the season in front of the home fans and sparks a lengthy mid-game celebration on the field.

(i) Hank Aaron broke another significant record earlier in the game when he scored his 2,063rd career run to surpass Willie Mays' National League mark for runs scored.

1975   Future Hall of Famer Frank Robinson becomes the first black manager in major league history when he debuts as player-manager of the Cleveland Indians. The 39-year-old Robinson celebrates the historic event in grand style by drilling a home run in his first plate appearance.

(i) Frank Robinson's memorable blast gave him a major league-record eight Opening Day home runs, surpassing by one the career marks of Babe Ruth, Willie Mays and Eddie Mathews.

2016  At Coors Field, Colorado Rockies shortstop Trevor Story homers twice against the San Diego Padres to become the first rookie to hit home runs in each of his first four major league games and the first player to hit six home runs in the first four games of a major league season.

# 9

1916  Following a prolonged salary dispute, the Boston Red Sox trade star centerfielder Tris Speaker to the Cleveland Indians on the last day of Spring Training. In exchange, the Indians send pitcher Sad Sam Jones, minor league infielder Fred Thomas and $55,000 to the Red Sox. Speaker will go on to lead the American League in batting average (.386), hits (211), doubles (41), on-base percentage (.470), slugging percentage (.502) and total bases (287) this season.

1965  With United States President and Texas native Lyndon Johnson among a crowd of nearly 48,000 on hand for the official opening of Houston's Astrodome, the host Astros claim a 2-1 exhibition win over the New York Yankees in Major League Baseball's first indoor game.

> ⓘ  Yankees slugger Mickey Mantle hit the first-ever indoor home run when he went deep in the sixth inning.

1966  On Opening Day at Washington's D.C. Stadium, Emmett Ashford becomes the first black umpire in major league history. The 51-year-old Ashford, who started his professional umpiring career 15 years earlier in the low minor leagues and most recently served as the Pacific Coast League's Umpire-in-Chief, will ump for five seasons in the American League before retiring in 1970.

> DID YOU KNOW?  In 1951, Emmett Ashford became the first black umpire in Organized Baseball when he worked games in the Southwestern International League.

1981  The phenomenon soon to be known as "Fernandomania" has its genesis when Los Angeles Dodgers rookie pitcher Fernando Valenzuela impresses with a complete game, five-hit shutout against the Houston Astros. The 20-year-old lefty will bolt to an 8-0 start (with a 0.50 ERA and 68 strikeouts) and quickly gain a legion of fans on his way to becoming the first rookie recipient of the Cy Young Award.

2001  Wilver Dornell "Willie" Stargell, nicknamed "Pops" in the later years of his career, dies at age 61 in Wilmington, North Carolina. A beloved member of the Pittsburgh Pirates for his entire 21-year career, Stargell was best known for his tremendous power and great leadership. The 1988 Baseball Hall of Fame inductee won the 1979 National League MVP award, hit 475 career home runs and led the Pirates to World Series titles in 1971 and 1979.

# 10

**1947**  Jackie Robinson becomes the first black player of the 20th century to sign a major league contract when he agrees to a one-year deal with the Brooklyn Dodgers. The 28-year-old Robinson, personally recruited by Dodgers GM Branch Rickey for his exceptional character as well as his skill, will officially topple Major League Baseball's long-standing color barrier when he makes his Brooklyn debut five days later.

**1989**  Nineteen-year-old sensation Ken Griffey Jr. of the Seattle Mariners hits his first major league home run, a first inning opposite field blast off White Sox starter Eric King at the Kingdome. Griffey will hit 630 homers during his brilliant 22-year career, ranking him fifth on the all-time home run list at the time of his retirement.

> (i) Griffey's father was an outfielder with the Cincinnati Reds at the time, making the two the first father-son duo to play in the major leagues simultaneously.

**2000**  Cincinnati Reds star Ken Griffey Jr. belts his 400th major league home run in a 7-5 loss at Colorado, becoming the youngest player to date to reach that milestone. At 30 years, 141 days of age, Griffey Jr. eclipses Hall of Famer Jimmie Foxx's previous standard by 107 days.

> (i) The historic home run served as a special 50th birthday present for Ken Griffey Sr., who witnessed the event while serving as the Reds bench coach.

# 11

**1906**  On the eve of Opening Day, New York Giants charismatic star "Turkey Mike" Donlin marries Mabel Hite, a stunning 21-year-old vaudeville sensation. Donlin, a .337 career hitter with an adoring fan base, will soon leave baseball for several years to tour and perform with Hite, setting aside a baseball career that had Hall of Fame potential.

**1907**  On Opening Day, New York Giants catcher Roger Bresnahan causes a stir when he takes his position behind home plate wearing leg guards similar to those used by cricket players. The safety measure is initially met with derision, but soon shin guards will become standard catching equipment.

(i) Later that season, Bresnahan also developed the first leather batting helmet after suffering a near-fatal beaning on June 18.

DID YOU KNOW ? This game also holds the distinction of being the only Opening Day forfeit in major league history. After eight innings of play, umpire Bill Klem ordered the game forfeited to the Philadelphia Phillies after rowdy fans at the Polo Grounds threw snowballs onto the field.

1917 Boston Red Sox star Babe Ruth tosses a complete game three-hitter, earning a 10-3 Opening Day victory over the New York Yankees. For Ruth, the performance is a harbinger of good things to come as he'll post a career-best 24 wins in 1917 while leading the American League with 35 complete games.

1996 Atlanta Braves pitcher Greg Maddux sees his major league record streak of 18 consecutive road victories come to an end in a 2–1 loss to the San Diego Padres.

(i) During the streak, Maddux posted a sparkling 0.99 ERA and .70 WHIP and allowed three or fewer earned runs in all 20 of his starts.

## 12

1877 Harvard star James Tyng becomes the first catcher to wear a facemask in a game. Despite controversy surrounding who invented the mask, Harvard manager/law student Fred Thayer claims it as his own and wisely patents it the following year.

1965 The Harris County Domed Stadium, better known as the Astrodome, hosts its first regular-season Major League Baseball game. The Philadelphia Phillies defeat the hometown Houston Astros 2-0 as reigning National League Rookie of the Year Richie Allen hits the first official indoor home run in major league history.

1970 At Yankee Stadium, iconic center fielders Joe DiMaggio and Mickey Mantle are in attendance for a dedication ceremony held in their honor as their plaques are enshrined in the stadium's historic Monument Park.

## 13

1926 In perhaps the greatest Opening Day pitchers' duel ever, Walter Johnson of the Washington Senators defeats knuckleballer Eddie Rommel and the Philadelphia Athletics 1-0 in 15 innings. The victory marks a record sixth Opening Day shutout for the 38-year-old Johnson.

1954   Twenty-year-old Hank Aaron makes his major league debut. Batting fifth and playing left field for the Milwaukee Braves, Aaron goes hitless in five at-bats in a 9–8 loss to the Cincinnati Redlegs.

1962   St. Louis Cardinals legend Stan Musial breaks Mel Ott's National League record for runs scored when he crosses the plate for the 1,860th time in his career in the Cardinals' 8-5 win over the Chicago Cubs at Wrigley Field.

1963   After 16 hitless plate appearances to start the season, Cincinnati Reds second baseman Pete Rose records his first major league hit when he triples off Bob Friend in the Reds' 12-4 loss to the visiting Pittsburgh Pirates.

(i)   The future all-time hits leader went on to claim Rookie of the Year honors this season after batting .273 and scoring 101 runs.

1984   Pete Rose of the Montreal Expos records his 4,000th career hit when he doubles off Philadelphia Phillies veteran Jerry Koosman. Rose, whose 4,000th hit comes exactly 21 years after his first, joins Ty Cobb as the only members of the 4,000 Hit Club.

2019   Baltimore Orioles first baseman Chris Davis ends his major league-record streak of 54 consecutive hitless at-bats when he singles off Rick Porcello in the first inning of the Orioles' 9-5 win over the Boston Red Sox.

(i)   Davis' run of futility easily surpassed the previous mark of 46 straight hitless at-bats established by Eugenio Vélez in 2010-2011.

# 14

1910   At League Park in Washington, D.C., William Howard Taft becomes the first United States president to open a season with a ceremonial first pitch. Washington Senators ace Walter Johnson, who momentarily doubled as Taft's catcher, adds to the special day by throwing a 3-0 one-hit shutout against future Hall of Famer Eddie Plank and the Philadelphia Athletics.

1922   Future Hall of Famer Adrian Constantine "Cap" Anson dies at age 69 in Chicago, Illinois. Regarded as baseball's first superstar, Anson managed the Chicago White Stockings to five National League pennants and became the first major leaguer to amass 3,000 career hits, ending with a total of 3,435.

1941   Pete Rose, Major League Baseball's Hit King, is born in Cincinnati, Ohio.

1953   Cleveland Indians right-hander Bob Lemon becomes the first pitcher in major league history to throw a shutout and homer in an Opening Day game. The future Hall of Famer hits a solo shot in four at-bats and dominates on the mound, allowing just a first-inning single to Minnie Minoso in a 6-0 win over the visiting Chicago White Sox.

1969   At Montreal's Parc Jarry, the expansion Expos defeat the visiting St. Louis Cardinals 8–7 in the first regular-season major league game played outside the United States. The first home run hit in Canada is recorded in the opening inning when Expos outfielder Mack Jones launches a three-run shot off Nelson Briles.

# 15

1883   Francis Richter publishes the first issue of *Sporting Life*, a weekly newspaper which will quickly become early baseball's most influential publication.

1942   At Sportsman's Park, Hiram "Hi" Bithorn becomes the first Puerto Rican to appear in a major league game, pitching two scoreless innings in relief for the Chicago Cubs in a 4-2 loss to the St. Louis Cardinals.

1947   Jackie Robinson breaks Major League Baseball's color barrier when he debuts for the Brooklyn Dodgers against the Boston Braves at Ebbets Field. Robinson goes 0-for-3 but plays flawlessly at first base and scores the deciding run in a 5–3 victory.

1958   In the first Major League Baseball game played on the West Coast, a park-record crowd of 23,448 at San Francisco's Seals Stadium watches Rubén Gómez of the hometown Giants toss an 8-0 shutout against Don Drysdale and the Los Angeles Dodgers.

2000   Cal Ripken Jr. of the Baltimore Orioles becomes the 24th player to reach the 3,000-hit plateau when he singles in the seventh inning of the Orioles' 6-4 win over the Minnesota Twins at the Metrodome.

# 16

1938   The Chicago Cubs take a gamble on former MVP Dizzy Dean, acquiring him from the St. Louis Cardinals for pitchers Curt Davis and Clyde Shoun, outfielder Tuck Stainback and $185,000. Considered by some to be washed up following his career-threatening toe injury, Dean will recover to help lead the Cubs to the World Series this season by compiling a 7-1 record with a team-best 1.81 ERA.

1940   Cleveland Indians ace Bob Feller begins the season by tossing the first Opening Day no-hitter in major league history. Weathering chilly temperatures and a brisk wind at Chicago's Comiskey Park, the 21-year-old Feller shuts down the White Sox, winning 1–0.

1983   A capacity crowd at Dodger Stadium sees San Diego Padres first baseman and longtime Dodgers star Steve Garvey eclipse Billy Williams' National League record of 1,117 consecutive games played.

> ⓘ Garvey's streak ended at 1,207 games later that season when he dislocated his thumb in a home plate collision on July 29.

# 17

1953   New York Yankees 21-year-old outfielder Mickey Mantle hits the longest home run in Griffith Stadium history. The mammoth shot off Washington Senators lefty Chuck Stobbs clears the leftfield bleachers and nestles in an adjacent housing complex. After using a tape measure to estimate how far the ball traveled, Yankees publicist Red Patterson reports an astonishing distance of 565 feet.

> ⓘ Mantle's blast entered lore as one of baseball's greatest feats of strength, and gave rise to the fascination with "tape measure" home runs.

1960   Cleveland Indians GM "Trader" Frank Lane sends outfielder Rocky Colavito, the defending American League home run leader, to the Detroit Tigers for 1959 AL Batting Champ Harvey Kuenn. Colavito, a huge fan favorite while in Cleveland, will average 35 home runs and 108 RBIs in four prime seasons with the Tigers while Kuenn will spend one injury-shortened season with the Indians before being traded away.

1976   With the wind blowing out at Wrigley Field, Philadelphia Phillies third baseman Mike Schmidt becomes just the 10th player in major league history to hit four home runs in one game. Schmidt's extraordinary power display helps the Phillies overcome an 11-run deficit to beat the Chicago Cubs 18–16 in ten innings.

2012   In the Colorado Rockies' 5–3 victory over the San Diego Padres at Coors Field, left-hander Jamie Moyer, at 49 years, 150 days of age, becomes the oldest pitcher in major league history to earn a win. Moyer eclipses the previous mark set in 1932 by Jack Quinn of the Brooklyn Dodgers.

# 18

**1899**  John McGraw makes his managerial debut for the National League's Baltimore Orioles in a 5–3 win over the New York Giants - the team he will later manage for more than 30 years.

**1923**  Yankee Stadium, known as "The House That Ruth Built," opens to a major league-record crowd of 74,217. Fittingly, Babe Ruth christens the park with a third-inning, three-run home run, leading the New York Yankees to a 4-1 victory over the Boston Red Sox.

 On this same day future Yankees star Lou Gehrig, then a standout for Columbia University, struck out seventeen Williams College batters to set a school record.

**1946**  Six months after joining the Brooklyn Dodgers organization, Jackie Robinson breaks Organized Baseball's longstanding color barrier as he makes his first regular season appearance with the Montreal Royals of the International League. The 27-year-old trailblazer makes an immediate impression with a home run and three singles on his way to winning the league batting title.

**1981**  Cincinnati Reds pitcher Tom Seaver fans Keith Hernandez of the St. Louis Cardinals to become only the fifth pitcher in major league history to reach 3,000 career strikeouts, joining Walter Johnson, Bob Gibson, Gaylord Perry and Nolan Ryan.

**1987**  Mike Schmidt of the Philadelphia Phillies hits his 500th career home run in an 8–6 win over the Pittsburgh Pirates at Three Rivers Stadium. Schmidt's three-run shot comes off Don Robinson with two outs in the ninth inning, lifting the Phillies to a come-from-behind victory.

# 19

**1949**  The New York Yankees dedicate a granite monument in center field to the recently deceased Babe Ruth prior to their Opening Day game at Yankee Stadium. The Yankees also unveil plaques honoring Lou Gehrig and former manager Miller Huggins.

ⓘ After the ceremony, Tommy Henrich's two-out, ninth-inning solo home run gave the Yankees a 3–2 walk-off win over the Washington Senators.

1960   Roger Maris goes 4-for-5 with two home runs and four RBIs in his New York Yankees debut, leading his new club to an 8–4 win over the Boston Red Sox at Fenway Park. Maris will total 39 home runs and 112 RBIs this season on his way to earning American League MVP honors.

1965   The ceiling of the newly-opened Houston Astrodome is painted white in order to improve fielding conditions by reducing the sun's glare. This alteration will eventually cause the grass playing surface to die, necessitating the use of artificial turf - soon to be known as AstroTurf - next season.

2013   In Boston, the Red Sox game against the Kansas City Royals is postponed when a massive manhunt for the second of two suspects in the Boston Marathon bombings prompts a lockdown of the city.

# 20

1889   Al Spalding and a group of Chicago White Stockings and National League All-Stars complete their unprecedented world baseball tour, playing one final game at West Side Park in Chicago. The troupe had spent the previous six months promoting baseball - and Spalding's sporting goods - while visiting 14 countries and five continents.

1908   Baseball pioneer and future Hall of Famer Henry Chadwick dies at age 83 in Brooklyn, New York. A renowned sportswriter, statistician and baseball historian, Chadwick is credited with developing the modern baseball box score and introducing statistics such as Earned Run Average and Batting Average. He also helped strengthen and popularize early baseball through his work as editor of the Spalding and Reach annual guides and his service as chairman of baseball's early rules committees.

1912    Boston's newly built Fenway Park plays host to its first professional game as the hometown Red Sox claim a thrilling 7-6 come-from-behind victory over the New York Highlanders. Star Tris Speaker ends the game with an RBI single in the eleventh inning. Minutes later, the Detroit Tigers defeat the Cleveland Naps 6-5 to christen their new home - Navin Field.

(i)   Both park openings were overshadowed in the news by the continuing coverage of the sinking of the *Titanic*, an event which occurred five days earlier.

1939   Ted Williams makes his major league debut for the Boston Red Sox, going 1-for-4 with a double in a 2–0 road loss to the New York Yankees on

Opening Day. Only six games from the end of his career, Lou Gehrig goes hitless and commits an error in the only matchup to feature the two iconic sluggers.

1982 At Atlanta-Fulton County Stadium, the host Braves become the first team in major league history to start a season with twelve straight victories as they claim a 4-2 come-from-behind win over the Cincinnati Reds.

> (i) Atlanta added a 13th and final win to their historic streak when they defeated the Reds again the following night.

2006 At 47 years, 240 days of age, Julio Franco of the New York Mets becomes the oldest player in major league history to hit a home run when he lines a pinch-hit, two-run homer in the Mets' 7–2 victory over the San Diego Padres. The record had belonged to Philadelphia Athletics pitcher Jack Quinn, who was 46 years, 357 days old when he homered on June 27, 1930.

# 21

1880 One of Organized Baseball's early stars becomes the first player victimized by the newly implemented reserve system when George Wright, now bound to the Providence Grays under the new league agreement, is restricted from signing with another club despite not being able to come to terms with the Grays. Wright instead opts to temporarily retire and focus on his burgeoning sporting goods business rather than play the upcoming season with Providence.

1966 The Chicago Cubs acquire 23-year-old pitcher Ferguson Jenkins in a five-player trade with the Philadelphia Phillies. The deal will prove to be one of the best in Cubs history as Jenkins will soon reel off a franchise-record six consecutive 20-win seasons and finish with 167 victories in 10 seasons with Chicago.

1996 At The Ballpark in Arlington, Brady Anderson of the Baltimore Orioles extends his own record by hitting a leadoff home run in a fourth consecutive game.

> (i) Despite Anderson's exploits, the Orioles lost all four games.

2000 Mo Vaughn, Tim Salmon and Troy Glaus become the first trio of teammates to hit home runs in the same inning twice in one major league game. The three Angels reach the seats in the fourth and ninth innings, leading Anaheim to a 9–6 win over the Tampa Bay Devil Rays.

# 22

**1876**  Boston Red Stockings star and future Hall of Famer George Wright becomes the first batter in National League history when he steps to the plate against the host Philadelphia Athletics.

> DID YOU KNOW? Two of George Wright's sons were tennis greats. Beals Wright won an Olympic gold medal and U.S. National Championship, and Irving Wright claimed a U.S. mixed doubles National Championship.

**1897**  Louis Sockalexis, a member of the Penobscot Indian tribe of Maine, becomes the first recognized minority to play in the National League when he takes the field for the Cleveland Spiders in a 3-1 loss to the host Colonels at Louisville's Eclipse Park.

**1914**  Nineteen-year-old Babe Ruth makes his professional pitching debut, hurling a six-hit, 6–0 shutout for the International League's Baltimore Orioles against the Buffalo Bisons.

> (i) The second batter Ruth faced was Joe McCarthy, Ruth's future manager with the New York Yankees.

**1970**  Following a pregame ceremony in which he received his 1969 Cy Young Award, Tom Seaver of the New York Mets wows the Shea Stadium crowd with a sensational complete-game, 2-1 victory over the San Diego Padres, rewriting the record books in the process. "Tom Terrific" fans the last 10 batters he faces - a record for consecutive strikeouts in one game - and notches 19 total strikeouts to tie Steve Carlton's single-game record.

> (i) Seaver topped the Mets single-game strikeout record of 15, a mark that was set just five days earlier by fellow flamethrower Nolan Ryan.

**2008**  Atlanta Braves 40-year-old starter John Smoltz becomes the 16th pitcher in major league history to reach 3,000 career strikeouts when he fans the Washington Nationals' Felipe Lopez in the third inning of the Braves' 6-0 loss at Turner Field.

# 23

**1939**  At Fenway Park, rookie Ted Williams of the Boston Red Sox slugs his first major league home run and adds three more hits in a 12-8 loss to the Philadelphia Athletics.

1952   In the New York Giants' 9-5 defeat of the Boston Braves, knuckleballing reliever Hoyt Wilhelm earns his first career victory and homers in his first big league at-bat. Wilhelm will win 142 more games during his 21-year Hall of Fame career, but he'll never hit another home run.

1954   Hank Aaron of the Milwaukee Braves hits the first home run of his major league career in a 7-5 loss to the St. Louis Cardinals at Sportsman's Park. The blast comes off pitcher Vic Raschi, who also gave up Aaron's first big league hit eight days earlier.

1999   St. Louis Cardinals third baseman Fernando Tatis becomes the first player in major league history to hit two grand slams in one inning, connecting twice in an 11-run third inning against Chan Ho Park of the Los Angeles Dodgers.

2000   Bernie Williams and Jorge Posada become the first pair of teammates to homer from both sides of the plate in the same game as they power the New York Yankees to a 10–7 win over the Blue Jays.

# 24

1901   In the first-ever American League game, the Chicago White Sox claim an 8-2 victory over the Cleveland Blues. Cleveland outfielder Ollie Pickering becomes the first player to bat in the new league, and Roy Patterson earns the first win.

1962   Los Angeles Dodgers pitcher Sandy Koufax matches Bob Feller's single-game strikeout record when he fans 18 Chicago Cubs in a 10–2 win at Wrigley Field.

# 25

1976   Midway through a Chicago Cubs-Los Angeles Dodgers game, Cubs center fielder Rick Monday, a former Marine Corps reservist, races into left field and grabs an American flag away from two protesters who were about to set it on fire. The Dodger Stadium crowd gives Monday a standing ovation for his act of patriotism, then spontaneously breaks out into the singing of "God Bless America."

1984   At Olympic Stadium in Montreal, Dwight Gooden of the New York Mets becomes the first teenager to strike out ten or more batters in a major league game since the Minnesota Twins' Bert Blyleven accomplished the feat in 1970.

> ⓘ  By season's end, the 19-year-old phenom would post 15 double-digit strikeout games and finish with a major league rookie-record 276 strikeouts.

2001 Rickey Henderson of the San Diego Padres breaks Babe Ruth's career walks record when he draws free pass No. 2,063 in the Padres' 5–3 loss to the Philadelphia Phillies.

# 26

1904 Seventeen-year-old Ty Cobb makes his professional debut, smashing a double and home run for the Augusta Tourists of the South Atlantic League.

1959 Sadaharu Oh of the Yomiuri Giants hits the first home run of his Nippon Professional Baseball career. Oh will go on to hit a professional baseball-record 868 home runs across 22 seasons with the Giants.

1990 Texas Rangers star Nolan Ryan ties Bob Feller's career record with his 12th and final one-hitter. The 43-year-old Ryan strikes out 16 and allows only a check-swing single to Ron Kittle, leading his team to a 1–0 win over the Chicago White Sox.

# 27

1947 Babe Ruth Day is celebrated throughout Major League Baseball. An ailing Ruth, now nearing the end of his life due to throat cancer, gives an emotional farewell speech to a capacity crowd at Yankee Stadium.

1971 At Atlanta Stadium, Hank Aaron notches his 600th career home run when he hammers a third inning shot off San Francisco Giants starter Gaylord Perry. The Atlanta Braves slugger edges closer to Babe Ruth (714) and Willie Mays (633) on the all-time home run list.

1983 Houston Astros flamethrower Nolan Ryan fans the 3,509th batter of his career, breaking Walter Johnson's 56-year-old career strikeout record. The new strikeout king is coronated when he catches pinch-hitter Brad Mills looking in the eighth inning of the Astros' 4-2 defeat of the Montreal Expos.

# 28

1930 Independence, Kansas hosts the first night game in the history of Organized Baseball as the Muskogee Chiefs earn a 13-3 victory over the Independence Producers in Western Association action.

1956 Frank Robinson of the Cincinnati Redlegs hits the first home run of his Hall of Fame career in a 9-1 defeat of the Chicago Cubs. The 20-year-old slugger will unanimously earn National League Rookie of the Year honors this season after clouting a rookie record-tying 38 home runs.

1961    Milwaukee Braves 40-year-old ace Warren Spahn becomes the second oldest major leaguer (behind only Cy Young, 41) to pitch a no-hitter to date when he shuts down the San Francisco Giants 1-0 at Milwaukee's County Stadium.

> (i) Spahn threw his first no-hitter just six starts earlier on September 16, 1960.

1989   Rickey Henderson of the New York Yankees sets a record when he leads off a game with a home run for the 36th time in his major league career, breaking the mark previously held by Bobby Bonds.

# 29

1931    In a stellar all-around performance against his brother Rick and the St. Louis Browns, 23-year-old Wes Ferrell of the Cleveland Indians becomes the first pitcher in big league history to homer and throw a no-hitter in the same game. Ferrell blanks St. Louis 9-0 while collecting a home run, double and four RBIs.

> (i) Wes Ferrell slugged nine home runs in 1931, setting a single-season major league record for pitchers.

>  Hall of Fame catcher Rick Ferrell hit 28 home runs in 7,076 major league plate appearances while younger brother Wes belted 38 homers - an all-time record for pitchers - in just 1,344 career plate appearances.

1936   In the first game ever played in the Japan Professional Baseball League, Nagoya claims an 8-5 victory over Dai Tokyo at Koshien Stadium. Harris McGalliard, Nagoya's starting catcher, becomes the first American to play professional baseball in Japan.

1981    Philadelphia Phillies hurler Steve Carlton becomes the sixth major league pitcher - and first left-hander - to reach 3,000 career strikeouts when he fans Tim Wallach of the Montreal Expos in the Phillies' 6–2 victory.

1986   Right-hander Roger Clemens of the Boston Red Sox strikes out a major league-record 20 batters in a 3–1 win over the Seattle Mariners at Fenway Park. The 23-year-old ace breaks the mark of 19 strikeouts previously set by Steve Carlton, Nolan Ryan and Tom Seaver.

> (i) The attendance total for this historic game was just 13,414, in part because the eventual NBA World Champion Boston Celtics were hosting a playoff game across town.

2006 Slugging superstar Albert Pujols of the St. Louis Cardinals hits his 14th homer of April to set a new major league home run record for the month. The tie-breaking solo shot lifts the Cardinals to a 2-1 victory over the Washington Nationals.

2019 Los Angeles Dodgers star Cody Bellinger breaks the major league mark for most runs batted in by May 1 when he collects his 37th RBI of the season in the Dodgers' 3-2 loss to the San Francisco Giants. The previous record was set in 1998 by both Juan Gonzalez and Mark McGwire.

> (i) Bellinger also set the record for most total bases by May 1 (97), and tied the home run mark (14).

# 30

1922 In just his fourth big league start, 26-year-old rookie Charlie Robertson of the Chicago White Sox pitches a 2-0 perfect game against the Detroit Tigers at Navin Field. It is the fifth perfect game in major league history, and the last until Don Larsen accomplished the feat in Game 5 of the 1956 World Series.

1923 Columbia University star Lou Gehrig signs with the New York Yankees for $1,500 and a salary of $400 per month. The 19-year-old Gehrig had convinced Yankees scout Paul Krichell of his worth earlier in the day when he backed his own complete game victory over New York University with a mammoth home run.

1939 Playing in his 2,130th consecutive game, Lou Gehrig of the New York Yankees goes hitless in four at-bats against the Washington Senators to drop his season batting average to .143. It will be the final game of Gehrig's career.

1961 Willie Mays becomes the ninth player in major league history to hit four home runs in one game as he leads the San Francisco Giants to a 14-4 victory over the host Milwaukee Braves. Mays misses a chance at a fifth homer when the game ends with him on deck.

> (i) Mays accomplished the feat despite recovering from a bout of food poisoning likely caused by an order of spare ribs that he and roommate Willie McCovey shared the night before.

2019 CC Sabathia of the New York Yankees records his 3,000th career strikeout when he fans John Ryan Murphy in the second inning of the Yankees' 3-1 loss to the Arizona Diamondbacks. The 38-year-old Sabathia becomes the 17th pitcher - and third left-hander - to reach the 3,000-strikeout plateau.

# MAY

## 1

**1884** Catcher Moses Fleetwood Walker becomes the first full-time black player in major league history when he takes the field for the Toledo Blue Stockings in an American Association game against the Louisville Eclipse. Walker will be released by the Blue Stockings after he sustains an injury in mid-July, and no other African American player will see action in the majors until Jackie Robinson joins the Brooklyn Dodgers in 1947.

**1926** Satchel Paige makes his professional debut at the age of 19 in the Negro Southern League. Paige and the Chattanooga Black Lookouts defeat the Birmingham Black Barons 5-4.

**1951** Nineteen-year-old phenom Mickey Mantle of the New York Yankees belts his first major league home run, a two-run shot off reliever Randy Gumpert in an 8-3 win over the Chicago White Sox at Comiskey Park.

**1959** Early Wynn of the Chicago White Sox strikes out 14 and allows just one hit in a 1–0 win over the Boston Red Sox. At the plate, Wynn supports himself with a home run and a double. The 39-year-old hurler will go on to earn Cy Young Award honors this season after leading the White Sox to their first pennant since 1919.

**1991** Nolan Ryan of the Texas Rangers extends his own record by throwing his seventh career no-hitter in a 3–0 defeat of the Toronto Blue Jays at Arlington Stadium. The 44-year-old Ryan also earns distinction by becoming the oldest pitcher in major league history to throw a no-hitter, surpassing the mark he set one year earlier.

**1991** Oakland Athletics outfielder Rickey Henderson passes Lou Brock to become baseball's all-time steals leader when he swipes his 939th base during the Athletics' 7-4 win over the New York Yankees at Oakland-Alameda County Coliseum.

# 2

**1876**   At Avenue Grounds in Cincinnati, Ross Barnes of the Chicago White Stockings hits the first home run in National League history, going deep off Cherokee Fisher in the fifth inning of a 15-9 victory over the Reds.

> (i)   Barnes led the league in nearly every offensive category in 1876, including batting average (.429), hits (138), runs scored (126), doubles (21), triples (14), total bases (190), on-base percentage (.462) and slugging percentage (.590).

**1917**   In a pitching duel for the ages, Fred Toney of the Cincinnati Reds and the Chicago Cubs' Hippo Vaughn each carry no-hitters into the 10th inning at Chicago's Weeghman Park before Vaughn falters, giving up two hits and a run. Toney completes his no-hitter, leading the Reds to a 1-0 victory.

> (i)   Fred Toney, no stranger to marathon masterpieces, pitched a 17-inning no-hitter eight years earlier for Winchester in the Blue Grass League.

> DID YOU KNOW?   In perhaps the greatest pitching duel in major league history, it was Olympic champion Jim Thorpe who drove in the lone run.

**1920**   The Indianapolis ABCs host the Chicago American Giants in the first-ever Negro National League game. The ABCs, featuring Oscar Charleston, defeat the Rube Foster-managed Giants 4–2.

**1939**   New York Yankees first baseman Lou Gehrig ends his record streak of 2,130 consecutive games played when he removes himself from the lineup prior to a game with the Detroit Tigers at Briggs Stadium. The Yankees captain tells manager Joe McCarthy he cannot play due to ongoing weakness, which doctors later diagnose as amyotrophic lateral sclerosis, a fatal muscular disease. Already in rapidly declining health, Gehrig never plays again.

**1954**   Stan Musial of the St. Louis Cardinals hits a record five home runs in a doubleheader against the New York Giants, launching three homers in the first game and two more in the nightcap. The record will later be matched by Nate Colbert who, coincidentally, is in attendance at Sportsman's Park on this day and witnesses his idol's historic feat.

**1995**   Hideo Nomo debuts with the Los Angeles Dodgers, becoming the first Japanese native to play in the major leagues since 1965. The five-time Nippon Professional Baseball All-Star will produce a sensational rookie campaign, fashioning a 13-6 record with a league-leading 236 strikeouts. Nomo's eye-opening success will pave the way for a large number of Japanese-born players who will soon follow him to the major leagues.

> (i) In 1997, Nomo became the fastest pitcher in major league history to date to reach 500 career strikeouts, doing it in only 444 $^2/_3$ innings.

**2002** Seattle Mariners outfielder Mike Cameron becomes the 13th player in major league history to hit four home runs in one game as the Mariners rout the Chicago White Sox 15-4. Cameron and Bret Boone also become the first teammates in history to hit back-to-back home runs twice in the same inning, performing the feat in Seattle's 10-run first.

# 3

**1927** Jesse and Virgil Barnes become the first pair of brothers to oppose each other as starting pitchers in a major league game. Virgil and the New York Giants secure a 7-6 win over older brother Jesse and the Brooklyn Robins.

**1936** At Yankee Stadium, 21-year-old Joe DiMaggio makes his much-anticipated major league debut. Batting third in front of slugger Lou Gehrig, DiMaggio triples and singles twice in New York's 14-5 pummeling of the St. Louis Browns.

# 4

**1869** The Cincinnati Red Stockings debut as baseball's first openly all-professional club, claiming a 45-9 victory over the amateur Great Westerns of Cincinnati. Led by player-manager Harry Wright, the Red Stockings will win an additional 56 straight games this year during an undefeated barnstorming tour across America.

**1871** The Fort Wayne Kekiongas host Forest City of Cleveland in the first major league game ever played, with Fort Wayne earning a 2-0 victory over their National Association opponent. Future Hall of Famer Deacon White of Forest City records the first major league hit when he doubles in the opening inning.

**1960** The Chicago Cubs engineer an unusual trade that sees WGN broadcaster Lou Boudreau come down from the radio booth to switch places with manager Charlie Grimm.

> (i) After guiding the Cubs to a 54-83 record, Lou Boudreau returned to his broadcasting role at WGN after the season and remained there until 1987.

1966  Willie Mays of the San Francisco Giants hits his 512th career homer to establish a new National League record. Mays' blast, which moves him past former New York Giants great Mel Ott on the all-time home run list, helps the Giants beat the Los Angeles Dodgers 6-1.

1975  At Candlestick Park, Bob Watson of the Houston Astros scores the one millionth run in Major League Baseball history as the San Francisco Giants top the Astros 8-6.

2010  Beloved broadcaster William Earnest "Ernie" Harwell dies of cancer at age 92 in Novi, Michigan. Harwell is best remembered for his warm, southern accent and relaxed style as the "voice" of the Detroit Tigers, for whom he announced games for over four decades. In 1981, he became just the fifth recipient of the Ford C. Frick Award from the Baseball Hall of Fame.

2018  Los Angeles Angels slugger Albert Pujols becomes the 32nd member of the 3,000 Hit Club when he singles off Mike Leake in the Angels' 5-0 win over the Seattle Mariners.

> ⓘ The historic hit also allowed Pujols to join Hank Aaron, Willie Mays and Alex Rodriguez as the only players in major league history to amass 3,000 hits and 600 home runs.

# 5

1904  Cy Young pitches the first perfect game in Major League Baseball's modern era as the Boston Americans defeat Rube Waddell and the Philadelphia Athletics 3-0.

1949  Charlie Gehringer, former star second baseman of the Detroit Tigers and 1937 American League MVP, earns enshrinement in the Baseball Hall of Fame, garnering 159 of 187 votes (85%) from the Baseball Writers Association of America.

> DID YOU KNOW? Charlie Gehringer played in every inning of the first six All-Star Games, batting a remarkable .500 in 20 at-bats.

1978  Pete Rose of the Cincinnati Reds becomes the 14th player in major league history to reach 3,000 career hits when he singles off Steve Rogers in a 4-3 loss to the Montreal Expos at Riverfront Stadium.

2004  New York Mets slugger Mike Piazza establishes a major league record for home runs by a catcher when he goes deep in the Mets' 8-2 win over the

San Francisco Giants at Shea Stadium. The historic homer, Piazza's 352$^{nd}$ as a catcher, moves him past Carlton Fisk on the all-time list.

2018   After closing out a 6-5 win over the Texas Rangers, Craig Kimbrel of the Boston Red Sox reaches 300 career saves in record time, setting new marks in terms of age (29), fewest appearances (494) and fewest save opportunities (330).

# 6

1915   Boston Red Sox rookie pitcher Babe Ruth hits his first major league home run, a solo shot off Jack Warhop of the New York Yankees at the Polo Grounds.

1925   New York Yankees shortstop Everett Scott's record streak of 1,307 consecutive games played comes to an end when he's benched in favor of rookie Pee Wee Wanninger in New York's 6-2 home loss to the Philadelphia Athletics.

> (i) Scott held the consecutive games played record until fellow Yankee Lou Gehrig surpassed it in 1933.

1931   Superstar center fielder Willie Mays, baseball's one and only "Say Hey Kid," is born in Westfield, Alabama.

1953   St. Louis Browns rookie Bobo Holloman tosses a no-hitter in his first major league start, blanking the Philadelphia Athletics 6-0 at Sportsman's Park. The 30-year-old Holloman will never pitch another complete game in the majors and will win only two more games during his brief big league career.

1982   Gaylord Perry of the Seattle Mariners becomes the 15th major league pitcher to reach 300 career wins when he beats the New York Yankees 7–3 at the Kingdome.

1998   Chicago Cubs rookie Kerry Wood makes history when he strikes out 20 batters in a 2–0 win over the Houston Astros at Wrigley Field. The 20-year-old Wood joins Roger Clemens as the only major leaguers to fan 20 batters in a nine-inning game and eclipses Bill Gullickson's single-game rookie record of 18 strikeouts.

# 7

1957   Cleveland Indians star pitcher Herb Score suffers a career-altering injury when he's struck in the face by a line drive off the bat of Gil McDougald of the New York Yankees. The 23-year-old lefty leaves the game with a broken nose and a damaged right eye, injuries which will force him to miss the remainder of the season.

(i) After returning to action in 1958, Score went 17-26 with a 4.43 ERA in parts of five seasons before retiring in 1962, never again approaching the spectacular start to his career that produced two All-Star selections, two strikeout titles and a 38-20 record.

1959   A major league record-breaking crowd of 93,103 packs the Los Angeles Memorial Coliseum for Roy Campanella Night, an event held in honor of the former Dodgers star catcher who was paralyzed in a car accident in 1958. The Los Angeles Dodgers play an exhibition game against the New York Yankees as part of the festivities, losing 6-2.

2009   Major League Baseball suspends Los Angeles Dodgers outfielder Manny Ramirez 50 games for use of a banned substance. Ramirez becomes the most prominent player suspended under the league's current drug policy.

2010   Jamie Moyer of the Philadelphia Phillies becomes the oldest pitcher in major league history to throw a shutout when he blanks the visiting Atlanta Braves 7–0. At 47 years, 170 days of age, Moyer eclipses by almost a year the previous record held by Phil Niekro. Moyer also becomes the first pitcher to throw shutouts in four different decades.

2016   Just 17 days shy of his 43rd birthday, New York Mets pitcher Bartolo Colon becomes the oldest player to hit his first major league home run when he goes deep against James Shields of the San Diego Padres at Petco Park. Colon surpasses the previous mark set by Hall of Fame pitcher Randy Johnson, who was 40 years and nine days old when he hit his first (and only) career homer.

# 8

1871   Third baseman Ezra Sutton of the Cleveland Forest Citys hits the first home run in professional baseball history, a fourth-inning blast in Cleveland's 14-12 loss to the Chicago White Stockings.

1963   St. Louis Cardinals legend Stan Musial surpasses Babe Ruth's all-time record of 1,356 extra base hits when he homers off former teammate Bob Miller of the Los Angeles Dodgers in an 11–5 Cardinals win.

1968   At Oakland-Alameda County Coliseum, Athletics pitcher Catfish Hunter tosses the first American League regular-season perfect game in 46 years, blanking the Minnesota Twins 4–0.

(i) At the plate, Hunter went 3-for-4 and drove in three runs.

1984  Kirby Puckett collects four singles in his major league debut, leading the Minnesota Twins to a 5–0 win over the California Angels. Puckett becomes just the ninth player in history to record four or more hits in his first nine-inning major league game.

2001  Arizona Diamondbacks star Randy Johnson strikes out 20 in the D'backs' 4–3, 11-inning win over the Cincinnati Reds. Johnson, who was relieved after the ninth inning, becomes the first left-hander to record 20 strikeouts in a major league game.

2012  At Baltimore's Camden Yards, Josh Hamilton of the Texas Rangers hits four two-run home runs and collects an American League-record 18 total bases in the Rangers' 10–3 win over the Orioles.

2018  Seattle Mariners lefty James Paxton, a Ladner, British Columbia native, becomes just the second Canadian to throw a major league no-hitter and the first to do so in Canada when he blanks the Toronto Blue Jays 5-0.

# 9

1871  Twenty-one-year-old Cuban infielder Esteban Bellán becomes the first Latin American in the major leagues, playing as Steve Bellan for the Troy Haymakers of the National Association.

1973  Cincinnati Reds star catcher Johnny Bench belts three home runs off Steve Carlton for the second time in his young career, leading the Reds to a 9-7 win over the Philadelphia Phillies at Veterans Stadium. Having homered in his final plate appearance the previous night, Bench ties a major league record with four consecutive home runs.

1999  Florida State University junior second baseman Marshall McDougall sets NCAA single-game records when he hits six home runs and collects 16 RBIs in a 26–2 rout of Maryland.

2019  Albert Pujols of the Los Angeles Angels records the 2,000th RBI of his career when he belts a solo home run in the third inning of the Angels' 13-0 win over the Detroit Tigers. The 39-year-old slugger becomes just the third player to reach the 2,000-RBI plateau, joining Hank Aaron and Alex Rodriguez.

# 10

1909  Fred Toney, pitching for the Blue Grass League's Winchester Hustlers, throws the longest no-hitter in Organized Baseball history, blanking the

Lexington Colts for 17 innings in a 1-0 victory. Toney walks just one batter while striking out 19.

> ⓘ Toney entered his name in the record books again later in his career when, while with the Cincinnati Reds, he and the Chicago Cubs' Hippo Vaughn threw the only double no-hitter in major league history on May 2, 1917.

1936   New York Yankees phenom Joe DiMaggio hits his first major league home run in a 7–2 win over the Philadelphia Athletics. The victory propels the Yankees into first place, where they will remain the rest of the season.

1970   Atlanta Braves 46-year-old reliever Hoyt Wilhelm becomes the first pitcher in major league history to amass 1,000 career appearances when he pitches the ninth in a 6-5 loss to the St. Louis Cardinals.

# 11

1904   Midway through another fantastic performance, Boston Americans star Cy Young sees his record streak of hitless innings come to an end at 25 1/3 when Sam Crawford of the Detroit Tigers singles with one out in the seventh inning. Prior to this game, Young had pitched no-hit baseball during successive appearances on April 25 (final three innings), April 30 (seven innings of relief) and May 5 (perfect game).

> ⓘ Cy Young was nearly untouchable again on this day, throwing a 15-inning shutout to defeat Ed Killian and the Tigers 1-0.

1977   With his team in the throes of a 16-game losing streak, Atlanta Braves owner Ted Turner places skipper Dave Bristol on sabbatical and takes over managerial duties himself. It doesn't help, as the Braves lose 2-1 to the Pittsburgh Pirates in Turner's debut. The National League will soon intervene and boot Turner from the dugout, ending his managerial career after just one game.

1980   Pete Rose of the Philadelphia Phillies steals second base, third base and home in the seventh inning of a 7–3 win over the Cincinnati Reds at Riverfront Stadium. The 39-year-old Rose becomes the first National League player to accomplish this feat since Jackie Robinson in 1954.

1998   After fanning 20 Houston Astros five days earlier, Kerry Wood of the Chicago Cubs strikes out 13 in a 4-2 win over the Arizona Diamondbacks. The 20-year-old's total of 33 strikeouts over consecutive games breaks the previous record of 32 shared by Luis Tiant, Nolan Ryan, Dwight Gooden and Randy Johnson.

**2003** At the Ballpark in Arlington, Rafael Palmeiro of the Texas Rangers becomes the 19th major leaguer to reach 500 career home runs when he hits a two-out, seventh-inning blast off Dave Elder in a 17–10 victory over the Cleveland Indians.

**2016** In an overwhelming performance at Nationals Park, Washington pitcher Max Scherzer joins Roger Clemens, Kerry Wood and Randy Johnson as the only major league pitchers to notch 20 strikeouts in a nine-inning start. Scherzer misses his chance for strikeout No. 21 when Detroit Tigers catcher James McCann, who had fanned in his three previous at-bats, grounds into a game-ending force out to seal the Nationals' 3-2 win.

> (i) Scherzer, like Clemens, Wood and Johnson before him, completed his 20-strikeout game without issuing a walk.

# 12

**1926** Washington Senators star Walter Johnson joins Cy Young as the only major leaguer pitchers to reach 400 career wins when he records a complete-game, 7-4 victory over the visiting St. Louis Browns.

**1970** At Wrigley Field, Ernie Banks of the Chicago Cubs becomes the eighth member of the 500 Home Run Club when he launches a solo shot off Atlanta Braves pitcher Pat Jarvis in the second inning of a 4-3 Cubs win.

**2000** Boston Red Sox ace Pedro Martinez ties the American League record for most strikeouts over two consecutive games when he fans 15 in a 9-0 defeat of the Baltimore Orioles after recording 17 strikeouts versus the Tampa Bay Devil Rays in his previous start on May 6.

# 13

**1942** In a 6-5 win over the visiting Chicago Cubs, Jim Tobin of the Boston Braves becomes the only pitcher in modern major league history to hit three home runs in a single game.

> (i) Tobin's attempt at a fourth homer in his final at-bat was caught against the left-field fence.

**1952** Ron Necciai of the Appalachian League's Bristol Twins rewrites the record books when he strikes out 27 batters in a 7-0 no-hitter against the Welch Miners.

1958  Stan Musial of the St. Louis Cardinals becomes the eighth major leaguer to reach 3,000 career hits when he lines a pinch-hit double off Moe Drabowsky in the Cardinals' 5–3 come-from-behind win over the Chicago Cubs at Wrigley Field.

1976  George Brett of the Kansas City Royals ties the major league record of six consecutive games with three or more hits when he goes 3-for-4 against the White Sox at Royals Stadium. The 22-year-old third baseman notched 18 hits in 26 at-bats during the streak, raising his season batting average from .277 to .396.

> ⓘ  Brett would go on to claim his first batting title in 1976 after leading the American League with a .333 average.

2006  Major League Baseball introduces a new Mother's Day tradition when players and umpires wear bright pink wristbands and several players use pink bats. The items are auctioned off following the day's play, raising $350,000 for Susan G. Komen, a breast cancer awareness organization.

# 14

1913  During a 10-5 win over the St. Louis Browns, Washington Senators ace Walter Johnson breaks Jack Coombs' major league record of 53 consecutive scoreless innings when he stretches his own streak to 55 2/3 straight before finally giving up a run in the 4th inning. Johnson's mark will stand until Don Drysdale surpasses it by 2 1/3 innings in 1968.

1920  Walter Johnson records his 300th major league win as he shuts down the Detroit Tigers over the final 3 2/3 innings of the Washington Senators' 9-8 come-from-behind victory at Griffith Stadium.

>   The Big Train is the only pitcher in major league history to earn his 300th career win while working in relief.

1939  Lena Feller is struck by a foul ball off the bat of Chicago White Sox third baseman Marv Owen on Mother's Day. Lena's son, pitcher Bob Feller of the Cleveland Indians, threw the pitch that resulted in his mother needing seven stitches above her right eye. With his mother at the hospital, Feller completes a 9–4 Indians win.

1967  Mickey Mantle of the New York Yankees becomes the sixth major leaguer to reach 500 career home runs when he belts a seventh-inning solo shot off Stu Miller in a 6–5 victory over the Baltimore Orioles at Yankee Stadium.

# 15

1941   New York Yankees star Joe DiMaggio launches his historic 56-game hitting streak when he singles in the first inning of a 13-1 loss to the Chicago White Sox.

1951   The Boston Red Sox celebrate the American League's 50th Anniversary as 29 former players, managers and umpires, including Cy Young, Connie Mack, Tom Connolly, Hugh Duffy and Clark Griffith, gather for a special ceremony at Fenway Park. In the game that follows, the Chicago White Sox upstage Ted Williams' 300th career home run by claiming a 9-7, 11-inning victory with the winning runs coming on Nellie Fox's first career homer.

1973   Nolan Ryan of the California Angels throws the first of his seven career no-hitters, blanking the host Kansas City Royals 3–0. Ryan strikes out 12 and gets some help from shortstop Rudy Meoli, who makes a fantastic over-the-shoulder catch in the eighth inning to help preserve the gem.

1976   Mark Fidrych of the Detroit Tigers wins his first major league start, tossing a complete game two-hitter in a 2-1 win over the Cleveland Indians. Known as "The Bird," Fidrych draws attention for talking to the ball and tamping down the mound with his hands before each inning.

1981   Len Barker of the Cleveland Indians pitches the 11th perfect game in major league history, blanking the Toronto Blue Jays 3-0 at Cleveland Stadium. The reigning American League strikeout champion fans 11 and never reaches a 3-ball count on the night.

2019   Right-hander Edwin Jackson establishes a major league record by appearing in a game for his 14th big league team when he takes the mound for the Toronto Blue Jays at San Francisco's Oracle Park.

# 16

1954   Boston Red Sox star Ted Williams is spectacular in his return from a broken collarbone, going 8-for-9 with two home runs and seven RBIs in a double-header against the Detroit Tigers.

1957   Following a 3-0 win over the Kansas City Athletics, a group of New York Yankees players celebrate Billy Martin's 29th birthday at the Copacabana night club in Manhattan, and mayhem ensues. Hank Bauer allegedly starts a fight that becomes well-publicized, and the Yankees fine Mickey Mantle, Hank Bauer, Yogi Berra, Whitey Ford, Johnny Kucks and Billy Martin for their involvement.

Martin, viewed by Yankee management as a troublesome influence, will be traded to Kansas City one month later.

1965  Nineteen-year-old pitcher Jim Palmer of the Baltimore Orioles earns his first big league win and hits his first major league home run in a 7-5 victory over the New York Yankees at Memorial Stadium.

2012  Colorado Rockies 49-year-old pitcher Jamie Moyer becomes the oldest player in major league history to collect an RBI when he drives in two runs in the Rockies' 6-1 victory over the Arizona Diamondbacks.

# 17

1925  Tris Speaker of the Cleveland Indians becomes the fifth major leaguer to reach 3,000 career hits when he singles off Tom Zachary in the Indians' 2-1 home loss to the Washington Senators.

1939  Columbia University and Princeton University square off in the first-ever televised baseball game. The contest is aired on W2XBS, an experimental station in New York City that will later become WNBC-TV. Bill Stern provides the historic play-by-play for the 2-1 Princeton victory.

1970  Hank Aaron of the Atlanta Braves becomes the ninth member of the 3,000 Hit Club when he singles off Wayne Simpson in a 7-6, 15-inning loss to the Cincinnati Reds.

1979  With winds gusting out at Wrigley Field, the Philadelphia Phillies outlast the Chicago Cubs 23–22 in a wild slugfest. Dave Kingman of the Cubs hits three home runs while Philadelphia's Mike Schmidt slugs two, including the game-winner in the 10th inning.

1998  New York Yankees lefty David Wells fires the 15th perfect game in major league history, downing the Minnesota Twins 4-0 in front of a raucous crowd at Yankee Stadium. Wells' perfecto is the first by a Yankees pitcher since Don Larsen's gem in Game 5 of the 1956 World Series.

> (i) Coincidentally, Don Larsen and David Wells attended the same high school - Point Loma High School in San Diego, California.

2011  Harmon Clayton Killebrew, nicknamed "Killer", dies at age 74 in Scottsdale, Arizona. The soft spoken Killebrew was power personified during his 22-year Hall of Fame career. The 13-time All-Star captured six home run titles and amassed 573 lifetime homers, figures which ranked him second only to Babe Ruth in American League history at the time of his retirement.

# 18

1968  Washington Senators slugger Frank Howard establishes a new major league record for most home runs hit in a week when he belts his 10th homer since May 12 in the Senators' 8-4 win over the Detroit Tigers.

2004  Forty-year-old Randy Johnson of the Arizona Diamondbacks becomes the oldest pitcher to throw a perfect game when he blanks the Atlanta Braves 2-0 at Turner Field. The big lefty also joins Jim Bunning, Hideo Nomo, Nolan Ryan and Cy Young as the only hurlers to record no-hitters in both major leagues.

# 19

1962  Stan Musial of the St. Louis Cardinals becomes the National League's all-time hits leader during an 8–1 win over the Los Angeles Dodgers. The 41-year-old's ninth-inning single is the 3,431st hit of his major league career, moving him past Pittsburgh Pirates great Honus Wagner.

# 20

1871  Former National Association pitcher Mort Rogers introduces the first in a series of collectible "photographic score cards" at a Boston Red Stockings home game against the Philadelphia Athletics, pioneering the concept that would ultimately evolve into baseball cards.

1919  Babe Ruth of the Boston Red Sox belts his first career grand slam and pitches a complete game in Boston's 6-4 win over the St. Louis Browns at Sportsman's Park.

1984  Roger Clemens earns the first of his 354 career wins as he pitches the Boston Red Sox to a 5-4 defeat of the Minnesota Twins.

2000  Rickey Henderson of the Seattle Mariners joins Ted Williams and Willie McCovey as the only major leaguers to homer in four different decades when he goes deep in the first inning of a 4-3 loss to the Tampa Bay Devil Rays.

> ⓘ  The historic long ball was also Henderson's 76th career leadoff homer, extending his own major league record. He hit No. 77 the following day.

# 21

1981  Yale's Ron Darling and Frank Viola of St. John's square off in what many consider the greatest pitchers' duel in college baseball history. The two aces match zeroes through eleven innings, with Darling maintaining a no-hitter to go along with 16 strikeouts. St. John's finally prevails 1-0 one inning later when Steve Scafa bloops a single and then steals second, third and home.

(i) Darling's masterpiece remains the longest single-game string of no-hit innings in NCAA history.

2013  In a 12-0 rout of the Seattle Mariners, Los Angeles Angels of Anaheim 21-year-old star Mike Trout becomes the youngest player in American League history to hit for the cycle. After recording a single in the third inning, a triple in the fourth and a double in the sixth, Trout homers to deep right-center field in the eighth inning to complete the feat.

(i) At 21 years, 288 days of age, Trout surpassed by three weeks the record previously held by former Mariner Alex Rodriguez.

# 22

1942  Despite receiving a draft deferment, Boston Red Sox star Ted Williams opts to enlist in the Navy to support the United States war effort. The 23-year-old will finish out this season before joining the Navy's V-5 program to become a fighter pilot.

1949  Brooklyn Dodgers righty Don Newcombe makes a splash in his first major league start, going the distance in a 3-0 victory over the Cincinnati Reds to become the first National League pitcher in 11 years to throw a shutout in his first start. Newcombe shines at the plate as well, driving in two of the three Dodgers runs.

1975  Hall of Famer Robert Moses "Lefty" Grove dies at age 75 in Norwalk, Ohio. One of the most dominant pitchers in major league history, Grove led the American League in ERA a record nine times and won seven consecutive strikeout titles while compiling a spectacular 300-141 record in 17 seasons with the Philadelphia Athletics and Boston Red Sox.

1990  Andre Dawson of the Chicago Cubs sets a new major league record when he draws five intentional walks in a 2–1, 16-inning win over the Cincinnati Reds.

# 23

1901  On his way to winning the 1901 American League Triple Crown, Philadelphia Athletics star Nap Lajoie becomes the first player in major league history to receive an intentional walk with the bases loaded when Chicago White Sox player-manager Clark Griffith issues the free pass while leading 11-7 in the ninth inning. The strategy pays off when the next three Athletics are retired in order, giving the White Sox an 11-9 win.

2000 Rickey Henderson of the Seattle Mariners draws the 2,000th walk of his career in a 4-2 loss to the Baltimore Orioles. Henderson joins Babe Ruth and Ted Williams as the only players in major league history to date to reach the 2,000-walk plateau.

2002 Los Angeles Dodgers outfielder Shawn Green goes 6-for-6 with four home runs, six runs scored and seven RBIs in the Dodgers' 16–3 win over the Milwaukee Brewers at Miller Park. Green becomes the 14th major leaguer to hit four home runs in one game and sets a big league record with 19 total bases.

# 24

1928 A major league-record 13 future Hall of Famers play in the New York Yankees' 9-7 victory over the Philadelphia Athletics at Shibe Park when Earle Combs, Leo Durocher, Lou Gehrig, Waite Hoyt, Tony Lazzeri and Babe Ruth see action for the Yankees while Ty Cobb, Mickey Cochrane, Eddie Collins, Jimmie Foxx, Lefty Grove, Al Simmons and Tris Speaker appear for Philadelphia.

ⓘ Managers Miller Huggins of the Yankees and Connie Mack of the Athletics were also Cooperstown-bound, as were two of the umpires for the star-studded affair - Tom Connolly and Bill McGowan.

1935 The first official night game in major league history takes place at Cincinnati's Crosley Field as 25,000 watch the host Reds defeat the Philadelphia Phillies 2-1. President Franklin D. Roosevelt kicks off the historic event by ceremoniously turning on the ballpark lights by throwing a switch at the White House.

1936 Tony Lazzeri sets a new American League mark by driving in 11 runs in the New York Yankees' 25-2 dismantling of the Philadelphia Athletics at Shibe Park. The slugging second baseman's big day includes a triple and three home runs, two of which are grand slams.

 On this day, Tony Lazzeri became the first player in major league history to hit two grand slams in one game.

1984 The Detroit Tigers achieve the best 40-game start in major league history when they improve to 35-5 after defeating the host California Angels

5-1. The Tigers also establish a new American League mark by earning their 17th consecutive road victory.

# 25

1935  Showing one last glimpse of his past glory, Babe Ruth of the Boston Braves goes 4-for-4 with three home runs and six RBIs in an 11–7 loss to the Pittsburgh Pirates. The 40-year-old's third home run, the 714th and last of his career, is the first to clear the roof of Pittsburgh's Forbes Field.

1937  At Yankee Stadium, Detroit Tigers player-manager Mickey Cochrane sees his stellar 13-year playing career come to an abrupt end when he suffers a near fatal beaning from Bump Hadley of the New York Yankees.

> ⓘ The 34-year-old Cochrane eventually recovered and made his return as bench manager later in 1937, but he proved to be a less effective leader without his on-field responsibilities. Cochrane's .320 career batting average, two MVP awards and a well-deserved reputation as one of baseball's greatest catchers and leaders earned him induction into the Baseball Hall of Fame in 1947.

1982  Ferguson Jenkins of the Chicago Cubs becomes the seventh pitcher in major league history to reach 3,000 career strikeouts when he fans Garry Templeton of the San Diego Padres in a 2-1 loss at Jack Murphy Stadium.

1989  Just weeks after debuting Ken Griffey Jr., the Seattle Mariners add another key piece to their young nucleus by acquiring future Hall of Fame pitcher Randy Johnson from the Montreal Expos in a five-player deal that sees lefty ace Mark Langston head to the Expos.

# 26

1956  Aloysius Harry "Al" Simmons (born Aloys Szymanski) dies at age 54 in Milwaukee, Wisconsin. A premier hitter and outfielder during his 20-year career, Simmons batted over .300 and drove in more than 100 runs in each of his first eleven major league seasons. He was a key member of the Philadelphia Athletics World Championship teams of 1929 and 1930, and was inducted into the Baseball Hall of Fame in 1953.

1959  In one of the most remarkable pitching performances in baseball history, Pittsburgh Pirates lefty Harvey Haddix pitches twelve perfect innings to start the game against the Milwaukee Braves before finally faltering. Haddix loses his perfect game in the 13th when Felix Mantilla reaches first base on a

Don Hoak throwing error to start the inning, then loses the game one out later when Joe Adcock drives in Mantilla for the contest's only run.

1993   Texas Rangers outfielder Jose Canseco unintentionally aids his opponent during a 7-6 loss to the Cleveland Indians when a long fly ball hit by Carlos Martinez caroms off Canseco's head and sails over the Cleveland Stadium fence for a home run.

> (i) Three days later in a 15-1 loss to the Boston Red Sox, Canseco blew out his arm when he was allowed to throw 33 pitches in mop-up duty.

# 27

1937   New York Giants ace Carl Hubbell picks up the 24th and final victory of his major league-record winning streak when he pitches two perfect innings of relief in the Giants' 3-2 road win over the Cincinnati Reds. Slugger Mel Ott homers in the ninth to provide the winning margin.

1953   Jesse Cail Burkett, nicknamed "Crab" because of his serious demeanor, dies at age 84 in Worcester, Massachusetts. During his 16-year major league career, the 1946 Hall of Fame inductee compiled a .338 lifetime average while twice batting over .400 in a season.

1968   A pair of future Hall of Fame first basemen are born on the same day 1,200 miles apart - Jeff Bagwell in Boston, Massachusetts and Frank Thomas in Columbus, Georgia.

1997   Seattle Mariners star Ken Griffey Jr. breaks his own major league mark for home runs hit through May when he launches his 23rd of the season in the Mariners' 11-10 loss to the Minnesota Twins.

# 28

1951   After going 0-for-12 to start his major league career, New York Giants rookie Willie Mays blasts a 450-foot home run off ace Warren Spahn in a 4-1 loss to the Boston Braves.

>  Over the course of his big league career, Willie Mays hit more home runs against Warren Spahn (18) than any other pitcher.

1956   Pittsburgh Pirates first baseman Dale Long establishes a new major league record by homering in his eighth consecutive game when he takes Carl Erskine deep in the Pirates' 3-2 defeat of the Brooklyn Dodgers at Forbes Field.

2006 Barry Bonds of the San Francisco Giants passes Babe Ruth on the all-time home run list when he belts the 715th homer of his major league career, a two-run shot off Byung-Hyun Kim in the Giants' 6-3 victory over the visiting Colorado Rockies.

# 29

1922 The U.S. Supreme Court famously rules that Major League Baseball is not interstate commerce and, therefore, is exempt from federal antitrust laws. As a result, major league players will continue to be bound by the reserve clause for the next five decades.

1962 Former Negro League player-manager Buck O'Neil becomes the first black coach in Major League Baseball history when he takes on that role with the Chicago Cubs.

1971 Cincinnati's Big Red Machine adds more horsepower, acquiring 22-year-old outfielder George Foster from the San Francisco Giants for shortstop Frank Duffy and pitcher Vern Geishert. Foster will develop into a dominant offensive force with the Reds, earning the 1977 National League MVP award and five All-Star selections during his eleven seasons in Cincinnati.

1990 Oakland Athletics star Rickey Henderson breaks Ty Cobb's 62-year-old American League stolen base record when he swipes his 893rd career base during a 2-1 home loss to the Toronto Blue Jays. After sliding safely into third, Henderson pulls the base from its moorings and raises it over his head in celebration of the accomplishment.

2010 Roy Halladay of the Philadelphia Phillies tosses the 20th perfect game in major league history, defeating the Florida Marlins 1-0 at Sun Life Stadium.

# 30

1884 At Chicago's tiny Lakeshore Park, White Stockings third baseman Ned Williamson becomes the first player in National League history to hit three home runs in one game, leading his team to a 12-2 victory over the Detroit Wolverines. Williamson will clout 27 homers this season (25 at home) - a major league record that will stand until Babe Ruth surpasses it in 1919.

1894  Boston Beaneaters second baseman Bobby Lowe becomes the first major leaguer to hit four home runs in one game during a 20–11 drubbing of the Cincinnati Reds at Boston's Congress Street Grounds.

1935  At Philadelphia's Baker Bowl, 40-year-old Babe Ruth of the Boston Braves makes his final major league appearance as a player, grounding out in one at-bat against Philadelphia Phillies pitcher Jim Bivin.

1956  In the fifth inning of a 4-3 win over the Washington Senators, star outfielder Mickey Mantle of the New York Yankees comes within 18" of becoming the first player to hit a home run out of Yankee Stadium when his left-handed blast off starter Pedro Ramos hits the roof's facade in deep right field.

1982  Cal Ripken Jr. of the Baltimore Orioles begins his historic streak of 2,632 consecutive games played by going 0-for-2 with a walk in a 6–0 loss to the Toronto Blue Jays.

# 31

1890  George Gore and future Hall of Famers Buck Ewing and Roger Connor become the first major league trio to homer consecutively, leading the Players' League New York Giants to a 23-3 mauling of the Pittsburgh Burghers.

1937  A massive crowd at the Polo Grounds sees Carl Hubbell's major league-record 24-game win streak come to an end as the visiting Brooklyn Robins hand King Carl and the New York Giants a 10-3 loss.

2008  Manny Ramirez of the Boston Red Sox becomes the 24th member of the 500 Home Run Club when he launches a solo shot off Chad Bradford in Boston's 6-3 road victory over the Baltimore Orioles.

# JUNE

## 1

1917   Boston Braves catcher Hank Gowdy becomes the first active major leaguer to enlist in World War I. The 1914 World Series star will serve with distinction in the Great War as a key member of the famed "Rainbow Division," the Fighting 42nd.

> (i) Gowdy also participated in World War II as a major in the United States Army, becoming the only big league player to serve in both world wars.

1925   Lou Gehrig of the New York Yankees launches his iconic record streak of 2,130 consecutive games played when he flies out as a pinch-hitter against legendary pitcher Walter Johnson in a 5-3 loss to the Washington Senators.

> (i) This game also marked Babe Ruth's return to baseball following his famous illness, coined the "Bellyache Heard 'Round the World."

1975   California Angels star Nolan Ryan ties Sandy Koufax's career record of four no-hitters when he blanks the Baltimore Orioles 1-0 at Anaheim Stadium. The win is the 100th of Ryan's career.

2012   Johan Santana tosses the first no-hitter in the 50-year history of the New York Mets, defeating the St. Louis Cardinals 8-0. Outfielder Mike Baxter seriously injures himself when he makes a highlight reel catch against the left field fence in the seventh to preserve Santana's gem.

## 2

1891   Charles "Old Hoss" Radbourn of the Cincinnati Reds becomes the fourth pitcher to reach 300 major league wins when he defeats the host Boston Beaneaters 10-8 at South End Grounds. Radbourn will retire later this season, finishing his 11-year career with a 309-194 record.

1925  Twenty-one-year-old Lou Gehrig makes his way into the New York Yankees starting lineup for the first time when manager Miller Huggins pencils him in at first base to replace longtime starter Wally Pipp. Columbia Lou responds by going 3-for-5 to help lead the Yankees to an 8-5 win over the Washington Senators. Gehrig will hold on to his starting spot for the next 14 seasons, while the usurped Pipp will play only sparingly before being sold to the Cincinnati Reds in the offseason.

1935  Aging icon Babe Ruth, batting just .181 in 28 games this season with the Boston Braves, officially announces his retirement from baseball.

> (i) The Sultan of Swat finished his spectacular major league career with 714 home runs, a figure which at that time was more than twice that of any other player (Gehrig, 353).

1941  Hall of Famer Henry Louis "Lou" Gehrig, nicknamed "The Iron Horse," dies at age 37 in New York City, New York. One of the best and most admired players in baseball history, Gehrig established himself as a devastating offensive force during his 17-year career with the New York Yankees, scoring and driving in 100-plus runs in thirteen consecutive seasons while amassing a .340 lifetime batting average, 493 home runs and 1,995 RBIs. He dominated the postseason too, batting .361 while powering the Yankees to seven pennants and six World Series titles. Gehrig's career and memorable consecutive games-played streak ended prematurely when he was debilitated by amyotrophic lateral sclerosis, the neurodegenerative disease that ultimately took his life.

2010  Detroit Tigers pitcher Armando Galarraga's bid for a perfect game against the Cleveland Indians falls one out short when first base umpire Jim Joyce makes an incorrect call, turning an obvious Galarraga putout at first into a Jason Donald infield single. Galarraga finishes with a one-hit, 3-0 victory when the next batter grounds out to end the game. Upon seeing the video replay after the game and realizing his error, Joyce issues an emotional apology and Galarraga graciously accepts, simply stating "Nobody's perfect."

# 3

1888  The baseball poem Casey at the Bat, written by Ernest Lawrence Thayer, is first published in the San Francisco Examiner.

1925  Eddie Collins of the Chicago White Sox becomes the sixth player in major league history to reach 3,000 career hits when he singles against Rip Collins in a 4-1 victory over the Detroit Tigers at Navin Field.

1932  New York Yankees slugger Lou Gehrig becomes the first American League player - and the first major leaguer since Ed Delahanty in 1896 - to hit four home runs in one game as the Bronx Bombers blast the Philadelphia Athletics 20–13 at Shibe Park. A great catch by centerfielder Al Simmons in the ninth robs Gehrig of a potential fifth home run.

> (i)  This slugfest rewrote the record books as the Yankees tallied a major league-record 50 total bases and the two teams combined to establish a new major league high for extra base hits with 41.

> (i)  Gehrig, accustomed to playing second fiddle to Babe Ruth, was again overshadowed on his record-setting day when John McGraw, another New York baseball legend, announced his retirement from baseball.

1932  Faced with a worsening sinus condition, 59-year-old John McGraw, baseball's pugnacious "Little General," retires as manager of the New York Giants after guiding the team for 31 seasons, ending a 33-year managerial career that produced a 2,763-1,948 record, 10 pennants and three World Series titles.

> DID YOU KNOW? John McGraw became the first manager to win four straight pennants when he led the Giants to the World Series in each season from 1921-1924.

1995  In the Montreal Expos' 1-0, ten-inning victory over the San Diego Padres, Expos ace Pedro Martinez pitches nine perfect innings before allowing a leadoff double to Bip Roberts in the 10th. Martinez joins Harvey Haddix as the only pitchers in major league history to have a perfect game broken up in extra innings.

2017  Los Angeles Angels of Anaheim slugger Albert Pujols becomes the ninth player in major league history to reach 600 career home runs when he slugs a grand slam against starter Ervin Santana in the Angels' 7-2 defeat of the Minnesota Twins.

> (i)  The 37-year-old Pujols became the fourth youngest player to reach the milestone, and the first to do so with a grand slam.

2017  For the first time in major league history, seven grand slams are hit on the same day. Contributing to the record are Matt Adams of the Atlanta Braves, Ian Desmond of the Colorado Rockies, Albert Pujols of the Los Angeles Angels of Anaheim, Travis Shaw of the Milwaukee Brewers, Kyle Schwarber of the Chicago Cubs, Chris Taylor of the Los Angeles Dodgers and Mike Zunino of the Seattle Mariners.

# 4

**1890**  Tim Keefe of the New York Giants becomes the second pitcher to amass 300 major league victories when he and the Giants defeat the Boston Reds 9-4. The 33-year-old Keefe joins fellow future Hall of Famer Pud Galvin in the exclusive club.

**1964**  Los Angeles Dodgers ace Sandy Koufax throws his major league record-tying third career no-hitter, leading the Dodgers to a 3-0 defeat of the Philadelphia Phillies. Koufax strikes out 12 and issues only one walk, narrowly missing his first perfect game.

**1968**  Don Drysdale of the Los Angeles Dodgers blanks the Pittsburgh Pirates 5-0 for his sixth consecutive shutout, in the process breaking both Doc White's 64-year-old record of five straight shutouts and Carl Hubbell's 1933 mark of 54 consecutive scoreless innings.

> (i)  Drysdale's remarkable scoreless innings streak ended at 58 $^2/_3$ in his next start.

**1974**  The Cleveland Indians hold a 10-cent beer promotion when the Texas Rangers visit Cleveland Municipal Stadium for a night game. Alcohol-fueled mayhem and violence ensue, and the Indians are forced to forfeit the game when the crowd spills onto the field.

**1986**  At Atlanta-Fulton County Stadium, site of Hank Aaron's historic 715th homer, future home run king Barry Bonds of the Pittsburgh Pirates launches his first major league homer during a 12-3 victory over the Braves.

**2009**  Randy Johnson of the San Francisco Giants becomes the 24th pitcher in major league history to reach 300 career wins as he surrenders just two hits over six innings in a 5-1 victory over the Washington Nationals.

# 5

**1989**  Toronto's SkyDome hosts its first major league game as the hometown Blue Jays drop a 5-3 decision to the Milwaukee Brewers. The state-of-the-art facility is the first to utilize a fully retractable roof and also features the world's largest video display board.

**2008**  Atlanta Braves third baseman Chipper Jones joins Mickey Mantle and Eddie Murray as the only switch hitters in major league history to amass 400 career home runs when he goes deep in the sixth inning of a 7-5 home win over the Florida Marlins. The historic homer is part of a four-hit night for Jones, whose .418 batting average leads the majors.

# 6

1892  Benjamin Harrison becomes the first sitting U.S. President to attend a major league game as he watches the Washington Senators fall 7-4 to the Cincinnati Reds at nearby Boundary Field.

1939  In Williamsport, Pennsylvania, the first-ever Little League game takes place as Lundy Lumber tops Lycoming Dairy 23–8.

> (i) Lycoming Dairy recovered to win the league title, defeating Lundy Lumber in a three-game championship series.

1971  Willie Mays extends his major league record for extra-inning home runs when he clubs the 22nd of his career, a solo shot off Joe Hoerner that gives the San Francisco Giants a 4–3 walk-off victory over the Philadelphia Phillies.

2017  During a 13-1 rout of the St. Louis Cardinals at Cincinnati's Great American Ballpark, Scooter Gennett of the host Reds becomes the 17th player in major league history to hit four home runs in one game. The 27-year-old utility man drives in a run with a single in the first inning, then follows with a grand slam in the third, a two-run homer in the fourth, a solo home run in the sixth and another two-run shot in the eighth.

 On June 6, 2017, Scooter Gennett became the first player in history to collect five hits, four home runs and 10 RBIs in a major league game.

# 7

1884  At Boston's South End Grounds, Providence Grays 21-year-old pitcher Charlie Sweeney sets a new major league record by striking out 19 batters in a 2-1 complete game victory over the defending National League champion Boston Beaneaters.

> (i) Sweeney's mark for strikeouts in a nine-inning game stood for 102 years until Roger Clemens surpassed it by one.

1906  The burgeoning dynasty in Chicago takes possession of first place in the National League as the Cubs hand the reigning World Champion New York Giants a humiliating 19-0 loss at the Polo Grounds, scoring 11 of those runs in the first inning off Christy Mathewson and Joe McGinnity. The defeat is the worst in Giants franchise history.

> (i) The Cubs went 82-21-3 (.796) the rest of the way, winning the pennant by a staggering 20 games over the second-place Giants.

**1966** The New York Mets, picking first in the June Amateur Draft, bypass Arizona State University outfielder Reggie Jackson and select Steve Chilcott, a left-handed-hitting catcher from Antelope Valley High in Lancaster, California. Chilcott will retire from baseball after six injury-riddled seasons in the minors while Jackson, whom the Kansas City Athletics select with the second overall pick, will blossom into a major league star and eventual Hall of Famer.

**1973** The Milwaukee Brewers and San Diego Padres each bring a future first-ballot Hall of Famer into the fold at Major League Baseball's June Amateur Draft as the Brewers select high school shortstop Robin Yount with the third overall pick while the Padres choose reigning College World Series Most Outstanding Player Dave Winfield with the following selection.

> DID YOU KNOW? Dave Winfield, a multi-sport athlete while at the University of Minnesota, became the only person in history to be drafted by teams in four professional sports leagues when he was chosen by the National Basketball Association's Atlanta Hawks, the American Basketball Association's Utah Stars and the National Football League's Minnesota Vikings in addition to his selection by the San Diego Padres.

# 8

**1965** The Kansas City Athletics select Arizona State's Rick Monday with the top overall pick in Major League Baseball's first amateur draft. Other notable picks include Johnny Bench in the second round by the Cincinnati Reds and Nolan Ryan in the 10th round by the New York Mets.

**1982** Legendary pitcher Leroy Robert "Satchel" Paige dies of a heart attack at age 75 at his home in Kansas City, Missouri. A renowned gate attraction and one of the greatest pitchers in baseball history, Paige wowed fans and batters alike with his blazing fastball and pinpoint control. After a phenomenal Negro League career, the star right-hander debuted in Major League Baseball at the age of 42 and, despite his age, made two All-Star teams and won 28 games in parts of six seasons. In 1971, five years after completing his amazing 40-year playing career, Paige became the first African American pitcher to be inducted into the Baseball Hall of Fame.

**2005** New York Yankees 29-year-old third baseman Alex Rodriguez becomes the youngest player in major league history to join the 400 Home Run Club when he hits a solo shot in the eighth inning of the Yankees' 12–3 win over the Milwaukee Brewers.

# 9

1907 After throwing a no-hitter in his previous outing, 19-year-old Walter Johnson pitches the only perfect game of his professional career, leading Weiser to an 11-0 win over Southern Idaho League foe Emmett.

1914 Pittsburgh Pirates star Honus Wagner joins Cap Anson in the 3,000 Hit Club when he rips a ninth-inning double off Erskine Mayer in the Pirates' 3-1 road loss to the Philadelphia Phillies.

2008 Ken Griffey Jr. of the Cincinnati Reds hits career home run No. 600, a towering two-run shot in the first inning of a 9-4 road win over the Florida Marlins. Griffey becomes only the sixth player to reach the historic milestone, joining Barry Bonds, Hank Aaron, Babe Ruth, Willie Mays and Sammy Sosa.

# 10

1892 In a 25-4 drubbing of the St. Louis Browns, Wilbert Robinson of the Baltimore Orioles establishes two major league records when he tallies seven hits in seven at-bats and drives in 11 runs.

1944 Joe Nuxhall, at 15 years, 10 months and 11 days of age, becomes the youngest major leaguer in history when he pitches two-thirds of an inning for the Cincinnati Reds in an 18-0 loss to the St. Louis Cardinals at Crosley Field.

1959 Cleveland Indians outfielder Rocky Colavito becomes the eighth player in major league history to hit four home runs in one game as the Indians beat the Baltimore Orioles 11-8 at Memorial Stadium.

1981 Before a crowd of 57,386 at Veterans Stadium, Pete Rose of the Philadelphia Phillies ties Stan Musial's National League record of 3,630 career hits when he singles off Nolan Ryan in the first inning of the Phillies' 5-4 win over the Houston Astros.

> (i) Rose's quest for historic hit No. 3,631 was temporarily put on hold two days later when the players began a two-month strike.

2019 The Arizona Diamondbacks and the Philadelphia Phillies set a single-game major league record when they combine to launch 13 home runs in Arizona's 13-8 victory at Citizens Bank Park. The D'backs open the game with three straight homers, and finish with a franchise-record eight.

> (i) The Diamondbacks-Phillies historic home run barrage topped by one the previous mark set in 1995 by the Chicago White Sox and Detroit Tigers and matched in 2002 by the same two teams.

# 11

1927  At Shibe Park, the Philadelphia Athletics field a team that includes a record seven future Hall of Famers when pinch-hitter Mickey Cochrane and pitcher Lefty Grove join starters Ty Cobb (LF), Eddie Collins (2B), Jimmie Foxx (1B), Al Simmons (CF) and Zack Wheat (LF) in the 9th inning of a game with the Detroit Tigers.

> (i)  The Athletics matched this feat on May 24, 1928 when they combined with the New York Yankees to field a record 13 future Hall of Famers.

1990  Texas Rangers pitcher Nolan Ryan extends his own major league record by throwing his sixth career no-hitter, a 14-strikeout, 5–0 gem against the Oakland Athletics. The 43-year-old Ryan becomes the first to throw no-hitters in three different decades, the first to throw no-hitters for three different teams and the oldest pitcher to date to throw a no-hitter.

# 12

1880  Lee Richmond tosses the first perfect game in major league history, leading the National League's Worcester Ruby Legs to a 1-0 victory over the Cleveland Blues.

> (i)  The 23-year-old lefty got a big assist from his defense when right fielder Lon Knight erased a potential base hit by throwing out a runner at first.

1939  The official dedication of the National Baseball Hall of Fame and Museum takes place at Cooperstown, New York, the supposed place of baseball's birth 100 years earlier. As part of the gala event, living legends Grover Cleveland Alexander, Ty Cobb, Eddie Collins, Walter Johnson, Nap Lajoie, Connie Mack, Babe Ruth, George Sisler, Tris Speaker, Honus Wagner and Cy Young are present to accept their plaques as members of the Hall's first induction classes.

1959  The Japanese Baseball Hall of Fame and Museum officially opens in Tokyo.

1981  One day after meeting with Major League Baseball owners, Marvin Miller of the MLB Players Association announces, "We have accomplished nothing. The strike is on.", thus beginning the longest baseball work stoppage to date. When play resumes on August 10, the strike will have wiped out 38 percent of the schedule.

1990   Cal Ripken Jr. of the Baltimore Orioles plays in his 1,308th consecutive game, moving him past Everett Scott for second place on the all-time list.

1997   Major League Baseball's first-ever official regular season interleague game takes place at the Ballpark in Arlington as the Texas Rangers host the San Francisco Giants.

# 13

1905   New York Giants superstar Christy Mathewson throws his second career no-hitter, beating Mordecai Brown and the Chicago Cubs 1-0 at Chicago's West Side Park. Only a pair of infield errors prevents Mathewson from recording a perfect game.

1912   Christy Mathewson of the New York Giants earns his 300th major league victory, beating the Chicago Cubs 3–2. Mathewson becomes the eighth member of the 300 Win Club and the first to record all of his victories in the 20th century.

1948   An ailing Babe Ruth makes an emotional final appearance at Yankee Stadium as his iconic uniform number three is retired by the New York Yankees during a special ceremony that also commemorates the 25th anniversary of the Stadium.

(i) Just two months later on August 16, the 53-year-old Ruth died after losing his battle with throat cancer.

1984   The division-leading Chicago Cubs fortify their roster by acquiring pitchers Rick Sutcliffe and George Frazier and catcher Ron Hassey from the Cleveland Indians in exchange for future RBI Champ Joe Carter, outfielder Mel Hall and two others. The trade will yield immediate dividends for Chicago as Sutcliffe's 16-1 record the rest of the way will help propel the Cubs to their first ever National League East crown.

2003   Roger Clemens of the New York Yankees strikes out his 4,000th career batter during the second inning of his 300th career win, a 5–2 defeat of the St. Louis Cardinals. The 40-year-old right-hander becomes the 21st pitcher to reach 300 major league wins, and he joins Nolan Ryan and Steve Carlton in the 4,000 Strikeout Club.

2012   Matt Cain of the San Francisco Giants tosses the 22nd perfect game in major league history, defeating the Houston Astros 10–0. His 14 strikeouts match Sandy Koufax's mark for most in a perfect game.

**2019** In the Los Angeles Angels' 5-3 victory over the Tampa Bay Rays, Angels designated hitter Shohei Ohtani becomes the first Japanese-born player in major league history to hit for the cycle.

# 14

**1870** The Cincinnati Reds, baseball's first all-professional team, see their 84-game winning streak come to an end when the Brooklyn Atlantics defeat them 8-7 in an 11-inning thriller before a crowd of 20,000 at Capitoline Grounds.

**1949** While in Chicago to play in a series against his former team, first baseman Eddie Waitkus of the Philadelphia Phillies is nearly murdered by a deranged fan named Ruth Ann Steinhagen. The 19-year-old Steinhagen, who had been obsessed with Waitkus since his playing days with the Cubs, successfully lured Waitkus to her room at the Edgewater Beach Hotel and shot him in the chest with a .22 caliber rifle, narrowly missing his heart. Waitkus survived the blow but nearly died during surgery before making a near-miraculous recovery.

> (i) While his assailant was confined to a mental institution, Eddie Waitkus returned to the diamond in 1950 and helped lead Philadelphia's "Whiz Kids" Phillies to an improbable pennant.

**1952** Boston Braves ace Warren Spahn ties Jim Whitney's National League record for strikeouts in a game when he whiffs 18 in a 15-inning, 3-1 loss to the Chicago Cubs. Spahn's only run support in the contest was his own home run.

> (i) Help was on the way for Spahn and his teammates as this was also the day that the Braves signed 18-year-old Hank Aaron.

**1969** Oakland Athletics slugger Reggie Jackson pounds out two home runs, a double and two singles in six at-bats while driving in a career-high 10 runs in a 21-7 rout of the Boston Red Sox at Fenway Park.

> (i) The 23-year-old Jackson finished the 1969 season with career bests in several categories, including home runs (47), RBIs (118), runs scored (123) and slugging percentage (.608).

**1974** Nolan Ryan strikes out 19 Boston Red Sox batters (including Cecil Cooper six times) in 13 innings of work as the California Angels win 4-3 in 15 innings.

# 15

**1928** Forty-one-year-old Ty Cobb of the Philadelphia Athletics extends his own major league record when he steals home for the 54th and final time of his career in the Athletics' 12-5 win over the Cleveland Indians.

1938    Four days after no-hitting the Boston Bees, 23-year-old lefty Johnny Vander Meer of the Cincinnati Reds becomes the first major leaguer to throw consecutive no-hitters when he holds the Brooklyn Dodgers hitless in a 6-0 victory at Ebbets Field.

1964    The St. Louis Cardinals acquire 24-year-old outfielder Lou Brock along with pitchers Jack Spring and Paul Toth from the Chicago Cubs for veteran hurlers Ernie Broglio and Bobby Shantz and outfielder Doug Clemens. The trade will become substantially lopsided in the Cardinals' favor when Brock develops into a star and eventual Hall of Famer while Broglio, a former 21-game winner, disappoints in Chicago, going just 7-19 in three seasons with the Cubs.

1977    It's a dark day for many New York Mets fans as the club agrees to trade Tom Seaver, a three-time Cy Young Award winner and the face of the Mets franchise, to the Cincinnati Reds for infielder Doug Flynn, outfielders Steve Henderson and Dan Norman and pitcher Pat Zachry just moments before the trade deadline. The move, in conjunction with an earlier deal that sent slugger Dave Kingman to the San Diego Padres, becomes known in Mets lore as the "Midnight Massacre."

1983    The New York Mets make a key acquisition, adding first baseman Keith Hernandez in a trade that sends pitchers Neil Allen and Rick Ownbey to the St. Louis Cardinals. Hernandez will excel in his time in New York, adding defense, run production and leadership to a team that will quickly develop into one of baseball's best.

DID YOU KNOW?    Keith Hernandez became the Mets' first team captain on May 6, 1987.

2016    On his quest for 3,000 major league hits, Miami Marlins 42-year-old outfielder Ichiro Suzuki accomplishes another historic feat when his ninth-inning double against the San Diego Padres pushes his combined total of hits in Japan's Pacific League (1,278) and Major League Baseball (2,979) to 4,257, one more than that of MLB's all-time hits leader Pete Rose.

# 16

1978    After several near-misses, Tom Seaver of the Cincinnati Reds throws his first and only no-hitter, blanking the St. Louis Cardinals 4-0 at Riverfront Stadium.

1996    Legendary broadcaster Mel Allen dies at age 83 in Greenwich, Connecticut. Primarily known as the "Voice of the New York Yankees" because of his play-by-play duties in the 1940s-1960s, Allen also earned recognition later in life as the first host of the television show *This Week in Baseball*. In 1978, he and Red Barber became the first recipients of the Baseball Hall of Fame's Ford C. Frick Award.

2014   Tony Gwynn, San Diego's beloved "Mr. Padre," dies from salivary gland cancer at age 54 in Poway, California. Considered one of the finest pure hitters in baseball history, Gwynn won a record-tying eight National League batting titles during his 20-year career with the Padres and finished with 3,141 hits and a .338 lifetime batting average. Admired both on and off the field, the 15-time All-Star was inducted into the Baseball Hall of Fame in 2007.

# 17

1880   Just six days after Lee Richmond threw the first perfect game in major league history, Providence Grays ace John Montgomery Ward records the second as he defeats Pud Galvin and the Buffalo Bison 5-0.

(i)   Ward's gem stood as the National League's last perfect game until Jim Bunning matched the feat on June 21, 1964.

1960   Ted Williams of the Boston Red Sox hits his 500th career home run, a two-run shot off Wynn Hawkins in a 3–1 win over the Cleveland Indians. Williams becomes the fourth player in major league history to reach the 500-home run plateau, joining Babe Ruth, Jimmie Foxx and Mel Ott.

1970   The San Francisco Giants' Willie Mays and Ernie Banks of the Chicago Cubs both homer in the eighth inning of a 6-1 Cubs victory at Candlestick Park, marking the first time two members of the 500 Home Run Club go deep in the same game.

1978   In a 4-0 win over the California Angels, Ron Guidry of the New York Yankees strikes out 18 to set a new American League single-game mark for left-handers. Guidry's electrifying performance raises his record to 11–0 and inspires Yankees announcer Phil Rizzuto to call the southpaw by a new nickname — "Louisiana Lightning."

2009   Ivan Rodriguez of the Houston Astros breaks Carlton Fisk's major league record by catching his 2,227th game in Houston's 5-4, 10-inning road loss to the Texas Rangers.

(i)   Rodriguez began his major league career as a 19-year-old in 1991 with these same Texas Rangers and, coincidentally, opposed Carlton Fisk of the Chicago White Sox in his debut.

# 18

1953   The Boston Red Sox set a major league record when they score 17 runs in the seventh inning of a 23–3 win over the Detroit Tigers at Fenway Park. Red Sox rookie outfielder Gene Stephens doubles and singles twice in the historic frame, setting a new American League mark for most hits in one inning by a single player.

1975   Boston Red Sox prized rookie Fred Lynn ties an American League record with 16 total bases as he goes 5-for-6 with three home runs, a triple and 10 RBIs in a 15–1 drubbing of the host Detroit Tigers. The 23-year-old center fielder will go on to win Rookie of the Year and Most Valuable Player honors this season.

1977   At Fenway Park, a national television audience witnesses an ugly confrontation between New York Yankees manager Billy Martin and Yankees outfielder Reggie Jackson. The incident starts when Martin pulls Jackson off the field in the sixth inning for alleged loafing, then escalates in the dugout when a heated argument between the two nearly turns physical before Yankees coaches Yogi Berra and Elston Howard restore order. The Boston Red Sox win the game 10-4, moving a game and a half ahead of the second-place Yankees in the American League East.

1986   Don Sutton of the California Angels records his 300th career win in an impressive 3-hit, 5–1 victory over the league-leading Texas Rangers. The 41-year-old right-hander becomes the 19th pitcher to reach the 300-win plateau.

2003   Hall of Famer Lawrence Eugene "Larry" Doby, the man who broke the American League's color barrier, dies at age 79 in Montclair, New Jersey. Despite shouldering the burdens of a racial trailblazer, Doby won two home run titles and garnered seven All-Star selections during his 13-year major league career. The power-hitting center fielder was a key contributor on the Cleveland Indians' World Championship club in 1948 and pennant-winner in 1954.

2014   In one of the most dominant pitching performances in major league history, Los Angeles Dodgers ace Clayton Kershaw fires a no-hitter while striking out 15 and walking none in an 8-0 home win over the Colorado Rockies. Only a seventh inning Hanley Ramirez throwing error prevents Kershaw from recording a perfect game.

# 19

1846   In what was once accepted as the first baseball match ever played, a team called the New York Nine claims a 23-1, 4-inning victory over the

Knickerbocker Club of New York at Elysian Fields in Hoboken, New Jersey. The game is played using rules documented by Knickerbocker club member Alexander Cartwright, who also serves as umpire for the event.

> (i) While this game's historical import has diminished as new evidence now points to earlier matches, it remains a significant event in the evolution of early baseball.

1903  Star slugger Lou Gehrig, baseball's beloved "Iron Horse," is born in New York City, New York.

1942  Paul Waner of the Boston Braves joins the exclusive 3,000 Hit Club with a fifth-inning single to center off former teammate Rip Sewell during a 7-6 home loss to the Pittsburgh Pirates. The game is stopped momentarily following the historic hit as the 39-year-old Waner is congratulated by members of both teams.

> (i) Paul Waner was the only major leaguer to reach 3,000 career hits during a 33-year stretch from 1925 (Eddie Collins) to 1958 (Stan Musial).

1989  New York Mets 24-year-old ace Dwight Gooden records his 100th career victory, defeating the Montreal Expos 5-3 at Shea Stadium. Gooden becomes the third youngest pitcher in the modern era to reach the 100-win plateau, and does so with a 100-37 win/loss total that is second only to Whitey Ford's 100-36.

2015  Alex Rodriguez of the New York Yankees becomes the 29th major leaguer to amass 3,000 career hits when he homers off Justin Verlander in the first inning of the Yankees' 7-2 win over the Detroit Tigers at Yankee Stadium.

# 20

1912  Owen "Chief" Wilson of the Pittsburgh Pirates hits two triples in the opener of a doubleheader at Cincinnati and another in the nightcap to give him a record-tying five consecutive games with at least one three-bagger. The slugging outfielder will end the season with a major league-record 36 triples.

1950  The New York Giants outbid several other clubs and sign Birmingham Black Barons star Willie Mays to a $15,000 contract. The Giants were persuaded by scout Eddie Montague, who called the 19-year-old Mays the best player he had ever seen.

2004  Cincinnati Reds 34-year-old slugger Ken Griffey Jr. becomes the 20th major leaguer to reach the 500-home run plateau when he hits a solo shot against St. Louis Cardinals starter Matt Morris in the Reds' 6-0 win at Busch Stadium.

ⓘ The historic homer was also Junior's 2,143rd major league hit, matching his father's career total.

**2007** Sammy Sosa hits the 600th home run of his major league career, leading the Texas Rangers to a 7-3 home win over his former team, the Chicago Cubs. Sosa joins Hank Aaron, Barry Bonds, Willie Mays and Babe Ruth in the 600 Home Run Club.

**2015** Washington Nationals ace Max Scherzer is one strike away from throwing a perfect game when he hits Jose Tabata of the Pittsburgh Pirates with an errant slider. Scherzer retires the next batter on a long fly out to garner his first career no-hitter, leading the Nationals to a 6-0 win.

ⓘ Scherzer joined Hooks Wiltse of the 1908 New York Giants as the only pitchers in major league history to lose a perfect game by hitting the 27th batter.

# 21

**1959** Hank Aaron of the Milwaukee Braves blasts three two-run homers in a 13–3 win over the San Francisco Giants at Seals Stadium. It will be the only three-home run game of Aaron's career.

**1964** On Father's Day at Shea Stadium, Philadelphia Phillies right-hander Jim Bunning fans ten, drives in two runs and pitches the first regular-season perfect game in 42 years as the Phillies beat the New York Mets 6-0. Having already thrown a no-hitter for the Detroit Tigers six years earlier, the 32-year-old ace becomes the first pitcher to toss no-hitters in both major leagues.

**1970** Detroit Tigers shortstop Cesar "Cocoa" Gutierrez becomes the first player in American League history to go 7-for-7 in a game when he collects a double and six singles in the Tigers' twelve-inning, 9-8 win over the Cleveland Indians.

ⓘ Gutierrez, who coincidentally wore #7, totaled just seven hits in all of 1971 and 128 hits in his four-year major league career.

# 22

**1947** Ewell Blackwell of the Cincinnati Reds falls just short of tossing consecutive no-hitters when Brooklyn Dodgers second baseman Eddie Stanky lines a clean single up the middle with one out in the ninth inning. Blackwell allows another single to Jackie Robinson before closing out the 4-0 victory. The near miss comes four days after Blackwell pitched a 6-0 no-hitter against the Boston Braves.

1976  In a 4-2 win over the San Francisco Giants, pitcher Randy Jones of the San Diego Padres matches Christy Mathewson's National League mark of 68 consecutive innings without issuing a base on balls. Jones' walk of Marc Hill in the 8th inning ends the record-tying streak.

> (i) Randy Jones earned the 1976 National League Cy Young Award after finishing the season with a 22–14 record and a 2.74 ERA.

1982  Philadelphia Phillies first baseman Pete Rose moves into second place on Major League Baseball's career hits list with a third-inning double against the St. Louis Cardinals. The historic hit is the 3,772nd of Rose's career, moving him one spot ahead of Hank Aaron.

# 23

1917  After Boston Red Sox pitcher Babe Ruth is ejected for arguing with home plate umpire Brick Owens following Ruth's walk to the game's first batter, Ernie Shore relieves and is perfect the rest of the way, earning a 4-0 win over the Washington Senators at Fenway Park. Shore is initially credited with a perfect game, but the ruling is later changed to a Ruth-Shore combined no-hitter.

1971  Rick Wise of the Philadelphia Phillies becomes the first pitcher in major league history to hit two home runs and throw a no-hitter in the same game as he shuts down the Cincinnati Reds 4-0 at Riverfront Stadium.

1984  In what will become known as "The Sandberg Game," Chicago Cubs second baseman Ryne Sandberg goes 5-for-6, collects seven RBIs and hits game-tying home runs off Bruce Sutter in both the ninth and 10th innings in the Cubs' 12–11, 11-inning victory over the St. Louis Cardinals at Wrigley Field.

2003  San Francisco Giants star Barry Bonds records his 500th career stolen base in a 3-2 win over the Los Angeles Dodgers, becoming the first player in major league history to amass both 500 stolen bases and 500 home runs.

2008  Felix Hernandez of the Seattle Mariners becomes the first American League pitcher to hit a grand slam since the designated hitter rule went into effect in 1973 when he goes deep off Johan Santana in a 5–2 win over the New York Mets.

# 24

1947 Brooklyn Dodgers rookie Jackie Robinson steals home for the first of 19 times in his major league career in the Dodgers' 4–2 defeat of the Pittsburgh Pirates.

1972 Following a prolonged legal battle in her attempt to enter professional baseball, Bernice Gera becomes the first female umpire in Organized Baseball history when she works a Class A New York-Penn League game between the Auburn Phillies and Geneva Senators. Gera faces harsh criticism during the game and resigns immediately afterward when she senses a lack of support from her fellow umpires.

1979 Rickey Henderson makes his major league debut for the Oakland Athletics in a 5-1 loss to the Texas Rangers. The future "Man of Steal" doubles and singles in four at bats, and records the first of his 1,406 career stolen bases.

1983 At County Stadium, Don Sutton of the Milwaukee Brewers becomes just the eighth major leaguer to reach 3,000 career strikeouts when he fans Alan Bannister in the eighth inning of a 3-2 win over the Cleveland Indians.

1991 Thirty-nine-year-old Dave Winfield of the California Angels becomes the oldest player in major league history to date to hit for the cycle when he accomplishes the feat in the Angels' 9–4 win over the Kansas City Royals.

1997 Seattle Mariners ace Randy Johnson sets a new American League single-game record for strikeouts by a left-hander when he fans 19 in a 4-1 loss to the Oakland Athletics at the Kingdome. Johnson allows 11 hits in the game, including a solo home run to Mark McGwire that travels an estimated 538 feet.

# 25

1998 Sammy Sosa of the Chicago Cubs sets a major league record for home runs in a month when he hits his 19th of June in a 6–4 loss to the Detroit Tigers. Rudy York of the Tigers set the previous mark when he hit 18 in August 1937.

1999 In the Baltimore Orioles' 9-8 loss to the New York Yankees, Orioles lefty Jesse Orosco breaks Kent Tekulve's all-time major league relief appearance record when he takes over on the mound for the 1,051st time in his career. Orosco will extend his mark to 1,248 relief appearances before retiring in 2003.

2019 In a 4-3 victory over the Toronto Blue Jays at Yankee Stadium, the New York Yankees set a major league record when they homer in their 28th consecutive game. The Bronx Bombers will extend their streak to 31 games before going homerless in a 4-2 loss to the New York Mets on July 2.

(i) The Yankees belted a franchise-best 306 home runs in 2019.

# 26

**1920** Seventeen-year-old Lou Gehrig of New York's Commerce High School earns his first national acclaim by hitting a ninth-inning grand slam in a 12–6 win over Chicago's Lane Tech. The special game between city championship teams takes place at Cubs Park, later known as Wrigley Field.

**1944** In a unique event held to support the Allied Forces in World War II, New York's three major league clubs face each other in the "Tri-Cornered Baseball Game" before a capacity crowd at the Polo Grounds. With each team taking equal turns at bat and in the field in the nine-inning contest, the final score is Dodgers 5, Yankees 1, Giants 0 as $5.5 million in war bonds are sold.

**1993** Hall of Famer Roy Campanella dies at age 71 in Woodland Hills, California. An exceptional catcher and dangerous slugger, "Campy" was an eight-time All-Star and three-time National League MVP for the Brooklyn Dodgers before his career was tragically cut short in 1958 when he was paralyzed in an automobile accident.

# 27

**1958** Chicago White Sox pitcher Billy Pierce misses a perfect game by inches in a 3-0 win over the Washington Senators at Comiskey Park. With two outs in the ninth, Senators pinch-hitter Ed Fitz Gerald connects on a double that falls just inside the left field line for the only hit that Pierce surrenders.

**1977** Willie McCovey of the San Francisco Giants becomes the first player in major league history to hit two home runs in one inning for a second time when he smashes a solo home run and a grand slam in the sixth inning of a 14–9 victory over the Cincinnati Reds. In addition, McCovey's bases-loaded blast gives him a National League-record 17 career grand slams.

**2002** In one of the best trades in Cleveland Indians history, general manager Mark Shapiro acquires prospects Cliff Lee, Brandon Phillips, and Grady Sizemore along with first baseman Lee Stevens from the Montreal Expos in exchange for staff ace Bartolo Colon and reliever Tim Drew. All three prospects netted by Cleveland will develop into major league All-Stars, with Lee ultimately surpassing Colon's production in the Indians rotation.

2003 In a 25-8 mauling of the Florida Marlins at Fenway Park, the Boston Red Sox set a major league record by scoring 10 runs before making their first out of the game. Red Sox leadoff hitter Johnny Damon ignites the offensive explosion, collecting a major league record-tying three hits in the first inning.

(i) The Marlins needed three pitchers, 91 pitches and 50 minutes to close out the historic half-inning.

2007 Reigning National League MVP Ryan Howard of the Philadelphia Phillies sets a new record when his majestic 500-foot blast in a 9–6 loss to the visiting Cincinnati Reds allows him to reach 100 career home runs in just his 325th major league game, surpassing the previous record of 385 games set by former Pittsburgh Pirates slugger Ralph Kiner.

# 28

1939 The New York Yankees set a single-game major league record when they pummel the Philadelphia Athletics with eight home runs in the first game of a double-header, then establish the mark of 13 homers in a double-header when they add five more in the nightcap. The Yankees win by scores of 23-2 and 10-0, with Joe DiMaggio, Babe Dahlgren and Joe Gordon each going deep three times.

1949 After missing the first 69 games of the season due to an injured heel, Joe DiMaggio returns to the New York Yankees lineup in time for a three-game set with the streaking Boston Red Sox at Fenway Park. DiMaggio homers and singles to lead New York to a 6-4 win on this day, and further pummels the rival Red Sox by hitting three more key home runs during the next two games to power the first-place Yankees' series sweep.

1962 Hall of Famer Gordon Stanley "Mickey" Cochrane, nicknamed "Black Mike" because of his competitive nature, dies at age 59 in Lake Forest, Illinois. An excellent all-around catcher and exceptional leader, Cochrane won two American League MVP awards and was a central figure on three World Series winners before a beaning prematurely ended his career in 1937.

1963 John Franklin "Home Run" Baker dies at age 77 in Trappe, Maryland. The slugging third baseman captured four consecutive home run titles from 1911-1914 and, as a member of the famed "$100,000 infield," helped the Philadelphia Athletics become World Champions in 1910, 1911 and 1913. Baker was inducted into the Baseball Hall of Fame in 1955.

1976 Detroit Tigers rookie sensation Mark "The Bird" Fidrych captivates a national television audience with his unique blend of animated quirkiness and excellence on the mound as he throws a complete game 7-hitter, leading the Tigers to a 5-1 win over the New York Yankees at Tiger Stadium.

(i) Fidrych won the American League Rookie of the Year Award and finished second in Cy Young Award voting in 1976 after fashioning a 19-9 record with a league-leading 2.34 ERA.

1991  Barry Larkin of the Cincinnati Reds hits three home runs in an 8–5 win over the Houston Astros, giving him a major league record-tying five homers in a two-game span. Larkin also joins Ernie Banks and Freddie Patek as the only shortstops to date to homer three times in a game.

2007  Toronto Blue Jays DH Frank Thomas becomes the 21st major leaguer to reach 500 career home runs when he clubs a three-run shot off Carlos Silva in an 8-5 road loss to the Minnesota Twins.

2007  Craig Biggio records his 3,000th major league hit during a 5-for-6 day, leading the Houston Astros to an 8–5 win over the Colorado Rockies at Minute Maid Park. The 41-year-old becomes the 27th major leaguer to reach 3,000 career hits and the first to do so with a five-hit game.

2009  New York Yankees closer Mariano Rivera earns his 500th career save in a 4–2 win over the New York Mets at Citi Field. Rivera joins Trevor Hoffman as the only pitchers to reach the 500-save milestone.

(i) Rivera had another reason to celebrate earlier in this game when he earned his first career RBI with a bases-loaded walk in the ninth.

# 29

1897  The Chicago Colts, led by 45-year-old player-manager Cap Anson, set a major league record for most runs scored in a game when they trounce the visiting Louisville Colonels 36-7 at West Side Park.

1941  New York Yankees star Joe DiMaggio surpasses George Sisler's American League-record 41-game hitting streak when he hits safely in both ends of a doubleheader with the Washington Senators.

1984  Pete Rose of the Montreal Expos plays in his 3,309th game, passing Carl Yastrzemski for the major league record. Rose's historic appearance comes in a 7–3 win against the Cincinnati Reds, the team with which Rose spent his first 16 seasons.

1990  No-hitters are thrown on the same day in each major league for the first time in history as the Oakland Athletics' Dave Stewart blanks the Toronto

Blue Jays 3-0 in American League play while Fernando Valenzuela of the Los Angeles Dodgers follows with a 6-0 gem against the St. Louis Cardinals in the National League.

**2004**  Arizona Diamondbacks 40-year-old ace Randy Johnson becomes just the fourth major leaguer to reach 4,000 career strikeouts when he fans Jeff Cirillo in the D'backs' 3-2 loss to the San Diego Padres.

> (i) The Big Unit needed fewer innings (3,327 1/3) to reach the milestone than Nolan Ryan (3,844 2/3), Roger Clemens (4,151) or Steve Carlton (4,991 1/3).

**2019**  At London Stadium, the Boston Red Sox and New York Yankees square off in Major League Baseball's first-ever official game in Europe. A capacity crowd of 59,659 that includes the Duke and Dutchess of Sussex sees the Yankees outslug the Red Sox 17-13.

# 30

**1894**  Future Hall of Famer Fred Clarke becomes the first player in history to record five hits in a major league debut when he triples and singles four times for the Louisville Colonels in a 13-6 loss to the Philadelphia Phillies.

**1908**  Boston Red Sox 41-year-old ace Cy Young throws the third and final no-hitter of his illustrious career, shutting down the New York Highlanders 8-0 at Hilltop Park. Only a leadoff walk prevents Young from registering his second career perfect game.

> (i) The iconic pitcher also contributed with his bat on this day, driving in half of his team's runs.

> (i) Young held the record as the oldest major leaguer to pitch a no-hitter for 82 years until Nolan Ryan surpassed his mark.

**1962**  Sandy Koufax of the Los Angeles Dodgers throws his first career no-hitter, blanking the New York Mets 5-0 at Dodger Stadium. Koufax strikes out 13 in his masterpiece, including the first three batters of the game on only nine total pitches.

**1978**  San Francisco Giants slugger Willie McCovey launches the 500th home run of his major league career in a 10-9 road loss to the Atlanta Braves.

**1995**  Eddie Murray of the Cleveland Indians becomes the 20th member of the 3,000 Hit Club when he singles in the sixth inning of a 4-1 win over the Minnesota Twins.

# JULY

## 1

**1859** The first known intercollegiate baseball game takes place in Pittsfield, Massachusetts as Amherst College claims a 73-32 victory over Williams College.

**1916** Pittsburgh Pirates 42-year-old shortstop Honus Wagner becomes the oldest player in major league history to hit an inside-the-park home run when he circles the bases in the fourth inning of a 2-1 win over the Cincinnati Reds at Crosley Field.

> (i) The historic hit was the 101st and final home run of Wagner's Hall of Fame career.

**1920** Walter Johnson throws the only no-hitter of his illustrious major league career, pitching the Washington Senators to a 1-0 victory over the Boston Red Sox at Fenway Park. Only a Bucky Harris error spoils the perfect game bid as the Big Train walks none while striking out 10.

**1941** Those who tune in to watch the television broadcast of the Brooklyn Dodgers-Philadelphia Phillies game at Ebbets Field witness the first television advertisement in United States history when Bulova runs a 10-second spot promoting their clocks and watches.

**1941** Before a crowd of 52,832 at Yankee Stadium, Joe DiMaggio of the New York Yankees equals Willie Keeler's major league-record 44-game hitting streak when he hits safely in both ends of a doubleheader sweep of the Boston Red Sox.

> (i) New York's Bronx Bombers scored seven runs in the opener but failed to homer, ending their record-setting streak of 25 consecutive games with at least one home run.

**1945** In a dramatic return to the majors after four years of military service, Hank Greenberg electrifies the Briggs Stadium crowd when he homers to help the first-place Detroit Tigers defeat the Philadelphia Athletics 9-5.

1949  Boston Red Sox star Ted Williams begins a record run of 84 straight games reaching base when he goes 1-for-4 against the Philadelphia Athletics.

1951  Bob Feller of the Cleveland Indians ties a major league mark by tossing his third career no-hitter in a 2-1 win over the Detroit Tigers at Cleveland Stadium.

# 2

1903  Washington Senators outfielder Ed Delahanty, one of baseball's greatest all-around players, dies mysteriously at age 35 in Niagara Falls, Canada. Hours before his death, "Big Ed" had abandoned the Senators in Detroit and boarded a train bound for New York, apparently in an attempt to jump to the Giants. The binge drinking and reckless behavior that had recently escalated in his life reared up again on the train, and Delahanty was ordered off at Bridgeburg, Ontario, just short of the United States border. Disoriented and possibly despondent over mounting financial concerns, Delahanty walked in the darkness onto the International Railway Bridge and, when approached by the bridge watchman, plunged into the Niagara River and drown. Whether he slipped or jumped remains a mystery.

1941  New York Yankees centerfielder Joe DiMaggio surpasses Wee Willie Keeler's record 44-game hitting streak when he belts a fifth-inning home run off Red Sox pitcher Dick Newsome at Yankee Stadium.

1963  A pitching duel for the ages takes place at Candlestick Park as San Francisco Giants ace Juan Marichal and Warren Spahn of the Milwaukee Braves match scoreless innings until Willie Mays hits a walk-off homer against Spahn in the 16th, giving the Giants a 1-0 victory.

1995  Rookie sensation Hideo Nomo of the Los Angeles Dodgers becomes the first Japanese-born player to be selected to a Major League Baseball All-Star team.

> (i) After going 6-1 with a 1.99 ERA and a league-leading 119 strikeouts in his first half-season in the majors, Nomo also became the first rookie pitcher to start the All-Star game since fellow first-year phenom Fernando Valenzuela did so in 1981.

2007  New York Yankees 44-year-old pitcher Roger Clemens wins his 350th major league game, giving up just two hits and a walk in eight innings during a 4-1 home victory over the Minnesota Twins. Clemens becomes the first pitcher to amass 350 career victories since Warren Spahn reached that milestone in 1963.

# 3

**1966**  In a 17-3 win over the San Francisco Giants, Tony Cloninger of the Atlanta Braves becomes the first National League player and only major league pitcher to hit two grand slams in one game. His total of nine RBIs also establishes a major league record for pitchers.

**1968**  Right-hander Luis Tiant of the Cleveland Indians sets a new modern major league record for strikeouts in a 10-inning game when he fans 19 in a 1-0 victory over the Minnesota Twins.

> (i) With runners on first and third with no one out in the top of the tenth, Tiant preserved a scoreless tie by striking out three straight batters.

> (i) In 1968, Tiant paced the American League with a 1.60 ERA and nine shutouts.

**1970**  At Anaheim Stadium, California Angels pitcher Clyde Wright is inducted into the National Association of Intercollegiate Athletics Hall of Fame during a special ceremony prior to his start against the Oakland Athletics. The former Carson-Newman College star then proceeds to no-hit the Athletics, leading the Angels to a 4-0 victory.

> (i) In 1965, Wright set the record for strikeouts in an NAIA World Series game with 22.

**2016**  In a special game created by Major League Baseball and the MLB Players Association to honor United States military personnel and their families, the Atlanta Braves and Miami Marlins face each other at a newly constructed 12,500-seat ballpark in Fort Bragg, North Carolina. The event, which includes an on-field baseball clinic for 250 children, is thought to be the first-ever regular season professional sporting contest held on an active military base.

# 4

**1904**  Spitballer Jack Chesbro of the New York Highlanders wins his 14th consecutive game, setting an American League record that will stand until Walter Johnson wins 16 straight for the Washington Senators in 1912.

**1908**  New York Giants pitcher Hooks Wiltse loses his bid for a perfect game when he hits pitcher George McQuillan of the Philadelphia Phillies with two outs in the 9th inning. Wiltse shuts down the Phillies the rest of the way, finishing with a 10-inning no-hitter in the Giants' 1-0 win.

**1911**   Ty Cobb's 40-game hitting streak is stopped by Chicago White Sox ace Ed Walsh in Chicago's 7-3 win over the Tigers at Detroit's Bennett Park. The streak will stand as the modern major league record until George Sisler surpasses it by one in 1922.

> DID YOU KNOW?   Ed Walsh's son, Ed Walsh Jr., stopped a significant hitting streak of his own 22 years later when, as a pitcher for the Oakland Oaks, he ended Joe DiMaggio's Pacific Coast League-record streak at 61 games.

**1932**   In International League play, Baltimore Orioles outfielder Buzz Arlett records a four-home run game against the Reading Keystones for the second time this season, having done so the first time just five weeks earlier on June 2.

**1934**   Pittsburgh Crawfords star Satchel Paige fires a 4-0 no-hitter against the Homestead Grays, walking just one while striking out a Negro National League-record 17 batters.

**1939**   The New York Yankees honor a terminally ill Lou Gehrig with a special ceremony at Yankee Stadium. Local dignitaries and former teammates - including Babe Ruth - are on hand to pay tribute to the beloved former Yankees captain. Despite being physically compromised by amyotrophic lateral sclerosis, a neurodegenerative disease that will ultimately bear his name, Gehrig describes himself as "the luckiest man on the face of the earth" in his famous address to the capacity crowd.

**1980**   Nolan Ryan of the Houston Astros reaches 3,000 career strikeouts when he fans Cesar Geronimo in an 8-1 road loss to the Cincinnati Reds. The 33-year-old Ryan joins Walter Johnson, Bob Gibson and Gaylord Perry as the only pitchers to date to reach the 3,000-strikeout plateau.

> (i)   Geronimo was also Bob Gibson's 3,000th strikeout victim when he fanned against him on July 17, 1974.

**1984**   Phil Niekro of the New York Yankees becomes the ninth pitcher to join the 3,000 Strikeout Club when he fans Larry Parrish in a 5-0 victory over the Texas Rangers. The 45-year-old knuckleballer tosses eight innings in the win, lowering his season ERA to 1.84 and improving his record to 11-4.

# 5

**1898**   Elizabeth Stroud becomes the first woman to play in Organized Baseball when she makes a mound appearance for the Atlantic League's Reading Coal Heavers, allowing two hits and a walk in one scoreless inning of work.

1947   Major League Baseball becomes fully integrated as former Negro League standout Larry Doby debuts for the Cleveland Indians, becoming the first black player in the American League. The 22-year-old slugger will strike out in one pinch-hitting appearance on this day, but will go on to fashion a 13-year Hall of Fame career that will include 1,515 hits and seven All-Star Game selections.

1998   Roger Clemens of the Toronto Blue Jays reaches 3,000 career strikeouts when he fans Randy Winn in a 2-1 victory over the Tampa Bay Devil Rays.

1998   Texas Rangers outfielder Juan Gonzalez becomes just the second player in major league history to eclipse the 100-RBI mark before the All-Star Game as he homers twice and plates four runs in the Rangers' 8-4 win over the Seattle Mariners. Gonzalez joins Hank Greenberg, who drove in 103 runs before the 1935 Midsummer Classic for the Detroit Tigers.

> (i) The 28-year-old Gonzalez garnered his second American League MVP award this season after finishing with a major league-best 157 RBIs.

2002   Theodore Samuel "Ted" Williams, considered by many to be the greatest hitter in baseball history, dies at age 83 in Inverness, Florida. Williams' quick, powerful swing, exceptional vision and scientific approach to hitting produced astounding career numbers despite his nearly five full seasons missed due to injuries and military service as a fighter pilot in World War II and the Korean War. During his 19-year tenure with the Boston Red Sox, "The Splendid Splinter" won two MVP awards, two Triple Crowns and six batting titles while garnering 17 All-Star selections. He finished his spectacular career with a .344 batting average and 521 home runs, and became a first-ballot Hall of Famer in 1966.

2004   Eric Gagne's consecutive saves streak ends at 84 when he blows a two-run lead for the Los Angeles Dodgers in their 10-inning, 6-5 win over the Arizona Diamondbacks. Gagne's remarkable run far outdistances the previous major league record of 54 straight saves set by Tom Gordon in 1999.

# 6

1932   Chicago Cubs rookie shortstop Billy Jurges is shot twice in his Chicago hotel room by a former girlfriend - 21-year-old showgirl Violet Popovich Valli - when Jurges attempts to stop her from committing suicide. Jurges will recover fully and rejoin the World Series-bound Cubs within 16 days while Valli will parlay her newfound notoriety into a 22-week contract to star in a local show billed as "Violet (What I Did for Love) Valli - the Most Talked About Girl in Chicago."

**1933** *Chicago Tribune* sports editor Arch Ward's brainchild comes to life as the first official Major League Baseball All-Star Game is held at Chicago's Comiskey Park. A crowd of nearly 50,000 watches Babe Ruth christen the event with a two-run homer in the third inning, leading the American League All-Stars to a 4-2 defeat of the National League squad.

 The first RBI in All-Star Game play was by a pitcher. The historic run batted in belongs to American League starter Lefty Gomez of the New York Yankees, who drove in third baseman Jimmy Dykes with a second-inning single.

**1936** In his first appearance against major league competition, 17-year-old wunderkind Bob Feller strikes out eight batters in three innings for the Cleveland Indians during an All-Star break exhibition game against the National League-leading St. Louis Cardinals. Feller will stay with the Indians for the rest of the season, compiling a 5-3 record with a 3.34 ERA and 76 strikeouts in 62 innings.

**1983** The American League celebrates the All-Star Game's 50th anniversary by routing the National League 13-3 for its first win since 1971. All-Star Game MVP Fred Lynn caps a seven-run fourth inning by launching a grand slam - the first ever hit in All-Star competition.

**1986** Bob Horner of the Atlanta Braves becomes the 11th player in major league history to hit four home runs in one game, accomplishing the feat in an 11–8 win over the Montreal Expos at Atlanta-Fulton County Stadium.

**2000** The American Sportscasters Association names Dodgers legend Vin Scully the No. 1 sportscaster of the 20th century. Scully, who called 25 World Series and 12 All-Star Games, is followed in the rankings by Howard Cosell, Mel Allen and Red Barber, respectively.

# 7

**1900** Kid Nichols earns his 300th major league win by pitching the Boston Beaneaters past the Chicago Orphans 11–4. In only his ninth season, the 30-year-old right-hander becomes the youngest to reach the 300-win mark.

**1906** Superstar pitcher and iconic Negro League legend Leroy Robert "Satchel" Paige is born in Mobile, Alabama.

**1914** Facing competition from the Federal League and in need of cash, Baltimore Orioles owner Jack Dunn offers to sell Babe Ruth, Ernie Shore and Ben Egan for $10,000 to old friend Connie Mack of the Philadelphia Athletics. Mack, pleading poverty, declines the offer.

**1936** New York Yankees phenom Joe DiMaggio becomes the first major league rookie to participate in an All-Star Game when he starts in right field for the American Leaguers in the fourth Midsummer Classic.

> (i) Despite DiMaggio's presence, the National League prevailed 4-3 to claim their first All-Star Game victory. Dizzy Dean pitched three hitless innings to earn the win.

**1937** With President Franklin D. Roosevelt on hand to witness the MLB All-Star Game at Washington's Griffith Stadium, slugger Lou Gehrig drives in four runs with a home run and a double, leading the American League to an 8-3 victory. In a fateful third inning, National League starter Dizzy Dean gives up a long two-run homer to Gehrig, then suffers a career-altering injury when his left big toe is fractured by a low line shot off the bat of outfielder Earl Averill.

**1948** With his team in a heated pennant race, Cleveland Indians owner Bill Veeck signs 42-year-old Negro League legend Satchel Paige to help bolster the Indians pitching staff. Though his signing is viewed by some as just another Veeck publicity stunt, Paige will quickly quiet the doubters by going 6-1 with a 2.48 ERA over the next three months to help propel Cleveland to a World Series victory.

**1991** Shortly after working a Texas Rangers-California Angels game, 41-year-old umpire Steve Palermo is shot and paralyzed from the waist down while foiling a robbery attempt outside a restaurant in Dallas, Texas.

> (i) Palermo soon regained partial use of his legs through intense rehabilitation, allowing him to stand and throw out the ceremonial first pitch of the 1991 World Series as Major League Baseball honored his unselfish act of heroism.

**2011** A heart-breaking incident occurs at Rangers Ballpark when Shannon Stone, a Brownwood, Texas firefighter who is in attendance with his 6-year-old son Cooper, suffers a fatal head injury when he falls twenty feet after tumbling over an outfield wall while trying to catch a baseball tossed to him by Texas Rangers star outfielder Josh Hamilton during a game with the Oakland Athletics.

# 8

1880   The Chicago White Stockings win their 21st consecutive game, setting a major league record that will stand until the New York Giants win 26 straight in 1916.

1902   After negotiating his release from the Baltimore Orioles, 29-year-old John McGraw signs on as manager of the New York Giants for a league-high salary of $10,000 per year. McGraw will manage the Giants for the next 30 seasons, winning ten National League pennants and three World Series titles during his tenure.

1941   In one of the most memorable moments in All-Star Game history, 22-year-old Boston Red Sox outfielder Ted Williams hits a three-run, walk-off home run to give the American League a dramatic 7-5 victory at Detroit's Briggs Stadium.

> (i)   Williams' heroics overshadowed a stellar performance by Pittsburgh Pirates shortstop Arky Vaughan, who launched two-run homers in both the seventh and eighth innings to give the National League a 5-3 lead heading into the bottom of the ninth.

1962   St. Louis Cardinals 41-year-old legend Stan Musial becomes the oldest player in major league history to hit three home runs in one game when he goes deep in his first three at-bats in the Cardinals' 15-1 drubbing of the New York Mets.

# 9

1914   Baltimore Orioles owner Jack Dunn sells nineteen-year-old Babe Ruth, Ernie Shore and Ben Egan for $25,000 to new Boston Red Sox owner Joe Lannin.

1946   At Boston's Fenway Park, Red Sox slugger Ted Williams is a star among stars at the 1946 All-Star Game as he collects two home runs, two singles, a walk, five RBIs and four runs scored to lead the American League squad to a 12-0 rout of the National Leaguers. Williams' three-run homer in the eighth inning is especially memorable as it comes off Rip Sewell's trademark blooper pitch.

1972   California Angels pitcher Nolan Ryan thoroughly dominates the Boston Red Sox, fanning 16 in a one-hit, 3-0 win. Following Carl Yastrzemski's one-out single in the first, Ryan reels off eight straight strikeouts (three on nine pitches in the second inning) and retires the final 26 batters consecutively.

1991    Baltimore Orioles star Cal Ripken Jr. drills a three-run homer in the All-Star Game, leading the American League club to a 4–2 victory. Ripken, who also won the All-Star Game's Home Run Derby, is selected as the game's Most Valuable Player.

2002  President George W. Bush presents the Presidential Medal of Freedom to Hank Aaron during a ceremony at the White House.

2011    Derek Jeter's 5-for-5 day includes his 3,000th career hit - a third-inning homer off David Price - as the New York Yankees claim a 5–4 win over the visiting Tampa Bay Rays. Jeter joins Wade Boggs as the only players to date to reach the 3,000-hit plateau with a home run.

# 10

1920  Cleveland Indians player-manager Tris Speaker extends his consecutive hits streak to 11 before finally making an out in a 7-2 win over the Washington Senators. Speaker's mark will stand as a major league record until Pinky Higgins of the Boston Red Sox bests it by one in 1938.

1932   During a historic slugfest between the Philadelphia Athletics and Cleveland Indians, Athletics veteran pitcher Eddie Rommel surrenders a record 29 hits in seventeen innings of relief and blows leads in the fourth, seventh, ninth and sixteenth innings, but eventually earns an 18-17 win thanks in large part to Jimmie Foxx's three home runs and eight RBIs. The Indians come up short despite belting out a record 33 hits, with shortstop Johnny Burnett leading the way, going 9-for-11 to set a new major league mark for most hits in a single game.

> ⓘ   This was Eddie Rommel's final major league win. The 34-year-old tried his hand at coaching for a few years before returning to the majors as an umpire in 1938.

 On April 18, 1956, Eddie Rommel became the first major league umpire to wear glasses in a regular season game.

1934   At Major League Baseball's second All-Star Game, New York Giants pitcher Carl Hubbell puts on a spectacular show, striking out future Hall of Famers Babe Ruth, Lou Gehrig, Jimmie Foxx, Al Simmons and Joe Cronin in succession.

1936   Philadelphia Phillies right fielder Chuck Klein becomes the fourth player in major league history to hit four home runs in one game. His final homer comes in the 10th inning and helps propel the Phillies to a 9–6 road win over the Pittsburgh Pirates.

 Klein narrowly missed hitting an additional home run when his second-inning blast to deep right field was caught against the fence by Paul Waner.

**1956**  Baseball's greatest stars illuminate the 1956 All-Star Game as Mickey Mantle, Willie Mays, Stan Musial and Ted Williams all homer in the 7-3 National League victory at Washington's Griffith Stadium.

**1984**  Fifty years after Carl Hubbell struck out five consecutive Hall of Famers in the 1934 All-Star Game, National League pitchers Fernando Valenzuela and Dwight Gooden combine to fan six straight batters in the National League's 3-1 win at Candlestick Park.

DID YOU KNOW?  At 19 years of age, New York Mets pitcher Dwight Gooden became the youngest participant in All-Star Game history when he pitched two scoreless innings in the 1984 Midsummer Classic.

# 11

**1914**  George Herman "Babe" Ruth makes his major league debut, pitching seven innings for the Boston Red Sox in their 4-3 win over the Cleveland Indians at Fenway Park.

**1917**  Boston Red Sox pitcher Babe Ruth has a memorable day on the mound as he throws a complete game one-hitter against a potent Detroit Tigers lineup, winning 1-0 at Navin Field. The 22-year-old Ruth gives up just a scratch single to shortstop Donie Bush in the eighth, and closes out the game by fanning Ty Cobb, Bobby Veach and Harry Heilmann in succession in the ninth.

**1961**  Candlestick Park's notoriously strong winds wreak havoc on the first All-Star Game of the season as a record seven errors and a wind-induced balk by Stu Miller of the hometown San Francisco Giants mark an eventful 5-4, 10-inning victory for the National League.

 After the American Leaguers pulled ahead with an unearned run in their half of the 10th, Willie Mays responded with a key double that drove in Hank Aaron, then scored on a Roberto Clemente single to complete the walk-off win.

**1967**  In the longest All-Star Game in major league history, Cincinnati Reds third baseman Tony Perez gives the National League a 2-1 victory when he launches a game-winning home run off the Kansas City Athletics' Catfish Hunter in the 15th inning.

1985   Nolan Ryan of the Houston Astros becomes the first pitcher to reach 4,000 career strikeouts when he fans Danny Heep in a 4–3 win over the New York Mets. The Astrodome crowd and players from both teams celebrate the moment by giving Ryan a two-minute standing ovation.

# 12

1921   After only a season and a half as a full-time position player, New York Yankees slugger Babe Ruth is recognized as baseball's new Home Run King after homering twice in the Yankees' 6-4 win over the St. Louis Browns at Sportsman's Park. The previous title holder was 19th century star Roger Connor, who was thought to have hit 136 home runs over his 18-year career.

1943   A team of United States Armed Forces all-stars featuring Joe DiMaggio and Ted Williams and managed by Babe Ruth face the Boston Braves in a fund-raising game at Fenway Park. Williams homers in the contest, leading the Armed Forces team to a 9-8 victory.

1949   At Ebbets Field, black players participate in the Major League Baseball All-Star Game for the first time as Jackie Robinson, Roy Campanella and Don Newcombe appear for the National League squad and Larry Doby for the American Leaguers.

1955   With the All-Star Game deadlocked in the bottom of the 12th inning, Stan Musial steps to the plate and tells opposing catcher Yogi Berra that he plans to end the game, then does just that, launching the first pitch he sees into the right field bleachers at Milwaukee's County Stadium to give the National League a dramatic 6-5, come-from-behind victory.

1979   On Disco Demolition Night at Chicago's Comiskey Park, the host White Sox are forced to forfeit the second game of a doubleheader with the Detroit Tigers after thousands of unruly attendees respond to the ill-fated promotion by storming the field and badly damaging the playing surface.

1996   After losing sight in his right eye due to glaucoma, 35-year-old Kirby Puckett of the Minnesota Twins announces his retirement from baseball. The 10-time All-Star and future Hall of Famer leaves the game as the Twins' all-time leader in hits (2,304), runs scored (1,071), doubles (414) and total bases (3,453).

# 13

1896  Ed Delahanty of the Philadelphia Phillies matches Bobby Lowe's single-game home run record when he slugs four homers in the Phillies' 9-8 road loss to the Chicago Colts.

1934  New York Yankees outfielder Babe Ruth becomes the first major leaguer to amass 700 career home runs when he takes Tommy Bridges deep in the third inning of a 4-2 win over the Detroit Tigers at Navin Field.

> ⓘ The Yankees moved into first place with the win despite the loss of star Lou Gehrig, who was forced to leave the game in the first inning with a severe bout of lumbago. Gehrig's record consecutive games played streak, which stood at 1,426, appeared to be in serious jeopardy.

1963  Cleveland Indians 43-year-old righty Early Wynn earns his 300th and final major league win in the Indians' 7–4 defeat of the Kansas City Athletics.

1971  In an All-Star Game that includes six home runs hit by six future Hall of Famers, 25-year-old Reggie Jackson steals the show when he launches what is likely the longest home run in All-Star Game history - a majestic fourth-inning shot to right off Dock Ellis that hits the base of a light tower on Tiger Stadium's roof.

> ⓘ The American Leaguers prevailed 6-4, marking their only victory between 1962 and 1983.

1999  Hank Aaron, Willie Mays and Stan Musial are among a constellation of former baseball stars gathered on the field at Boston's Fenway Park for a memorable and moving ceremony honoring the All-Century Team prior to the 70th All-Star Game. The loudest ovation is saved for Red Sox legend Ted Williams, who throws out the ceremonial first pitch.

> ⓘ Hometown ace Pedro Martinez earned MVP honors in the game that followed after he struck out five of the six batters he faced to lead the American League squad to a 4-1 victory.

2010  George Steinbrenner, prominent owner of the New York Yankees, dies of a heart attack at age 80 in Tampa, Florida. The bombastic Steinbrenner, nicknamed "The Boss," restored the Yankees to glory by overseeing seven World Series championship teams and 11 pennant winners during his tumultuous 38-year reign.

2014 San Francisco Giants catcher Buster Posey and pitcher Madison Bumgarner become the first battery mates to each hit a grand slam in the same major league game, leading the Giants to an 8-4 win over the Arizona Diamondbacks.

# 14

1934 Despite being stricken with an acute case of lumbago, star first baseman Lou Gehrig manages to extend his major league-record streak of 1,426 consecutive games played when the New York Yankees bat him leadoff and pull him after his first plate appearance in a game against the Detroit Tigers. It will be another four and a half seasons before Gehrig's iconic streak comes to an end at 2,130 games.

1967 Eddie Mathews of the Houston Astros slugs career home run No. 500, taking Juan Marichal deep in an 8–6 win over the San Francisco Giants. Mathews becomes the seventh member of the 500 Home Run Club and the first to reach the milestone while facing a future Hall of Fame pitcher.

1968 Atlanta Braves star Hank Aaron becomes the eighth major leaguer to reach 500 career home runs when he hits a three-run shot off Mike McCormick in the Braves' 4-2 victory over the San Francisco Giants.

1968 Don Wilson of the Houston Astros ties Bob Feller's major league single-game strikeout record when he fans 18 batters in a 6–1 win over the Cincinnati Reds. After a one-out walk in the first, the 23-year-old right-hander sets down the next eight batters on strikes, tying another modern mark.

1970 At Riverfront Stadium, hometown star Pete Rose ends a thrilling 5-4, come-from-behind All-Star Game win for the National League in the 12th inning when he bowls over catcher Ray Fosse at the plate while scoring the deciding run. Fosse, who had been Rose's dinner guest the previous night, is hospitalized with an injured shoulder.

ⓘ The Senior Circuit forced extra innings by scoring three runs in the bottom of the ninth off Catfish Hunter.

1992 The American Leaguers notch an All-Star Game-record 19 hits in a 13–6 win over the National League squad at Jack Murphy Stadium in San Diego. Twelve years after his father claimed All-Star Game MVP honors, 22-year-old Ken Griffey Jr. strokes a home run, double and single to earn the same award.

2005 The San Francisco Giants become the first major league franchise to reach 10,000 wins as they defeat their longtime rival Los Angeles Dodgers

4–3. The franchise, which began as the New York Gothams in 1883, improves to 10,000-8,511 with the landmark victory.

2008 At the All-Star Home Run Derby at Yankee Stadium, Texas Rangers outfielder Josh Hamilton steals the show with an electrifying power display that produces a record 28 home runs in the first round.

# 15

1901 New York Giants 20-year-old rookie Christy Mathewson throws the first of his two career no-hitters, blanking the St. Louis Cardinals 5–0 at Robison Field.

1952 Detroit Tigers first baseman Walt Dropo extends his string of consecutive hits to 12 in a doubleheader with the Washington Senators, tying Johnny Kling's major league record.

1973 California Angels fireballer Nolan Ryan throws his second no-hitter of the season, overpowering the Detroit Tigers in a 6-0 win before 41,411 fans at Tiger Stadium. Ryan finishes with 17 strikeouts, including three each in the second, fourth and seventh innings.

> ⓘ Tigers first baseman Norm Cash added some levity to the game by bringing a table leg to the plate in the ninth as a sign of surrender. Using his real bat shortly after, Cash flied out to end the game.

1993 In a 5-3 home victory over the Minnesota Twins, Cal Ripken Jr. of the Baltimore Orioles hits his 278th career home run as a shortstop, breaking the positional record previously held by Hall of Famer Ernie Banks.

2005 Rafael Palmeiro of the Baltimore Orioles becomes the 26th player in major league history to reach 3,000 career hits when he doubles in the Orioles' 6–3 road win over the Seattle Mariners. The 40-year-old first baseman also joins Hank Aaron, Willie Mays and Eddie Murray as the only players to date to amass both 3,000 hits and 500 home runs. In a matter of weeks, a positive test for performance-enhancing drugs will tarnish Palmeiro's accomplishments.

# 16

2006 Chipper Jones' two-run homer off Jake Peavy of the San Diego Padres gives the Atlanta Braves star at least one extra base hit in 14 straight games, tying Hall of Famer Paul Waner's 79-year-old record.

**2013**  New York Yankees closer Mariano Rivera earns MVP honors in his final All-Star Game appearance after throwing a perfect eighth inning to help preserve a 3-0 victory for the American League.

> DID YOU KNOW?  Mariano Rivera finished his Hall of Fame career with a 0.00 ERA in nine All-Star Game innings.

# 17

**1941**  Before a crowd of 67,468 at Cleveland Stadium, New York Yankees star Joe DiMaggio's iconic hitting streak comes to an end at 56 games when pitchers Al Smith and Jim Bagby Jr., aided by two stellar defensive plays by third baseman Ken Keltner, limit DiMaggio to three ground ball outs and a walk in the Yankees' 6-5 win.

**1961**  Tyrus Raymond "Ty" Cobb, nicknamed "The Georgia Peach," dies at age 74 in Atlanta, Georgia. One of baseball's fiercest competitors and true superstars, Cobb was an overwhelming offensive force during his 24-year major league career, winning a record 12 batting titles and hitting .320 or better for 22 consecutive seasons while pacing his league in steals six times and slugging percentage eight times. Upon retirement he held career records for hits, batting average, runs scored, total bases, games played and at bats. In 1936, Cobb was inducted into the Baseball Hall of Fame as a charter member after receiving the most votes of any player on the inaugural ballot, outdistancing the likes of Babe Ruth and Honus Wagner.

**1974**  At Busch Stadium, St. Louis Cardinals pitcher Bob Gibson joins Walter Johnson in the 3,000 Strikeout Club when he fans outfielder César Gerónimo of the Cincinnati Reds.

**1974**  Jay Hanna "Dizzy" Dean dies at age 64 in Reno, Nevada. The colorful, brash fireballer burst upon the scene for the St. Louis Cardinals in 1932 and won 120 games over his first five seasons while garnering four straight strikeout crowns and the 1934 National League MVP award. A broken toe suffered in the 1937 All-Star Game led to an arm injury that eventually shortened his playing career. Dean later embarked on a successful broadcasting career, and was inducted into the Baseball Hall of Fame in 1953.

**1990**  The Minnesota Twins make history in a 1-0 loss to the Boston Red Sox by becoming the first major league team to turn two triple plays in one game.

**2018**  At Nationals Park, a stunning power display takes place during the 89th All-Star Game as both teams combine to hit an ASG-record 10 home runs. Scooter Gennett of the Cincinnati Reds breaks the old mark of six with a game-tying, two-run shot in the bottom of the ninth, then Houston Astros teammates Alex Bregman and George Springer respond with back-to-back homers one half inning later. Cincinnati's Joey Votto hits the game's final home run in the bottom of the 10th, but the American League holds on to win 8-6, claiming its sixth straight All-Star Game victory.

# 18

1897   Chicago Colts player-manager Cap Anson becomes the first major leaguer to reach the 3,000-hit milestone when he singles off George Blackburn of the Baltimore Orioles.

1927   Ty Cobb of the Philadelphia Athletics becomes the first player in major league history to reach 4,000 career hits when he doubles off Sam Gibson in a 5-3 loss to the Detroit Tigers.

1948   At Philadelphia's Shibe Park, Pat Seerey of the Chicago White Sox becomes the fifth player in major league history to homer four times in one game. The rotund outfielder's fourth home run is an 11th-inning game-winner, handing the White Sox a 12-11 victory over the host Athletics.

1964   In the Cincinnati Reds' 14-4 victory over the Philadelphia Phillies at Crosley Field, Reds second baseman Pete Rose belts the only grand slam of his 24-year career. Dallas Green, Rose's future manager with the Phillies, serves up the homer.

1970   Willie Mays of the San Francisco Giants becomes the 10th major leaguer to amass 3,000 career hits when he singles in the second inning of a 10-1 win over the Montreal Expos at Candlestick Park.

1987   New York Yankees first baseman Don Mattingly matches Dale Long's 31-year-old record by homering in an eighth straight game as the Yankees fall to the host Texas Rangers 7-2.

> ⓘ  Mattingly hit two grand slams during the record-tying streak and eventually set a new major league mark by belting six grand slams over the course of the season. Oddly, these were the only grand slams Mattingly ever hit during his stellar 14-year career.

1999   On Yogi Berra Day at Yankee Stadium with Don Larsen in attendance to commemorate his 1956 World Series perfect game, New York Yankees pitcher David Cone makes history of his own when he throws just the 16th perfect game in major league annals, defeating the Montreal Expos 6-0.

# 19

**1910**  Cleveland Naps 43-year-old right-hander Cy Young becomes the first and only member of the 500 Win Club when he defeats the Washington Senators 5–2 in 11 innings.

**1912**  Ty Cobb sets a major league record when he pounds out 14 hits over the course of consecutive doubleheaders with the Philadelphia Athletics. The Detroit Tigers star will finish the month of July with 68 hits, establishing another major league mark.

**1920**  At the Polo Grounds, New York Yankees outfielder Babe Ruth breaks his own single-season home run record in just his 82nd game of the year when he slugs homer No. 30 in an 8-5 loss to the Chicago White Sox.

ⓘ  Ruth finished his breakout season with an astounding 54 home runs, outhomering six other American League clubs all by himself.

**1942**  In a 7-6, 11-inning loss to the St. Louis Cardinals, 23-year-old star centerfielder Pete Reiser of the Brooklyn Dodgers suffers a career-altering concussion when he crashes into the outfield wall at Sportsman's Park in an unsuccessful attempt to catch what turns out to be a walk-off, inside-the-park home run by Enos Slaughter. Reiser will miss just four games, but he'll struggle in his return, batting just .244 the rest of the way to drop his season average from .350 to .310. The Dodgers, who were 61-26 and leading the National League by seven games before Reiser's injury, will finish two games behind the 106-48 Cardinals at season's end.

**1955**  In the Southern League All-Star Game, Chattanooga Lookouts outfielder James Lemon hits four home runs against the host Birmingham Barons.

**1960**  In one of the most sensational pitching debuts in major league history, 22-year-old Juan Marichal of the San Francisco Giants fires a complete-game one-hitter while striking out 12 in the Giants' 2-0 win over the Philadelphia Phillies at Candlestick Park. The Dominican Dandy retires the first 19 batters he faces and carries a no-hitter into the eighth before Phillies catcher Clay Dalrymple breaks it up with a single.

ⓘ  Marichal was the first modern-era National League pitcher to debut with a one-hitter.

# 20

**1859**  Amateur All-Star teams from Brooklyn and New York square off at Queens' Fashion Park Race Course in the first baseball game in which admission is charged. The fifty cents paid by each of the 1,500 spectators goes to support New York area fire departments.

1922  St. Louis Cardinals star Rogers Hornsby breaks Gavvy Cravath's modern National League single-season home run record when he belts his 25th homer of the season. The historic three-run shot gives the Cardinals a 7-6 walk-off win over the Boston Braves.

1976  Hank Aaron of the Milwaukee Brewers launches his 755th and final home run, a seventh-inning solo shot in the Brewers' 6–2 win over the California Angels at Milwaukee's County Stadium.

1993  Slugger Fred McGriff, recently acquired by the Atlanta Braves in a trade with the San Diego Padres, makes an immediate impact with his new club by hitting a key two-run homer in the Braves' 8-5, come-from-behind win over the St. Louis Cardinals. With McGriff in tow, Atlanta will march from nine games back to capture the National League West title by one game over the San Francisco Giants, winning 51 of their final 68 games to finish with a major league-best 104-58 record.

# 21

1892  Tim Keefe of the Philadelphia Phillies defeats fellow 300-game winner Pud Galvin and the St. Louis Browns 2-0. This will be the last matchup of 300-win pitchers until Phil Niekro of the Cleveland Indians and the California Angels' Don Sutton face each other in 1986.

1941  Former University of Michigan standout Dick Wakefield becomes baseball's first "bonus baby" when he signs with the Detroit Tigers for an unprecedented sum of $52,000.

1967  Hall of Famer James Emory "Jimmie" Foxx, nicknamed "Double X" and "The Beast," dies at age 59 in Miami, Florida. One of the greatest sluggers in baseball history, Foxx won three American League MVP awards and a Triple Crown during his 20 major league seasons and ended his remarkable career with a .325 batting average, 534 home runs and 1,922 RBIs.

1969  At a banquet held in Washington, D.C. to celebrate Major League Baseball's centennial anniversary, Babe Ruth is announced as baseball's greatest all-time player and Joe DiMaggio as its greatest living player.

⊙ MLB's gala celebration was held just one day after Neil Armstrong and Buzz Aldrin walked on the moon.

**1973**   Hank Aaron of the Atlanta Braves joins Babe Ruth as the only major leaguers to amass 700 career home runs when he drives a Ken Brett fastball into the left-center field stands in an 8–4 loss to the Philadelphia Phillies. Aaron's two-run blast leaves him just 14 home runs behind Ruth's all-time record.

## 22

**1923**   Walter Johnson of the Washington Senators becomes the founding member of the 3,000 Strikeout Club in a 3-1 victory over the Cleveland Indians at Dunn Field. The Big Train will finish his Hall of Fame career with 3,508 strikeouts, a total that will remain unsurpassed for six decades.

## 23

**1896**   In the Cleveland Spiders' 2-0 win over the Philadelphia Phillies, Spiders ace Cy Young falls just short of throwing his first no-hitter when slugger Ed Delahanty lines a clean single with two outs in the ninth inning.

**1925**   At Yankee Stadium, 23-year-old Lou Gehrig belts his first major league grand slam, leading the New York Yankees to an 11-7 win over the Washington Senators. Gehrig will end his storied career with 23 grand slams, a big league record that will stand until Alex Rodriguez breaks it in 2013.

**1942**   Future Hall of Fame pitcher Leon Day of the Newark Eagles strikes out 18 Baltimore Elite Giants to set a new Negro National League record.

**1962**   Fifteen years after breaking Major League Baseball's color barrier, Jackie Robinson becomes the first African American to be enshrined in the Baseball Hall of Fame when he enters along with pitcher Bob Feller, manager Bill McKechnie and outfielder Ed Roush.

**2009**   Mark Buehrle of the Chicago White Sox pitches the 18th perfect game in major league history, shutting down the visiting Tampa Bay Rays 5–0. Dewayne Wise, a ninth-inning defensive replacement, makes a spectacular home run-robbing catch to help preserve the gem.

> (i) Following the game, Buehrle received a congratulatory phone call from noted White Sox fan President Barack Obama.

## 24

**1911**   The first "all-star" game in Major League Baseball history takes place at Cleveland's League Park as a team composed of American League stars, including Ty Cobb, Eddie Collins, Walter Johnson and Tris Speaker, defeats the Cleveland Naps 5-3 in a benefit game held in memory of the recently deceased Addie Joss, Cleveland's longtime ace pitcher. A crowd of over 15,000 raises $12,914 for the Joss family.

1983  In the memorable "Pine Tar Game" at Yankee Stadium, Kansas City Royals star George Brett hits an apparent two-run homer off New York Yankees reliever Goose Gossage with two outs in the ninth inning to give the Royals a 5-4 lead, only to have the home run disallowed when umpire Tim McClelland upholds Yankees manager Billy Martin's claim that the pine tar on Brett's bat exceeds the 18 inches permitted. Brett is called out and New York is granted the victory, prompting Brett to famously charge out of the dugout after McClelland. American League President Lee MacPhail eventually overturns the call, upsetting both the Yankees and his umpires. When the game resumes on August 18, the Royals will complete the 5-4 win.

1993  New York Mets reliever Anthony Young suffers his major league-record 27th straight defeat when he walks in the deciding run in a 5-4 loss to the Los Angeles Dodgers.

## 25

1916  Detroit Tigers outfielder Harry Heilmann dives into the Detroit River and saves three people from drowning after the car they were in backed off a dock. The heroic act will soon become headline news, and Heilmann will receive thunderous applause from Tigers fans at Bennett Park the next day.

> ⓘ  Heilmann's older brother Walter drowned eight years earlier when his sailboat capsized.

1941  Lefty Grove of the Boston Red Sox wins his 300th major league game, defeating the Cleveland Indians 10-6 at Fenway Park. The 41-year-old future Hall of Famer will make six more starts before retiring with a 300-141 record.

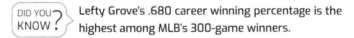

> DID YOU KNOW?  Lefty Grove's .680 career winning percentage is the highest among MLB's 300-game winners.

1956  At Forbes Field, Pittsburgh Pirates outfielder Roberto Clemente becomes the only player in major league history to hit a walk-off, inside-the-park grand slam when he clears the bases in the ninth inning to give the Pirates a dramatic 9-8 win over the Chicago Cubs.

1966  During his induction speech at Cooperstown, Boston Red Sox great Ted Williams calls for the inclusion of former Negro League stars in the Baseball Hall of Fame.

# 26

**1933**   San Francisco Seals 18-year-old star Joe DiMaggio sees his Pacific Coast League-record 61-game hitting streak come to an end when he goes hitless in five plate appearances against Oakland Oaks starter Ed Walsh Jr.

**1992**   Texas Rangers 45-year-old legend Nolan Ryan reaches 100 strikeouts in a season for a major league-record 23rd time during a 6–2 win over the Baltimore Orioles.

> (i)   Ryan also recorded his 319th career victory to pass Phil Niekro for 12th on the all-time wins list.

**2000**   The Arizona Diamondbacks acquire 33-year-old pitcher Curt Schilling from the Philadelphia Phillies in exchange for first baseman Travis Lee and pitchers Omar Daal, Nelson Figueroa and Vicente Padilla. During his four seasons with Arizona, Schilling will go 58-28 with a 3.14 ERA and team up with fellow ace Randy Johnson to lead the Diamondbacks to a World Series title in 2001.

**2005**   At Wrigley Field, Greg Maddux of the Chicago Cubs joins the 3,000 Strikeout Club when he fans Omar Vizquel in the Cubs' 3-2 loss to the San Francisco Giants.

# 27

**1904**   New York Giants owner John T. Brush and his manager John McGraw show their disdain for American League president Ban Johnson by publicly stating that their league-leading Giants will not participate in a postseason series with the victor of Johnson's "junior" league.

> (i)   When New York coasted to the National League pennant, Brush and McGraw stood firm in their refusal to play against the American League Champion Boston Americans, thus extinguishing any hope for a 1904 World Series.

**1959**   The Continental League, a proposed third major league, is formed by New York attorney William Shea with prominent baseball executive Branch Rickey as its president. The new loop plans to begin play in 1961 with franchises in New York City, Toronto, Atlanta, Buffalo, Dallas, Denver, Houston and Minneapolis.

> (i)   The league disbanded on August 2, 1960 when the American League and National League each agreed to expand into Continental League markets.

2008  While preserving a 6-5 victory over the Texas Rangers, reliever Brad Ziegler of the Oakland Athletics establishes a new major league mark with 27 consecutive scoreless innings to begin his career, topping the 101-year-old record of 25 set by the Philadelphia Phillies' George McQuillan.

# 28

1875  Joe Borden of the Philadelphia Whites pitches the first no-hitter in professional baseball history, blanking the Chicago White Stockings 4-0 at Philadelphia's Jefferson Park.

> ⓘ  While pitching for the Boston Red Stockings on April 22, 1876, Borden was also credited with the first win in National League history when he defeated the Philadelphia Athletics 6-5.

1989  St. Louis Cardinals outfielder Vince Coleman sees his record-setting stolen base streak end at 50 when catcher Nelson Santovenia of the Montreal Expos catches him trying to swipe second base.

> ⓘ  Coleman broke the previous record of 38 set by the Dodgers' Davey Lopes in 1975.

1993  At the Kingdome, Ken Griffey Jr. of the Seattle Mariners homers in his eighth consecutive game, tying the major league record held by Dale Long and Don Mattingly. Griffey's mammoth seventh-inning home run off starter Willie Banks accounts for the Mariners' lone run in their 5-1 loss to the Minnesota Twins.

# 29

1909  National League president Harry Pulliam, reportedly overwhelmed by the mounting strain of his job, dies several hours after shooting himself in his room at the New York Athletic Club.

1983  San Diego Padres first baseman Steve Garvey's National League-record consecutive games played streak ends at 1,207 after he dislocates his thumb during a home plate collision in the Padres' 2-1 loss to the Atlanta Braves.

# 30

1910  Connie Mack reluctantly trades 23-year-old prospect Shoeless Joe Jackson, sending him along with Morrie Rath to the Cleveland Naps for Bris

Lord and cash. After hitting just .150 in limited action with Mack's Philadelphia Athletics, Jackson will bat a rookie-record .408 in his first full season with Cleveland in 1911.

1933  St. Louis Cardinals right-hander Dizzy Dean sets a modern major league record by striking out 17 in an 8–2 win over the Chicago Cubs at Sportsman's Park.

1959  Willie McCovey of the San Francisco Giants impresses in his major league debut, going 4-for-4 with two triples, two RBIs and three runs scored against future Hall of Fame pitcher Robin Roberts of the Philadelphia Phillies. The 21-year-old McCovey earned the mid-season promotion by hitting .372 and belting 29 home runs at Triple-A Phoenix.

 Willie McCovey was the first player in National League history to triple twice in his major league debut.

1968  Bob Gibson of the St. Louis Cardinals defeats the New York Mets 7-1 to complete a run of 11 straight complete game wins in which he surrenders a total of just three runs. The phenomenal stretch lowers his ERA from 1.66 to 0.96.

ⓘ Gibson went on to capture both the National League Cy Young Award and Most Valuable Player award following his monumental 1968 season.

1980  While attempting to throw for the first time since being hospitalized for tests a week earlier, Houston Astros 30-year-old star pitcher J.R. Richard suffers a near fatal stroke that ends his career.

1990  MLB Commissioner Fay Vincent decrees that New York Yankees owner George Steinbrenner must resign as the club's general partner within three weeks and bans him from day-to-day operation of the team for life in light of evidence that Steinbrenner paid confessed gambler Howard Spira for damaging information about outfielder Dave Winfield and the Winfield Foundation.

ⓘ Vincent ultimately reinstated "The Boss," allowing for Steinbrenner's return on March 1, 1993.

2017  Third baseman Adrian Beltre of the Texas Rangers joins the 3,000 Hit Club when he doubles off pitcher Wade Miley in the fourth inning of a 10-6 home loss to the Baltimore Orioles. The 38-year-old Beltre becomes the

31st major leaguer to reach the historic milestone and the first Dominican-born player to do so.

# 31

**1891**   Twenty-year-old Amos Rusie of the New York Giants becomes the youngest pitcher in major league history to throw a no-hitter, blanking the Brooklyn Grooms 6-0 at the Polo Grounds.

**1954**   Using a borrowed bat, Milwaukee Braves slugger Joe Adcock hits four home runs and a double in the Braves' 15-7 victory over the Brooklyn Dodgers at Ebbets Field. Adcock becomes just the seventh major leaguer to hit four homers in one game and sets a new mark with 18 total bases.

**1978**   Cincinnati Reds 37-year-old third baseman Pete Rose singles off Phil Niekro of the Atlanta Braves to extend his hitting streak to 44 games, tying Willie Keeler for the longest streak in National League history.

**1981**   The bitter 50-day Major League Baseball strike ends as owners and players settle on issues related to free agent compensation. MLB's All-Star Game will be held on August 9, and its truncated regular season will resume on August 10.

**1990**   Nolan Ryan becomes the 20th major leaguer to amass 300 career wins when he pitches the visiting Texas Rangers past the Milwaukee Brewers 11–3.

**1997**   The St. Louis Cardinals trade for baseball's premier power hitter, acquiring first baseman Mark McGwire from the Oakland Athletics in exchange for young pitchers Eric Ludwick, T.J. Mathews and Blake Stein. McGwire will slug 24 home runs in two months with the Cardinals, finishing the season with a major league-leading 58 homers.

# AUGUST

## 1

**1925**  The New York Yankees purchase the contract of future Hall of Famer Tony Lazzeri from the Pacific Coast League's Salt Lake City Bees. Lazzeri will join the Yankees in 1926 after notching 60 home runs and 222 RBIs for the Bees this season.

**1945**  Mel Ott of the New York Giants joins Babe Ruth and Jimmie Foxx in the 500 Home Run Club when he hits a third-inning solo shot in the Giants' 9–2 home victory over the Boston Braves.

**1972**  Eighteen years after being in attendance at Busch Stadium as an eight-year-old to witness his childhood idol Stan Musial hit a major league-record five home runs in a doubleheader with the New York Giants, slugging first baseman Nate Colbert of the San Diego Padres matches the feat when he goes deep five times during a doubleheader sweep of the Atlanta Braves.

**1977**  Willie McCovey of the San Francisco Giants establishes a new National League record when he hits his 18th career grand slam in the third inning of a 9–2 win over the Expos at Montreal's Olympic Stadium.

**1978**  At Atlanta-Fulton County Stadium, Pete Rose's National League-record 44-game hitting streak comes to an end when he fans against Atlanta Braves reliever Gene Garber to close out the Braves' 16-4 win over the Cincinnati Reds.

**1986**  Bert Blyleven of the Minnesota Twins becomes the 10th pitcher in major league history to reach 3,000 career strikeouts when he fans Mike Davis in the Twins' 10–1 win over the Oakland Athletics. The 35-year-old right-hander strikes out 15 and allows just two hits in the complete-game victory.

**2005**  Baltimore Orioles slugger and new 3,000 Hit Club member Rafael Palmeiro is suspended for 10 days for violating Major League Baseball's new drug policy just five months after emphatically telling a Congressional reform committee "I have never used steroids. Period."

# 2

1906 The Chicago White Sox, baseball's famous "Hitless Wonders," launch their American League-record 19-game winning streak by defeating the visiting Boston Americans 3-0 at South Side Park. Chicago will make up 13 games on the league-leading Philadelphia Athletics during the historic run, moving from 7 1/2 games down in the standings to 5 1/2 games up.

> (i) The White Sox continued their winning ways in the postseason, claiming an improbable 1906 World Series title by defeating the powerhouse Chicago Cubs.

1907 Nineteen-year-old Walter Johnson makes his major league debut for the Washington Senators in a 3–2 loss to the Detroit Tigers. Ty Cobb's bunt single is the first hit off the future Hall of Famer.

1930 One of baseball's first great night games is played under a new portable light system at Kansas City's Muehlebach Field as Smokey Joe Williams, 45-year-old hurler for the Homestead Grays, and the Kansas City Monarchs' Chet Brewer hook up in a memorable pitcher's duel. Brewer strikes out 19, including 10 in a row, but loses in the 12th inning when Grays star Oscar Charleston scores the game's only run. The fireballing Williams is nearly untouchable, striking out 27 Monarchs while giving up just one hit in the complete-game victory.

1938 At Ebbets Field, the opening game of a doubleheader between the Brooklyn Dodgers and St. Louis Cardinals serves as a live experiment as a yellow-colored baseball is used in a major league regular season game for the first time in history. The test elicits an indifferent response, and the idea is soon scrapped.

1960 The Continental League, led by New York attorney William Shea and former Dodgers president Branch Rickey, ceases plans to create a third major league when the American League and National League each agree to expand into two of the existing Continental League markets. Shea's power play will result in new American League franchises in Los Angeles and Washington in 1961 and National League expansion into Houston and New York by 1962.

1979 New York Yankees 32-year-old star catcher Thurman Munson dies in Canton, Ohio while crash landing the small jet he was piloting. The beloved Yankees captain, a 7-time All-Star and 1976 American League MVP award winner, helped lead New York to World Championships in 1977 and 1978 and was one of the most revered competitors in the game.

> (i) Over 51,000 were on hand for his memorial tribute at Yankee Stadium the following day, and the entire Yankees team flew to Canton to attend his funeral on August 6.

# 3

**1921**   One day after eight Chicago White Sox players accused of throwing the 1919 World Series were acquitted by a jury, Judge Kenesaw Mountain Landis, the recently-appointed first Commissioner of Baseball, permanently bans the eight "Black Sox" from Organized Baseball, asserting that overwhelming evidence clearly shows the players' involvement in the fix.

**1933**   The New York Yankees suffer their first scoreless game in two years when they're shut out by Philadelphia Athletics ace Lefty Grove. Prior to Grove's gem the Yankees had scored at least one run in a major league-record 308 straight games.

**1948**   Former Negro League superstar Satchel Paige earns a win for the Cleveland Indians in his first major league start, beating Early Wynn and the Washington Senators 5-3 before a record night crowd of 72,434 at Cleveland Stadium.

**1960**   In an unprecedented move, general managers "Trader" Frank Lane of the Cleveland Indians and Bill DeWitt of the Detroit Tigers agree to swap managers, sending Joe Gordon to Detroit and Jimmy Dykes to Cleveland.

**1987**   In one of the most entertaining ejections in baseball history, Minnesota Twins knuckleballer Joe Niekro gets tossed after the umpiring crew catches him flinging an emery board from his pocket while they interrogate him on the mound about scuffed baseballs. Niekro's claim that he was using the board to file his fingernails convinces no one, including American League president Bobby Brown, who suspends him for 10 games.

**2012**   Brothers Justin and B.J. Upton hit their 100th career home runs on the same day. After Justin ripped a second-inning solo homer for the Arizona Diamondbacks in a 4–2 win over the Philadelphia Phillies, older brother B.J. hit his own solo shot an hour later for the Tampa Bay Rays in a 2–0 win over the Baltimore Orioles.

# 4

**1910**   Jack Coombs of the Philadelphia Athletics and future Hall of Famer Ed Walsh of the Chicago White Sox face off in a sensational 16-inning scoreless duel in Chicago. Coombs strikes out 18 and allows only three hits in what he calls his greatest game, while Walsh surrenders just six singles and strikes out 10.

**1945**   Bert Shepard, a World War II veteran who had his right leg amputated after his fighter plane was shot down in Germany, pitches an impressive

5 $\frac{1}{3}$ innings of relief for the Washington Senators in a 15-4 loss to the Boston Red Sox. The 25-year-old lefty strikes out two and allows just one run on three hits in what will be his only major league appearance.

**1982**  Joel Youngblood becomes the first player to record a hit for two different major league teams in different cities on the same day - and he does it against two future Hall of Famers. While still a member of the New York Mets, Youngblood goes 1-for-2 against Chicago Cubs pitcher Ferguson Jenkins in a day game at Wrigley Field, then singles off Steve Carlton of the Phillies later that night in Philadelphia after being traded to the Montreal Expos.

**1983**  While warming up before the fifth inning of a game at Toronto's Exhibition Stadium, outfielder Dave Winfield of the New York Yankees accidentally kills a seagull with an errant throw. Following the Yankees' 3–1 victory, Winfield is taken to the local police station and charged with cruelty to animals. The charge will be dropped the next day.

**1985**  Two longtime stars reach historic milestones on the same day as Rod Carew of the California Angels strokes career hit No. 3,000 in a 6-5 home defeat of the Minnesota Twins while Chicago White Sox pitcher Tom Seaver reaches 300 career wins with a 4-1 road victory over the New York Yankees.

**1989**  For the third time in 11 months, Dave Stieb of the Toronto Blue Jays loses a no-hitter with two outs in the ninth inning. New York Yankees outfielder Roberto Kelly plays spoiler on this day, doubling to end the perfect game bid. Stieb, who lost consecutive no-hit attempts the previous September, recovers to complete a 2–1 victory.

**2007**  New York Yankees third baseman Alex Rodriguez becomes the 22nd player in major league history to reach 500 career home runs when he belts a three-run shot in the first inning of a 16–8 win over the Kansas City Royals. Rodriguez, just eight days beyond his 32nd birthday, surpasses Jimmie Foxx as the youngest to reach the 500-homer plateau.

**2007**  Barry Bonds of the San Francisco Giants ties Hank Aaron's all-time home run record when he launches his 755th career homer in a 3–2 road loss to the San Diego Padres.

**2010**  On the third anniversary of his 500th career home run, Alex Rodriguez of the New York Yankees hits No. 600, a first-inning, two-run blast off Shaun Marcum in a 5–1 home win over the Toronto Blue Jays. At 35 years of age, Rodriguez becomes the youngest player to reach the rare milestone.

# 5

1921   Pittsburgh's KDKA becomes the first radio station to broadcast a Major League Baseball game. Harold Arlin handles the play-by-play duties as the Pittsburgh Pirates defeat the Philadelphia Phillies 8–5.

1922   St. Louis Cardinals star Rogers Hornsby breaks Ned Williamson's 38-year-old National League single-season home run record when he belts his 28th homer of the season in the Cardinals' 9-1 road loss to the Philadelphia Phillies.

1931   Detroit Tigers right-hander Tommy Bridges loses his bid for a perfect game with two outs in the ninth inning when he allows a bloop single to Washington Senators pinch-hitter Dave Harris. Bridges retires the next batter to close out the 13–0 win.

1986   Steve Carlton of the San Francisco Giants reaches 4,000 career strikeouts when he fans Eric Davis in an 11–6 loss to the Cincinnati Reds at Candlestick Park.

1999   St. Louis Cardinals slugger Mark McGwire launches his 500th career home run in the Cards' 10–3 loss to the San Diego Padres. McGwire becomes the 16th player to reach the 500-home run plateau and the first to hit his 400th and 500th homers in successive seasons.

2007   Tom Glavine of the New York Mets becomes just the fifth left-hander to join the 300 Win Club when he defeats the Chicago Cubs 8-3 at Wrigley Field.

# 6

1890   Twenty-three-year-old Cy Young takes the mound for the Cleveland Spiders in his major league debut and throws a three-hitter to earn a 6-1 victory over Cap Anson's Chicago Colts. During his 22-year Hall of Fame career Young will record an astonishing 511 career wins, nearly 100 more than any other pitcher in major league history.

1917   St. Louis Browns 41-year-old lefty Eddie Plank matches zeroes with Washington Senators ace Walter Johnson before finally faltering in the eleventh and losing 1-0. The brilliant performance turns out to be the last for the Hall of Fame-bound Plank, as he'll announce his retirement from the major leagues within a week.

> (i)   Eddie Plank finished his 17-year major league career with 326 wins, a record for lefties that stood for 45 years until Warren Spahn surpassed it.

**1979**   Just hours after attending Thurman Munson's funeral in Canton, Ohio, the New York Yankees return to Yankee Stadium and claim an emotional, come-from-behind 5-4 win in a nationally televised night game with the Baltimore Orioles. Veteran outfielder Bobby Murcer, a close friend of Munson's who eulogized the former Yankees captain earlier in the day, drives in all five New York runs with a three-run homer in the seventh inning and a two-run walk-off single in the ninth.

**1985**   The MLB Players Association initiates just the second midseason work stoppage in big league history when talks break down with the owners over issues relating to salary arbitration and the players' pension fund. The two sides will reach a new five-year agreement the following day, and all games missed during the two-day strike will be made up by season's end.

**1999**   San Diego Padres outfielder Tony Gwynn becomes the 22nd player in major league history to reach 3,000 career hits when he singles against Dan Smith of the Montreal Expos in the Padres' 12-10 victory.

# 7

**1956**   The Boston Red Sox fine star outfielder Ted Williams $5,000 for spitting at Boston fans for a third time in three weeks.

**1999**   One day after Tony Gwynn collected his 3,000th major league hit, Wade Boggs of the Tampa Bay Devil Rays does the same by homering off Chris Haney in Tampa Bay's 15-10 home loss to the Cleveland Indians.

**2001**   In a 6-5 win over the Houston Astros, Greg Maddux of the Atlanta Braves eclipses the National League record of 68 consecutive innings without allowing a walk when he pitches six clean innings to extend his mark to 70 1/3 innings.

> ⓘ   Maddux added two more innings to his record streak before issuing an intentional base on balls in his next start.

**2004**   Greg Maddux becomes the 22nd pitcher to reach 300 major league victories when he and the Chicago Cubs down the San Francisco Giants 8-4.

**2007**   At a packed AT&T Park, San Francisco Giants outfielder Barry Bonds lays claim to one of baseball's most cherished records when he surpasses Hank Aaron's career home run mark of 755 with a fifth-inning blast off Washington Nationals starter Mike Bacsik.

> ⓘ   Bacsik's father, Mike Sr., faced Hank Aaron as a reliever for the Texas Rangers on the day Aaron hit his 755th career home run.

**2016**   Ichiro Suzuki of the Miami Marlins records the 3,000th hit of his major league career when he lines a triple off Colorado Rockies reliever Chris Rusin in the Marlins' 10-7 win at Coors Field. The 42-year-old Suzuki becomes the 30th player to amass 3,000 major league hits, as well as the first Japanese player to do so.

# 8

**1903**   One of the greatest tragedies in MLB history occurs when a packed left-field balcony at Philadelphia's Baker Bowl collapses during a Phillies-Boston Braves doubleheader, killing 12 and injuring nearly 300.

**1957**   Dodgers owner Walter O'Malley confirms suspicions when he officially announces his plan to relocate his club from Brooklyn to Los Angeles prior to the 1958 season.

**1976**   At Comiskey Park, another Bill Veeck promotional stunt is put on display as his Chicago White Sox take the field against the Kansas City Royals wearing navy blue bermuda shorts, becoming the first team to wear shorts in a major league game.

**1988**   On 8/8/88, venerable Wrigley Field is readied for its first-ever major league night game as 91-year-old Chicago Cubs fan Harry Grossman pushes a button and proclaims "Let there be lights!" in a much-anticipated pregame ceremony. The Cubs-Philadelphia Phillies game that follows is wiped out by heavy rains after three innings, leading some to suggest that a higher power preferred the traditional day games at Wrigley.

**1997**   Seattle Mariners ace Randy Johnson fans 19 Chicago White Sox in a 5-0 win, becoming the first major leaguer to record two nine-inning, 19-strikeout games in the same season. Johnson's earlier 19-strikeout game came in a 4-1 loss to the Oakland Athletics on June 24.

**2019**   Less than two weeks into his major league career, Toronto Blue Jays shortstop Bo Bichette sets an MLB record when he doubles in his ninth consecutive game as his Blue Jays fall to the visiting New York Yankees 12-6. The hard-hitting 21-year-old also homered earlier in the contest to match Ted Williams' 1939 rookie record of hitting an extra-base hit in nine straight games.

# 9

**1975**   Los Angeles Dodgers second baseman Davey Lopes steals his 32nd consecutive base in a 2-0 win over the New York Mets, breaking the major league record set by Max Carey in 1922.

1998   Nicaraguan-born Dennis Martinez surpasses Juan Marichal's mark for most major league wins by a Latin American pitcher when he picks up his 244th career victory in the Atlanta Braves' 7-5 defeat of the San Francisco Giants.

2002   Barry Bonds of the San Francisco Giants joins Hank Aaron, Babe Ruth and his godfather Willie Mays in the exclusive 600 Home Run Club when he goes deep off Kip Wells in a 4-3 loss to the Pittsburgh Pirates at Pac Bell Park.

# 10

1888   New York Giants ace Tim Keefe registers his major league-record 19th consecutive victory when he and the Giants defeat the Pittsburgh Alleghenys 2-1.

> (i) Keefe surpassed by one the mark set by Old Hoss Radbourn during his remarkable 1884 season.

1944   Red Barrett of the Boston Braves sets a major league record when he needs only 58 pitches to earn a nine-inning, 2-0 win over the Cincinnati Reds. Barrett allows just two hits and does not walk or strikeout a batter in his remarkably efficient outing.

1960   In a 6-1 win over the Cleveland Indians, Ted Williams paces the Boston Red Sox with a double and two homers, the first of which is his 512th to move him into third place on the all-time home run list. After the game, the 41-year-old Red Sox icon announces that he'll retire at the end of the season.

1971   Sixteen baseball researchers gather at the National Baseball Hall of Fame Library and form the Society for American Baseball Research (SABR), with founder L. Robert Davids elected as president.

1981   In his first game since the end of the seven-week players strike, Pete Rose of the Philadelphia Phillies passes Stan Musial as the all-time National League hits leader when he singles against Mark Littell in the Phillies' 7-3 loss to the St. Louis Cardinals at Veterans Stadium. The hit is the 3,631st of Rose's career, placing him third on the career hits list behind only Ty Cobb (4,189) and Hank Aaron (3,771).

 On September 29, 1963, St. Louis Cardinals legend Stan Musial lined the last two hits of his career past Pete Rose, then a rookie second baseman with the Cincinnati Reds.

# 11

**1929**  Babe Ruth of the New York Yankees reaches another exclusive milestone when he slugs career home run No. 500, this one against Willis Hudlin in a 6-5 road loss to the Cleveland Indians.

**1940**  Stan Musial of the Florida State League's Daytona Beach Islanders ends his pitching career when he injures his throwing shoulder while making a diving catch in the outfield during a game with the Orlando Senators. The injury will be a blessing in disguise for the 19-year-old Musial, as he'll soon become a full-time outfielder and develop into a seven-time batting champion with the St. Louis Cardinals.

**1961**  Milwaukee Braves ace Warren Spahn becomes just the third left-hander and 13th pitcher overall to reach 300 major league wins when he tosses a complete game six-hitter in the Braves' 2-1 home win over the Chicago Cubs.

**1970**  Philadelphia Phillies right-hander Jim Bunning beats the Houston Astros 6-5 to become the first pitcher since Cy Young to amass 100 wins in both major leagues.

**1986**  Player-manager Pete Rose of the Cincinnati Reds notches a five-hit game for a National League-record 10th time in the Reds' 13–4 loss to San Francisco Giants.

**2003**  Kerry Wood of the Chicago Cubs becomes the fastest pitcher in major league history to date to strike out 1,000 batters when he reaches the mark in his 134th game, a 3–1 win over the Houston Astros. The 26-year-old breaks the record of Roger Clemens, who needed 143 games to reach the milestone.

# 12

**1936**  The 1936 Summer Olympics in Berlin, Germany provides the venue for the largest baseball crowd to date as more than 90,000 spectators watch a team of world amateurs claim a 6-5 victory over an American amateur club.

**1974**  California Angels fireballer Nolan Ryan breaks Bob Feller's American League record of 18 strikeouts in a game when he fans 19 in a 4-2 win over the Boston Red Sox. Ryan's historic output also matches the major league mark currently held by Steve Carlton and Tom Seaver.

**1987**  The Detroit Tigers, in search of pitching help for the stretch run, acquire veteran right-hander Doyle Alexander from the Atlanta Braves in exchange for 20-year-old minor league pitcher John Smoltz. Alexander will go 9-0 with a 1.53 ERA over the remainder of the season to help propel the

Tigers to a postseason berth, but Atlanta will reap the long-term rewards when Smoltz develops into a first-ballot Hall of Famer and helps lead the Braves to 14 straight division titles.

**1994**  Major League Baseball players initiate what will be the longest strike in big league history. The 232-day work stoppage will ultimately force the cancellation of the World Series for the first time in 90 years and will prematurely end the superb campaigns of Tony Gwynn (.394), Matt Williams (43 home runs) and the Montreal Expos (MLB-best 74-40 record).

# 13

**1906**  Chicago Cubs pitcher Jack Taylor's incredible "iron man" streak of 202 consecutive appearances without being relieved (187 complete games and 15 relief appearances) comes to an end when he's chased in the third inning of an 11-3 Cubs win over the Brooklyn Superbas.

**1948**  Former Negro League superstar Satchel Paige throws the first shutout of his major league career, leading the Cleveland Indians to a 5-0 win over the Chicago White Sox before a crowd of 51,013 at Comiskey Park. The 42-year-old rookie allows just five hits to improve his record to 5-1.

**1969**  Just four days removed from an extensive stint on the disabled list, Jim Palmer of the Baltimore Orioles no-hits the Oakland Athletics, winning 8-0 at Memorial Stadium. Palmer strikes out eight in the contest while issuing six walks, including three to slugger Reggie Jackson.

**1979**  St. Louis Cardinals outfielder Lou Brock reaches 3,000 career hits when he lines a single off Chicago Cubs pitcher Dennis Lamp in a 3-2 Cardinals win at Busch Stadium.

**1995**  Hall of Famer Mickey Charles Mantle, one of the greatest and most popular players in baseball history, dies at age 63 in Dallas, Texas. Mantle used his lightning speed and tremendous raw power to dominate the American League for much of his 18-year career. Despite a series of significant injuries, "The Mick" garnered 20 All-Star selections and won four home run titles, three MVP awards and a Triple Crown while leading the New York Yankees to seven World Series titles.

# 14

**1915**  Babe Ruth comes away the winner in his first mound matchup with legendary ace Walter Johnson when the Red Sox score two runs in the eighth inning to claim a 4-3 victory over the Washington Senators.

**1919**   Boston Red Sox slugger Babe Ruth clouts his 17th home run of the season, jump-starting a power surge that will produce seven home runs in the next 12 days. Ruth will hit his fourth grand slam of the season during this hot stretch, establishing an American League mark that will last for over four decades.

**1933**   Star slugger Jimmie Foxx strengthens his case for another league MVP award when he hits for the cycle and drives in an American League-record nine runs to lead the Philadelphia Athletics to an 11-5 road win over the Cleveland Indians.

 A record eight players, including Hall of Famers Earl Averill, Mickey Cochrane, Foxx, Chuck Klein and Arky Vaughn, hit for the cycle in 1933.

**1935**   In the Detroit Tigers' 18-2 win over the Washington Senators, All-Star pitcher Schoolboy Rowe supports his own mound effort by driving in four runs and scoring three more with a triple, double and three singles in five at-bats.

ⓘ Rowe helped lead the Tigers to a World Series title later this season after finishing with a 19-13 record (including a league-leading six shutouts) and batting .312 with 28 RBIs.

**1971**   Ten days after earning his 200th career victory, St. Louis Cardinals ace Bob Gibson throws his first and only no-hitter, downing the Pittsburgh Pirates 11-0 at Three Rivers Stadium.

**1986**   Cincinnati Reds player-manager Pete Rose records the 4,256th and final hit of his major league career in a 2–0 win over the San Francisco Giants at Riverfront Stadium.

**1987**   Mark McGwire of the Oakland Athletics establishes a new major league rookie record when he blasts his 39th home run of the season in a 7–6, 12-inning win over the California Angels.

ⓘ The 23-year-old slugger finished his record-breaking campaign with 49 homers.

# 15

**1886**   Pitcher Guy Hecker of the American Association's Louisville Colonels sets an all-time major league record when he scores seven runs in the Colonels' 22-5 win over the Baltimore Orioles at Louisville's Eclipse Park. Hecker also sets then-record marks of six hits, three home runs and 15 total bases in the game, all while tossing a complete-game, four-hitter.

 In 1886, Guy Hecker became the only pitcher in major league history to win a batting title when he finished one point ahead of teammate Pete Browning.

**1916** Boston Red Sox pitcher Babe Ruth improves to 3-0 lifetime against Walter Johnson after scattering eight hits in a 1–0, 13-inning win over the Washington Senators.

**1989** While in Montreal to face the Expos in his second start since recovering from cancer surgery, San Francisco Giants left-hander Dave Dravecky breaks his left arm while delivering a sixth-inning pitch to Tim Raines. The 33-year-old Dravecky will never pitch again, but the story of his courageous comeback will serve as inspiration for many.

**2011** Jim Thome of the Minnesota Twins becomes the eighth major leaguer to reach 600 career home runs when he goes deep twice in a 9-6 road win over the Detroit Tigers.

**2012** Seattle Mariners ace Felix Hernandez throws the 23rd perfect game in major league history, blanking the Tampa Bay Rays 1-0 at Safeco Field. Hernandez strikes out 12, including five of the last six batters he faces.

(i) King Felix's masterpiece followed perfect games tossed earlier in the year by Philip Humber and Matt Cain, marking the first time three perfect games were recorded in the same major league season.

# 16

**1920** The only on-field fatal incident in major league history occurs at the Polo Grounds as popular Cleveland Indians shortstop Ray Chapman suffers a fractured skull when he's beaned by submariner Carl Mays of the New York Yankees. The injury sends Chapman to nearby St. Lawrence Hospital, where he'll die twelve hours later.

(i) Ray Chapman's tragic death had a profound impact on the Cleveland Indians, who initially stumbled after the incident, then regrouped to make a stunning charge to a World Series title.

**1948** George Herman "Babe" Ruth, nicknamed "the Bambino" and "the Sultan of Swat," dies of cancer at age 53 in New York City, New York. Widely considered baseball's greatest player and one of the most celebrated athletes in the history of American professional sports, Ruth won three World Series titles with the Boston Red Sox as an ace pitcher and then won four more championships as a slugging outfielder with the New York Yankees. The charter Hall of Fame inductee led the American League in home runs a record twelve times, finishing with a career total of 714, and his unmatched popularity and power-hitting exploits changed baseball forever.

1996   Mexico hosts its first official Major League Baseball game when the San Diego Padres face the New York Mets at Estadio de Beisbol Monterrey. Mexican-born Fernando Valenzuela, a baseball legend in his home country, pitches six innings to earn the win for the Padres.

2009   Derek Jeter of the New York Yankees lines an RBI double off Seattle Mariners starter Doug Fister for his 2,674th hit as a shortstop, surpassing Hall of Famer Luis Aparicio's all-time record total for the position.

# 17

1882   In one of the greatest games of the 19th century, Providence Grays ace John Montgomery Ward records the longest shutout in major league history when he goes the distance in the Grays' 18-inning, 1-0 victory over the Detroit Wolverines. Renowned pitcher Old Hoss Radbourn, playing right field on this day, ends the game with a walk-off home run.

1933   New York Yankees first baseman Lou Gehrig plays in his 1,308th straight game, eclipsing Everett Scott's major league record.

> (i)   The Iron Horse went on to play 2,130 games in a row, setting a mark that would stand for over half a century.

1973   Willie Mays of the New York Mets hits the 660th and final home run of his spectacular career, a fourth-inning solo shot off Don Gullett in a 2-1, 10-inning loss to the Cincinnati Reds at Shea Stadium.

1986   While making the final appearance of his major league career, 45-year-old Pete Rose strikes out looking against San Diego Padres closer Goose Gossage to end a 9-5 home loss for the Cincinnati Reds. Rose finishes his storied career with 15,890 plate appearances, 14,503 at-bats and 3,562 games played - all major league records.

# 18

1934   Star outfielder, cultural icon and national hero Roberto Clemente is born in Carolina, Puerto Rico.

1960  Lew Burdette of the Milwaukee Braves no-hits the Philadelphia Phillies at County Stadium, winning 1-0 while facing the minimum 27 batters. His lone blemish - a fifth-inning hit batsman - is wiped out by a double play.

(i)  Burdette also came up big at the plate on this day, going two-for-three and scoring the game's lone run.

1967  At Fenway Park, 22-year-old star outfielder Tony Conigliaro of the Boston Red Sox suffers a gruesome, career-altering injury when an errant fastball from California Angels starter Jack Hamilton shatters Conigliaro's cheekbone and damages the retina of his left eye. The tragic accident will sideline the young slugger for the rest of Boston's "Impossible Dream" season of 1967 and all of 1968 as well. Conigliaro will make a successful return to the majors in 1969, and in 1970 he'll post career highs with 36 home runs and 116 RBIs, but worsening eyesight will soon force him into retirement, prematurely ending a career that seemed fated for stardom.

DID YOU KNOW?  In 1964, Tony Conigliaro set a record for most home runs hit by a teenager when he belted 24 as a 19-year-old rookie. The following season he became the majors' youngest home run champion when his 32 homers led the American League.

2011  Former major league first baseman Mike Jacobs, currently a Colorado Rockies farmhand, becomes the first athlete in any North American professional sport to be suspended for testing positive for human growth hormone when he receives a 50-game suspension from Major League Baseball.

# 19

1921  Detroit Tigers 34-year-old star Ty Cobb becomes the youngest player in major league history to reach 3,000 career hits when he singles against Boston Red Sox pitcher Elmer Myers in the Tigers' 10-0 win at Navin Field.

1931  Philadelphia Athletics ace Lefty Grove defeats the Chicago White Sox 4-2 to notch his 16th consecutive win, matching the American League record shared by Walter Johnson and Smoky Joe Wood.

1951  St. Louis Browns owner Bill Veeck pulls off his most memorable publicity stunt, sending 3'7" Eddie Gaedel to the plate as a pinch-hitter in a game against the Detroit Tigers. Wearing uniform number 1/8, Gaedel walks on four pitches in his only plate appearance and is immediately replaced by a pinch-runner.

(i) After calling the stunt a mockery of the game, American League president Will Harridge voided Gaedel's contract the following day, thus ending the career of the shortest player in major league history.

1957   Citing poor attendance as the reason, New York Giants team owner Horace Stoneham announces that his board of directors voted in favor of relocating his club to San Francisco to begin play in 1958. The decision ends the Giants' 74-year run in New York.

1965   Cincinnati Reds pitcher Jim Maloney throws a 10-inning no-hitter against the Chicago Cubs at Wrigley Field. Despite ten walks by Maloney, the game remains scoreless until shortstop Leo Cardenas homers in the tenth to give the Reds a 1-0 win.

(i) Earlier in the year, Jim Maloney also no-hit the New York Mets for ten innings before giving up a game-winning home run in the 11th.

1980   Kansas City Royals star George Brett's torrid 30-game hitting streak comes to an end when he's held hitless by Jon Matlack in the Royals' 4-3 win over the Texas Rangers. Brett collected 57 hits in 122 at-bats (.467) during the streak, raising his season average 38 points to .404.

# 20

1915   Cleveland Indians cash-strapped owner Charles Somers trades star Shoeless Joe Jackson and his .371 lifetime batting average to the Chicago White Sox for outfielder Braggo Roth, pitchers Ed Klepfer and Larry Chappell, and $31,500.

1919   Former major league outfielder Joe Wilhoit, now with the Western League's Wichita Jobbers, sees his Organized Baseball-record 69-game hitting streak come to an end when he's held hitless by the Tulsa Oilers.

(i) The only two serious threats to Wilhout's record in later years each came from Joe DiMaggio, who fashioned a 61-game hitting streak as a San Francisco Seals rookie in 1933 and a 56-game streak while with the New York Yankees in 1941.

1938   Lou Gehrig of the New York Yankees extends his own major league record when he hits the 23rd and final grand slam of his career in the Yankees' 11–3 win over the Philadelphia Athletics.

**1945**  Brooklyn Dodgers 17-year-old shortstop Tommy Brown homers off Preacher Roe in an 11–1 loss to the Pittsburgh Pirates, becoming the youngest player in major league history to hit a home run.

**1948**  At Cleveland Stadium, a major league-record night game crowd of 78,382 sees 42-year-old Satchel Paige fire a three-hitter in the Indians' 1-0 win over the Chicago White Sox.

> (i) Paige became the fourth consecutive Cleveland Indians pitcher to throw a shutout, following Gene Beardon, Sam Zoldak, and Bob Lemon.

**1960**  Ted Williams of the Boston Red Sox joins Babe Ruth as the only major leaguers to date to reach the 2,000-walk plateau when he draws a first-inning free pass from Chuck Estrada in an 8–6 win over the Baltimore Orioles.

> (i) Only weeks from retirement, the 41-year-old Williams followed his historic walk with two long three-run homers in the last multi-home run game of his career.

**1974**  Nolan Ryan of the California Angels records his third 19-strikeout game of the year in a 1–0, 11-inning loss to the Detroit Tigers. The 27-year-old fireballer will finish the season with 367 Ks, falling just 16 shy of the modern major league record he set the previous season.

**1985**  New York Mets 20-year-old ace Dwight Gooden becomes the first National League pitcher to reach 200 strikeouts in each of his first two seasons when he fans a season-high 16 in a 3-0 complete game win over the San Francisco Giants.

# 21

**1931**  Babe Ruth of the New York Yankees hits the 600th home run of his major league career, a three-run blast off George Blaeholder in an 11–7 win over the St. Louis Browns. Ruth will remain the only player to amass 600 career homers until Willie Mays reaches the mark in 1969.

**1947**  Little League Baseball hosts its inaugural National Little League Tournament in Williamsport, Pennsylvania. The local Maynard Midgets will win the 11-team tourney, defeating the Lock Haven All-Stars 16-7 in the championship game.

**1975**  At Wrigley Field, Chicago Cubs pitchers Rick and Paul Reuschel distinguish themselves as the first pair of brothers in major league history to throw a combined shutout when Rick starts and Paul finishes a 7-0 victory over the Los Angeles Dodgers.

1982  Rollie Fingers of the Milwaukee Brewers becomes the first pitcher in major league history to amass 300 career saves when he closes out a 3–2 win over the Seattle Mariners at the Kingdome.

2013  New York Yankees outfielder Ichiro Suzuki collects the 4,000th hit of his professional baseball career in the Yankees' 4-2 defeat of the Toronto Blue Jays at Yankee Stadium. The historic hit is Ichiro's 2,722nd as a major leaguer after recording 1,278 for the Japanese Pacific League's Orix Blue Wave from 1992 through 2000.

# 22

1965  An ugly incident breaks out in a game between the Los Angeles Dodgers and the San Francisco Giants when Giants pitcher Juan Marichal, thinking Dodgers catcher John Roseboro threw too close to his head when returning the ball back to pitcher Sandy Koufax, attacks Roseboro with his bat, igniting a 14-minute, bench-clearing brawl.

(i)  National League President Warren Giles responded by suspending Marichal for eight games and fining him $1,750.

1989  Nolan Ryan of the Texas Rangers becomes the first pitcher in major league history to reach 5,000 career strikeouts when he fans Rickey Henderson in the fifth inning of the Rangers' 2-0 home loss to the Oakland Athletics.

1999  In the first game of a doubleheader with the New York Mets, Mark McGwire of the St. Louis Cardinals launches two home runs, becoming the first major leaguer to hit 50 or more home runs in four consecutive seasons. Home run No. 49 travels over 500 feet and breaks a light bulb in the Shea Stadium scoreboard.

2007  The Texas Rangers establish a new American League record for most runs scored in a game when they rout the Baltimore Orioles 30–3 at Camden Yards.

(i)  The 30 runs scored by the Rangers were the most for a major league team since the Chicago Colts defeated the Louisville Colonels 36-7 on June 29, 1897.

# 23

1920  Thanks in large part to Babe Ruth's sensational play in his first year in New York, the Yankees become the first club in major league history to top one million in home attendance in a single season when a crowd of 20,000 sees them pound the Detroit Tigers 10-0 at the Polo Grounds.

1931 After winning his sixteenth game in a row to match an American League record in his previous start, Philadelphia Athletics ace Lefty Grove drops a 1-0 decision to pitcher Dick Coffman and the hapless St. Louis Browns. The lone run scores after reserve outfielder Jimmy Moore misjudges a routine fly ball with two outs in the third inning, allowing a runner to race all the way around from first. The volatile Grove, enraged not by Moore's blunder but rather by Al Simmons' absence due to injury, tears apart the clubhouse after the game.

1936 Seventeen-year-old phenom Bob Feller of the Cleveland Indians strikes out the first eight batters he faces in a 4-1 defeat of the St. Louis Browns. Rapid Robert finishes the game with 15 strikeouts, one short of the American League record.

1942 Retired legends Walter Johnson and Babe Ruth face off as a pregame attraction before the Washington Senators and New York Yankees play at Yankee Stadium. Ruth swats Johnson's fifth pitch into the right field stands and adds another homer before circling the bases. The event draws a crowd of 69,000 and raises $80,000 for Army-Navy relief.

# 24

1975 Los Angeles Dodgers second baseman Davey Lopes sees his major league-record streak of 38 consecutive stolen bases come to an end when rookie catcher Gary Carter throws him out in the 12th inning of the Dodgers' 5–3, 14-inning loss to the Montreal Expos.

1982 John Wathan of the Kansas City Royals breaks Ray Schalk's 66-year-old record for catchers when he steals his 31st base of the season in a 5–3 win over the Texas Rangers.

1989 Commissioner A. Bartlett Giamatti announces that Cincinnati Reds manager Pete Rose, baseball's all-time hits leader and one of the game's most iconic figures, is banned from baseball for life in response to evidence that Rose bet on baseball.

> (i) Rose became the 15th person to receive a lifetime banishment from baseball, and the first since 1943.

2001 In his major league debut, Jason Jennings of the Colorado Rockies hits a home run and two singles and tosses a complete game in the Rockies'

10–0 win over the New York Mets, becoming the first pitcher in baseball's modern era to pitch a shutout and hit a home run in his first major league game.

# 25

1922  At Cubs Park, the Chicago Cubs defeat the Philadelphia Phillies 26-23 in the highest-scoring game in major league history.

> (i) After trailing in this game by 19 runs after four innings, the Phillies nearly won after scoring 14 unanswered runs and leaving the bases full in the ninth.

1934  Rookie sensation Schoolboy Rowe of the Detroit Tigers wins his 16th straight decision, a 4–2 victory over the Washington Senators. The 24-year-old's winning streak ties the American League record shared by Walter Johnson, Smoky Joe Wood and Lefty Grove.

1939  New York Yankees third baseman Red Rolfe sets a modern major league record when he scores a run in his 18th consecutive game. Rolfe will finish the season with an American League-leading 139 runs scored.

1952  Virgil Trucks of the Detroit Tigers joins Johnny Vander Meer and Allie Reynolds as the only pitchers in major league history to throw two no-hitters in the same season when he blanks the New York Yankees 1-0.

> (i) In a highly dissonant statistical season, Trucks went just 5-19 in 1952 despite throwing two no-hitters and a one-hitter, largely because the last-place Tigers scored two or fewer runs in 15 of his starts. After leaving Detroit in an offseason trade, Trucks won 20 games in 1953.

1985  Dwight Gooden of the New York Mets records his 14th consecutive win and 20th victory of the season, defeating the San Diego Padres 9-3. At just 20 years and 9 months of age, Gooden surpasses Bob Feller as the youngest 20-game winner in major league history.

1996  The New York Yankees hold Mickey Mantle Day, during which a monument honoring the Yankee icon is dedicated. The statue is just the fourth to be housed in Yankee Stadium's Monument Park, joining those of Miller Huggins, Babe Ruth and Lou Gehrig.

2011  The New York Yankees become the first team in major league history to hit three grand slams in one game when Robinson Cano, Russell Martin and

Curtis Granderson each connect with the bases loaded during the Yankees' 22-9 rout of the Oakland Athletics.

# 26

1930  Chicago Cubs centerfielder Hack Wilson eclipses Chuck Klein's National League single-season home run record when he slugs his 44th homer of the season in the Cubs' 7-5 win over the Pittsburgh Pirates at Wrigley Field. Wilson will finish his historic season with 56 home runs and a major league-record 191 RBIs.

1939  At Ebbets Field, the first televised Major League Baseball game is broadcast, with Red Barber providing play-by-play coverage of a Brooklyn Dodgers-Cincinnati Reds doubleheader for local station W2XBS.

1980  Kansas City Royals star George Brett goes 5-for-5 in the Royals' 7-6 win over the Milwaukee Brewers to raise his batting average to a season-high .407. Brett will flirt with the .400 mark deep into September before finishing at .390.

1987  While watching from the on-deck circle, Paul Molitor of the Milwaukee Brewers sees his 39-game hitting streak come to an end when Rick Manning's RBI single clinches the Brewers' 1-0, 10-inning win over the Cleveland Indians. Molitor's streak is the longest in the American League since Joe DiMaggio hit safely in a record 56 straight games in 1941.

2002  An online audience of approximately 30,000 visits MLB.com to watch the New York Yankees face the Texas Rangers in the first-ever major league game streamed live on the internet.

> (i) Yankees shortstop Derek Jeter scored his 100th run of the season in the 10-3 New York win, joining Hall of Famers Earl Combs and Ted Williams as the only players in big league history to score at least 100 runs in each of their first seven seasons.

# 27

1955  Nineteen-year-old Sandy Koufax of the Brooklyn Dodgers earns his first major league win in impressive fashion, striking out 14 and allowing just two hits in a 7-0 defeat of the Cincinnati Redlegs.

> (i) The two teams tied a big league record when they combined to strike out 23 times.

1978   Cincinnati Reds second baseman Joe Morgan becomes the first major leaguer to reach 200 career home runs and 500 career stolen bases when he homers in a 7–1 loss to the Chicago Cubs.

1982   Oakland Athletics 23-year-old speedster Rickey Henderson breaks Lou Brock's single-season stolen base record when he steals his 119th base of the season in the Athletics' 5-4 loss to the Milwaukee Brewers.

(i)   Henderson finished his historic season with 130 stolen bases.

# 28

1884   New York Gothams right-hander Mickey Welch sets a major league record by striking out the first nine batters he faces in a 10–2 win over the Cleveland Blues.

1953   The Little League World Series is broadcast live for the first time as Jim McKay provides the play-by-play for CBS television while Howard Cosell announces the game for ABC radio.

2014   In the San Francisco Giants' 4-1 win over the Colorado Rockies, Giants pitcher Yusmeiro Petit retires his 46th consecutive batter, breaking the major league record previously set by Mark Buehrle of the Chicago White Sox in 2009.

# 29

1925   After being unruly throughout much of this season, New York Yankees star Babe Ruth is fined $5,000 and suspended indefinitely by manager Miller Huggins. A humbled Ruth will rejoin the team following a nine-game hiatus when he finally agrees to apologize and pay the enormous fine.

1977   St. Louis Cardinals outfielder Lou Brock breaks Ty Cobb's all-time stolen base record when he swipes the 892nd and 893rd bases of his career in a 4–3 loss to the San Diego Padres. Brock will extend his mark to 938 steals before retiring in 1979.

1993   George Brett of the Kansas City Royals joins Hank Aaron and Willie Mays as the only major leaguers in history to amass 3,000 hits, 300 home runs and 200 stolen bases when he steals a base in the Royals' 5–4 win over the Boston Red Sox.

# 30

**1905**  At Detroit's Bennett Park, eighteen-year-old Ty Cobb makes his major league debut for the Tigers in a 5–3 victory over the New York Highlanders.

 In his first plate appearance, Cobb lined an RBI double off future Hall of Famer Jack Chesbro.

Ty Cobb's big league debut came just three weeks after his mother accidentally shot and killed his father.

**1918**  Ted Williams, arguably the greatest hitter in baseball history, is born in San Diego, California.

**1965**  While still recovering from a broken hip suffered a month earlier, New York Mets 75-year-old manager Casey Stengel, one of baseball's legendary figures, announces his retirement.

 Stengel, who won 10 pennants and seven World Championships during his 12-year managerial tenure with the New York Yankees, was inducted into the Baseball Hall of Fame in 1966.

Having also played for both the Brooklyn Dodgers and New York Giants, among others, during his 14-year playing career, Casey Stengel holds the distinction of being the only person to have played for or managed all four of New York's major league clubs.

**1997**  Boston Red Sox shortstop Nomar Garciaparra's 30-game hitting streak, the longest streak ever for an American League rookie, comes to an end in a 15-2 loss to the Atlanta Braves.

**2006**  Curt Schilling of the Boston Red Sox becomes the 14th pitcher in major league history to reach 3,000 career strikeouts when he fans Nick Swisher in the first inning of Boston's 7-2 loss to the Oakland Athletics.

# 31

**1903**  In an unprecedented feat of durability and excellence, Joe McGinnity of the New York Giants completes and wins both games of a doubleheader for the third time in a calendar month, defeating the Philadelphia Phillies by scores of 4-1 and 9-2 today after previously claiming same-day sweeps of the Boston Beaneaters on August 1 and the Brooklyn Superbas on August 8.

> (i) The fabled Iron Man finished the 1903 season with a modern National League-record 434 innings pitched and led the league in wins (31) and complete games (44).

**1937** Detroit Tigers rookie Rudy York ties and then breaks Babe Ruth's one-month home run record when he slams his 17th and 18th homers of August in a 12–3 win over the Washington Senators.

**1950** Gil Hodges of the Brooklyn Dodgers smashes four home runs off four different pitchers and matches a major league record with 17 total bases in the Dodgers' 19–3 rout of the Boston Braves at Ebbets Field.

**1959** Playing in front of a record crowd of 83,000 at the Los Angeles Memorial Coliseum, Dodgers pitcher Sandy Koufax breaks Dizzy Dean's single-game National League strikeout record and ties Bob Feller's major league mark when he fans 18 in a 5-2 win over the league-leading San Francisco Giants.

**1990** Ken Griffey and Ken Griffey Jr. become the first father and son to play in the same major league game when they start for the Seattle Mariners against the Kansas City Royals. Both score runs in the 5–2 Mariners victory.

**1990** The Boston Red Sox and Houston Astros engage in a memorable swap when Boston acquires 37-year-old reliever Larry Anderson in exchange for minor league third baseman Jeff Bagwell, the Eastern League's reigning MVP. Anderson will pitch brilliantly in his 15 games with Boston, helping the Red Sox secure the American League East title, but the real prize of the deal is the 22-year-old Bagwell, who will soon establish himself as an offensive force in Houston, slugging 449 home runs and driving in 1,529 runs during a 15-year career spent entirely with the Astros.

**1998** Rickey Henderson of the Oakland Athletics scores the 2,000th run of his major league career in a 15–6 loss to the Cleveland Indians. Henderson joins Hank Aaron, Ty Cobb, Willie Mays, Pete Rose and Babe Ruth as the only players to date to reach the 2,000-run milestone.

**2017** The Houston Astros make one of the most crucial acquisitions in franchise history when they send a package of three prospects to Detroit for longtime Tigers star pitcher Justin Verlander just seconds before the waiver trade deadline. The 34-year-old Verlander, thought by some to be nearly washed up at the time of the trade, will go 5-0 (with a remarkable 1.06 ERA and .647 WHIP) down the stretch and 4-1 in the postseason, leading the Astros to their first-ever World Series title.

# SEPTEMBER

## 1

1902   The famed infield trio of Joe Tinker, Johnny Evers and Frank Chance take the field together for the first time when the Chicago Cubs call up Evers for today's doubleheader with the Philadelphia Phillies.

1916   Grover Cleveland Alexander of the Philadelphia Phillies notches his record-setting 14th shutout of the season, blanking the Brooklyn Robins 3-0. The losing pitcher in the game is Jack Coombs, who set the previous record of 13 shutouts while pitching for the Philadelphia Athletics in 1910.

1954   Joe Bauman of the Longhorn League's Roswell Rockets blasts four home runs in a 15–4 drubbing of the Sweetwater Spudders. Bauman will finish this season with a professional-record 72 home runs, a mark that will stand until Barry Bonds hits 73 for the San Francisco Giants in 2001.

1964   Twenty-year-old lefty Masanori Murakami becomes the first Japanese-born player to appear in a major league game when he debuts for the San Francisco Giants, pitching a scoreless inning of relief in the Giants' 4-1 loss to the New York Mets.

> ⓘ  Murakami was a key bullpen piece for the Giants in 1964 and again in 1965 before he returned home to continue his professional baseball career in Japan.

1971   At Three Rivers Stadium, the Pittsburgh Pirates make history by becoming the first major league team to field an all-minority starting lineup. The Pirates nine, which includes Rennie Stennett (2B), Gene Clines (CF), Roberto Clemente (RF), Willie Stargell (LF), Manny Sanguillén (C), Dave Cash (3B), Al Oliver (1B), Jackie Hernández (SS) and Dock Ellis (P), earns a 10-7 victory over the Philadelphia Phillies.

1975   Tom Seaver of the New York Mets reaches the 200-strikeout mark for a major league-record eighth consecutive season when he fans 10 in a 3-0 win over the Pittsburgh Pirates.

1989  Eight days after announcing his decision to ban Pete Rose from baseball for life, Commissioner A. Bartlett Giamatti dies suddenly at the age of 51 after suffering a heart attack at his summer home on Martha's Vineyard.

1998  With two home runs in a 7–1 win over the Florida Marlins, slugger Mark McGwire of the St. Louis Cardinals ties and then breaks Hack Wilson's 68-year-old National League record of 56 home runs in a season.

2019  At Toronto's Rogers Centre, Justin Verlander fires the third no-hitter of his illustrious career, leading the Houston Astros to a 2-0 victory over the host Blue Jays. The 36-year-old star right-hander allows just a first-inning walk and strikes out 14.

> ⓘ Verlander became just the sixth major leaguer to throw three or more no-hitters, joining Larry Corcoran (3), Bob Feller (3), Cy Young (3), Sandy Koufax (4) and Nolan Ryan (7).

# 2

1955  Chicago Cubs young star Ernie Banks breaks the single-season record for home runs by a shortstop when he smashes homer No. 40 in a 12–2 win over the St. Louis Cardinals.

1972  At Wrigley Field, Milt Pappas of the Chicago Cubs comes within one strike of pitching just the tenth perfect game in major league history before walking San Diego Padres pinch-hitter Larry Stahl. Pappas quickly regroups, retiring Garry Jestadt to complete the 8-0 no-hitter.

1990  After falling just short on numerous occasions, Toronto Blue Jays right-hander Dave Stieb finally adds a no-hitter to his resume after shutting down the Cleveland Indians 3-0.

2001  New York Yankees pitcher Mike Mussina narrowly misses throwing a perfect game when he surrenders a two-out, two-strike single to Carl Everett of the Boston Red Sox in the bottom of the ninth. Mussina settles for a one-hitter — the fourth of his career — as the Yankees win 1–0.

2006  Kevin Kouzmanoff of the Cleveland Indians becomes the first player in major league history to hit a grand slam on the first pitch he sees when he goes deep off Edinson Volquez in the first inning of the Indians' 6–5 win over the Texas Rangers.

# 3

1928   At Griffith Stadium, 41-year-old outfielder Ty Cobb of the Philadelphia Athletics records the 4,189th and final hit of his illustrious career when he lines a pinch-hit double in a 6–1 loss to the Washington Senators.

1961   New York Yankees outfielders Mickey Mantle and Roger Maris become the first pair of teammates in major league history to reach the 50-home run plateau in the same season when Mantle belts a ninth-inning homer in the Yankees' 8-5 win over the Detroit Tigers.

> (i) The slugging "M&M Boys" established a new single-season major league record by hitting a combined 115 home runs (61 for Maris, 54 for Mantle) in 1961.

1977   Sadaharu Oh of Japan's Yomiuri Giants hits his 756th career homer, breaking Hank Aaron's professional home run record.

> (i) Amidst national celebration, Oh was presented with the Japanese Medal of Honor the following day.

1993   Major League Baseball owners vote to split each league into three divisions and add another round to the playoffs, replacing the two-division setup that had existed since 1969.

2007   In his first appearance in nearly a year following offseason rotator cuff surgery, Pedro Martinez of the New York Mets becomes the 15th pitcher in major league history to reach 3,000 career strikeouts when he fans Aaron Harang in the Mets' 10-4 win over the Cincinnati Reds.

# 4

1986   Hall of Famer Henry Benjamin "Hank" Greenberg dies at age 75 in Beverly Hills, California. One of the greatest power hitters in baseball history, "Hammerin' Hank" led the American League in home runs and RBIs four times each and earned league MVP honors in 1935 and 1940. Greenberg is also recognized as the first Jewish superstar in American professional sports.

1993   Jim Abbott of the New York Yankees no-hits the Cleveland Indians, winning 4-0 at Yankee Stadium. Abbott accomplishes the impressive feat despite being born without a right hand.

> (i) As a sophomore at the University of Michigan in 1987, Jim Abbott beat out a field that included future NBA Hall of Famer David

Robinson to win the James E. Sullivan Award as the top amateur athlete in the United States, becoming the first-ever baseball player to claim the coveted honor.

1998 The New York Yankees win their 100th game on the earliest date in major league history, besting by five days the mark previously shared by the 1906 Chicago Cubs and 1954 Cleveland Indians.

1998 San Francisco Giants star Barry Bonds reaches base for a National League-record 15th straight time when he singles in the ninth inning of the Giants' 8-5 loss to the Los Angeles Dodgers. The streak, which includes two home runs, two doubles, five singles and six walks, eclipses the mark set by former Dodger Pedro Guerrero in 1983.

2017 At Dodger Stadium, J.D. Martinez becomes the 18th player in major league history to hit four home runs in one game, leading the Arizona Diamondbacks to their 11th straight victory. The slugging outfielder belts a two-run shot in the fourth, then follows with homers in the seventh, eighth and ninth innings of the 13-0 win.

ⓘ Martinez would go on to earn NL Player of the Month honors for September after becoming the first National Leaguer since Ralph Kiner in 1949 to hit 16 home runs in the month.

# 5

1914 Providence Grays 19-year-old pitcher Babe Ruth one-hits International League foe Toronto and aids his own cause by hitting his only minor league home run, a three-run blast off Ellis Johnson.

1948 Playing for the Amarillo Gold Sox of the hitter-friendly West Texas-New Mexico League, 29-year-old outfielder Bob Crues homers twice against the Lubbock Hubbers to reach 69 home runs on the season, matching the Organized Baseball record originally set by Joe Hauser of the American Association's Minneapolis Millers in 1933.

ⓘ Crues also established the single-season RBI mark with 254 while batting .404 and scoring 185 runs in just 140 games.

1971 Houston Astros flamethrower J.R. Richard matches Karl Spooner's record for most strikeouts in a major league debut when he fans 15 in a 5-3 win over the San Francisco Giants.

# 6

**1912**   In a highly-anticipated matchup at Boston's Fenway Park, an overflow crowd of 29,000 sees Smoky Joe Wood of the host Red Sox put his 13-game win streak on the line against the Washington Senators and star pitcher Walter Johnson, who himself fashioned an American League-record 16-game win streak just weeks before. Wood and the Red Sox prevail 1-0, with back-to-back doubles by Tris Speaker and Duffy Lewis producing the game's only run.

> (i) The Boston ace eventually matched Johnson's mark of 16 consecutive victories before dropping a game to the Detroit Tigers on September 20.

**1995**   In one of the most celebrated events in baseball history, Cal Ripken Jr. of the Baltimore Orioles plays in his 2,131st consecutive game to surpass Lou Gehrig's hallowed 56-year-old record. Ripken thrills the capacity crowd at Camden Yards with a fourth-inning home run off California Angels pitcher Shawn Boskie, then sets off an explosion of flash bulbs and applause one inning later when he takes a spontaneous victory lap after the game became official.

**1996**   Eddie Murray of the Baltimore Orioles becomes the 15th member of the 500 Home Run Club when he hits a solo shot off Felipe Lira in the seventh inning of a 5-4, 12-inning loss to the Detroit Tigers at Camden Yards. Murray's historic blast also allows him to join the select company of Hank Aaron and Willie Mays as the only major leaguers to date to amass both 500 homers and 3,000 hits.

**2010**   New York Yankees third baseman Alex Rodriguez reaches 100 RBIs for a major league-record 14th season when he hits a sacrifice fly in the sixth inning of the Yankees' 4–3 loss to the Baltimore Orioles.

> (i) Rodriguez had previously shared the record with iconic sluggers Jimmie Foxx, Lou Gehrig and Babe Ruth.

# 7

**1911**   Philadelphia Phillies rookie sensation Grover Cleveland Alexander fires a one-hitter to defeat 44-year-old Cy Young and the Boston Rustlers 1-0. With Young just weeks away from retirement, this marks the only matchup of the two pitching titans.

> (i) In 1911, the 24-year-old Alexander fashioned one of the greatest rookie seasons in major league history as he established modern

rookie records with 28 victories and 227 strikeouts while leading the National League in complete games (31) and innings pitched (367).

1975   The Cincinnati Reds clinch a division title earlier than any other team in history, securing the National League West with an 8–4 win over the San Francisco Giants. The Reds' victory leaves the second-place Los Angeles Dodgers 20 1/2 games out of first.

1978   Baseball's "Boston Massacre" begins at Fenway Park as the New York Yankees, who start the day just four games behind the division-leading Red Sox after trailing by as many as 14 games seven weeks earlier, pummel Boston 15-3. The World Series-bound Yankees will go on to sweep the Red Sox in the memorable four-game tilt, outscoring them 42-9.

1984   New York Mets 19-year-old phenom Dwight Gooden breaks Grover Cleveland Alexander's National League rookie strikeout record when he fans his 228th batter of the season during a 10-0, one-hit win over the Chicago Cubs.

1993   St. Louis Cardinals outfielder Mark Whiten becomes the 12th player in major league history to homer four times in one game in the Cardinals' 15-2 win over the Cincinnati Reds at Riverfront Stadium. Whiten's remarkable power display also produces 12 RBIs, tying Jim Bottomley's single-game record.

(i)   Prior to this game, Whiten had gone four weeks without homering.

1998   At Busch Stadium, slugger Mark McGwire of the St. Louis Cardinals matches Roger Maris' hallowed single-season home run record when he belts homer No. 61 against Chicago Cubs pitcher Mike Morgan in the first inning of the Cardinals' 3-2 win.

(i)   Big Mac hit his historic 61st home run on his father's 61st birthday.

# 8

1916   At Shibe Park, Philadelphia Athletics catcher Wally Schang becomes the first player in major league history to homer from both sides of the plate in the same game as the hapless Athletics defeat the New York Yankees 8-2. Few witness the historic achievement, though, as only 23 spectators are in attendance.

1919   Babe Ruth of the Boston Red Sox eclipses Buck Freeman's modern single-season home run record when he clouts his 26th homer of the season in a 3-1 win over the New York Yankees at the Polo Grounds.

1985  Cincinnati Reds player-manager Pete Rose ties Ty Cobb's major league record for career hits, presumed to be 4,191 at the time, when he lashes a fifth-inning single off Chicago Cubs starter Reggie Patterson at Wrigley Field.

1995  The Cleveland Indians defeat the Baltimore Orioles 3-2 to win the American League Central and earn their first playoff appearance since 1954, ending the longest postseason drought in the major leagues. The Indians secure the division faster than any other team in history, clinching in game No. 123 of the strike-shortened season.

1998  St. Louis Cardinals star Mark McGwire sets off a wild celebration at Busch Stadium when he breaks Roger Maris' single-season home run record by lining his 62nd homer of the season off Chicago Cubs pitcher Steve Trachsel in the fourth inning of the Cardinals' 6-3 win. The Cubs' Sammy Sosa, who hit his 58th home run earlier in the game, rushes in from right field to give Big Mac a congratulatory hug.

> ⓘ  In the great home run chase of 1998, both McGwire and Sosa eventually surpassed Maris' record, with each hitting eight more homers by season's end.

# 9

1915  Albert Goodwill Spalding dies of a stroke at age 65 in San Diego, California. Spalding was arguably the most important figure in early baseball, first as its premier pitcher, then as a highly successful manager, executive and promoter. He co-founded A.G. Spalding and Brothers, the most dominant sporting goods business in America in the 1800s, and in 1888 staged baseball's first world tour.

> ⓘ  For his efforts as the "organizational genius of baseball's pioneer days," Spalding was posthumously inducted into the Baseball Hall of Fame in 1939.

1918  In Game 4 of the World Series, Boston Red Sox pitcher Babe Ruth triples in two runs and extends his World Series-record scoreless innings streak to 29 2/3 before the Chicago Cubs tie the game at two in the eighth. The Red Sox respond with a run in the bottom of the eighth, and Ruth is credited with the win after Bullet Joe Bush pitches the ninth to secure the 3-2 victory.

1977  Shortstop Alan Trammell and second baseman Lou Whitaker make their big league debuts for the Detroit Tigers in an 8-6 loss to the Boston Red

Sox. The duo will go on to play 1,918 games together, more than any other middle infield tandem in major league history.

1992  Milwaukee Brewers 36-year-old center fielder Robin Yount becomes the third youngest player in major league history to amass 3,000 career hits when he singles off Jose Mesa in the seventh inning of the Brewers' 5–4 home loss to the Cleveland Indians. Only Ty Cobb and Hank Aaron reached the 3,000-hit plateau at a younger age.

2002  Randy Johnson of the Arizona Diamondbacks extends his own major league record by reaching 300 strikeouts for a fifth consecutive season when he fans seven in a 5–2 win over the San Diego Padres.

# 10

1881  With the Troy Trojans trailing the Worchester Ruby Legs by three runs and down to their last out, slugger Roger Connor powers the Trojans to an 8-7 walk-off victory when he hits what is believed to be the first grand slam in major league history.

1919  Just two weeks after being knocked unconscious by a lightning strike while on the mound, Cleveland Indians pitcher Ray Caldwell throws a no-hitter, blanking the New York Yankees 3-0 at the Polo Grounds.

 The Washington Senators' Clark Griffith thought so highly of Ray Caldwell that he reportedly offered to trade Walter Johnson for him in 1915.

1921  Walter Johnson of the Washington Senators breaks Cy Young's all-time record for strikeouts when he fans the 2,804th batter of his career during a 5–3 win over the Boston Red Sox.

1960  At Detroit's Briggs Stadium, New York Yankees star Mickey Mantle launches a prodigious home run that clears the right field roof and lands across Trumbull Avenue in the Brooks Lumber Yard. Twenty-five years later the blast, retroactively measured at 643 feet, will gain entry into the *Guinness Book of World Records*.

1969  After trailing in the National League East by as many as 10 games one month earlier and by five games just one week earlier, the New York Mets, baseball's perennial also-rans, take over the division lead from the Chicago Cubs with a doubleheader sweep of the Montreal Expos at Shea Stadium. The Mets, who had never finished higher than ninth place in their seven-year existence, will coast into the postseason, where they'll complete their truly "amazin'" season with a World Series title.

**1974**   Lou Brock of the St. Louis Cardinals breaks Maury Wills' single-season stolen base record when he steals his 104th and 105th bases of the season in the Cardinals' 8–2 loss to the Philadelphia Phillies at Busch Stadium. Brock also becomes the National League's new career leader in stolen bases, moving two ahead of Max Carey's total of 738.

**2000**   On his 37th birthday, Randy Johnson of the Arizona Diamondbacks becomes the 12th major leaguer to reach 3,000 career strikeouts when he fans a season-high 14 in a 4–3 loss to the Florida Marlins. With a first-inning K, the fireballing left-hander also reaches the 300-strikeout plateau for the fourth time in his career.

# 11

**1923**   Four days after throwing a no-hitter against the Philadelphia Athletics, Howard Ehmke of the Boston Red Sox one-hits the New York Yankees, giving up just an infield single to Whitey Witt to lead off the game. Ehmke's feat of surrendering just one hit over two straight complete games will stand as the major league record until Johnny Vander Meer surpasses it with consecutive no-hitters in 1938.

**1928**   Ty Cobb of the Philadelphia Athletics makes his last major league plate appearance, popping out as a pinch-hitter in the ninth inning of the Athletics' 5–3 road loss to the New York Yankees.

**1966**   New York Mets 19-year-old right-hander Nolan Ryan registers the first of his major league-record 5,714 strikeouts when he fans pitcher Pat Jarvis in the Mets' 8-3 loss to the Atlanta Braves.

**1985**   Before a packed house at Riverfront Stadium, Pete Rose of the Cincinnati Reds passes Ty Cobb to become Major League Baseball's new all-time leader in hits when he lines career hit No. 4,192 off San Diego Padres pitcher Eric Show in the first inning of the Reds' 2-0 win.

**2001**   In response to terrorist attacks on the World Trade Center, the Pentagon and Flight 93, Commissioner Bud Selig temporarily suspends the Major League Baseball season. Play will resume in six days, with the end of the season pushed back one week.

# 12

**1908**   Only one day after outdueling Philadelphia Athletics ace Eddie Plank, pitcher Walter Johnson of the Washington Senators is once again pressed into action when scheduled starter Charlie Smith comes down with a sore arm. Remarkably, the 20-year-old Johnson responds by tossing his fifth complete game victory in nine days, this time defeating the Athletics 5–4.

1911   Before a season-high crowd of 10,000 at Boston's South End Grounds, iconic pitchers Christy Mathewson of the New York Giants and the Boston Rustlers' Cy Young face each other for the only time in their careers. Matty and the World Series-bound Giants claim an easy 11-2 win, chasing the 44-year-old Young from the game in the third inning.

1932   When his New York Yankees clinch the American League pennant with an 8-3 victory over the Cleveland Indians, Joe McCarthy becomes the first manager in history to win pennants in both major leagues. "Marse Joe" had previously won a National League flag with the Chicago Cubs in 1929.

1954   A record-breaking crowd of 86,563 at Cleveland's Municipal Stadium sees the pennant-bound Indians sweep a doubleheader against the New York Yankees. Wins by future Hall of Famers Bob Lemon and Early Wynn all but end the Yankees' hopes for a sixth straight World Series title.

1962   Journeyman pitcher Tom Cheney of the Washington Senators sets a major league record when he strikes out 21 batters in a 16-inning, 2-1 win over the Baltimore Orioles.

1979   At Fenway Park, Carl Yastrzemski of the Boston Red Sox becomes the 15th member of the 3,000 Hit Club when he singles off Jim Beattie in Boston's 9–2 win over the New York Yankees.

1984   Dwight Gooden of the New York Mets breaks Herb Score's 29-year-old rookie record of 245 strikeouts when he fans a career-high 16 batters in a 2-0 shutout of the Pittsburgh Pirates.

2015   Boston Red Sox slugger David Ortiz becomes the 27th player in major league history to reach 500 career home runs when he goes deep for a second time off Tampa Bay Rays starter Matt Moore in Boston's 10-4 win at Tropicana Field.

# 13

1936   Cleveland Indians 17-year-old pitching sensation Bob Feller two-hits the Philadelphia Athletics and sets a new American League record by striking out 17 batters in the 5-2 victory.

1946   The Boston Red Sox clinch their first pennant in 28 years with a 1-0 win over the Cleveland Indians at League Park. Red Sox star Ted Williams hits the only inside-the-park home run of his career to account for the game's only run.

1965   Willie Mays of the San Francisco Giants becomes the fifth player in major league history to amass 500 home runs when he launches a fourth-inning solo shot in the Giants' 5-1 road win over the Houston Astros.

1971   Baltimore Orioles outfielder Frank Robinson becomes the eleventh member of the 500 Home Run Club when he hits a ninth-inning homer in a 10-5 home loss to the Detroit Tigers.

2008   Los Angeles Angels of Anaheim closer Francisco Rodriguez sets a major league record when he earns his 58th save of the season in the Angels' 5-2 win over the Seattle Mariners, breaking the mark set by Bobby Thigpen in 1990.

(i)   Rodriguez finished his record-breaking campaign with 62 saves.

2009   Seattle Mariners star Ichiro Suzuki reaches the 200-hit threshold for a major league-record ninth consecutive season when he legs out an infield single in the Mariners' 5-0 win over the Texas Rangers.

2017   With a 5-3 defeat of the Detroit Tigers at Progressive Field, the Cleveland Indians establish a new American League record with 21 consecutive wins, eclipsing the previous mark set by the 2002 Oakland Athletics.

(i)   The Indians added one more win to their record streak before losing to the Kansas City Royals on September 15.

# 14

1955   Cleveland Indians 22-year-old lefty Herb Score surpasses Grover Cleveland Alexander's rookie record of 227 strikeouts when he fans nine in the Indians' 3-2 loss to the Washington Senators.

1968   Right-hander Denny McLain of the Detroit Tigers claims his 30th win of the season, overcoming two Reggie Jackson home runs to beat the Oakland Athletics 5-4. The 24-year-old star becomes the first major leaguer to reach 30 wins in a season since Dizzy Dean in 1934.

1990   Ken Griffey and Ken Griffey Jr. of the Seattle Mariners become the first father-son duo to homer in the same game when they go back-to-back off Kirk McCaskill in a 7-5 loss to the California Angels.

**1994**  As the MLB players' strike extends to 34 days with no resolution in sight, team owners vote 26-2 to cancel the remainder of the 1994 season. The decision means there will be no World Series this year for the first time since 1904.

**2002**  At Coors Field, Chin-Feng Chen becomes the first Taiwanese player to appear in the major leagues as he walks and scores as a pinch-hitter for the Los Angeles Dodgers in their 16-3 rout of the Colorado Rockies.

> (i) As a 12-year-old, Chen was a member of the Tainan City, Taiwan team that won the 1990 Little League World Series.

# 15

**1914**  New York Yankees 23-year-old shortstop Roger Peckinpaugh becomes the youngest manager in major league history when he replaces Frank Chance at the Yankees' helm.

> (i) Peckinpaugh, known as "the calmest man in baseball," went 10-10 during his brief stint as Yankees player-manager.

**1931**  Lou Gehrig of the New York Yankees breaks his own American League record by driving in his 174th run of the season in a 9-2 win over the Detroit Tigers. The 28-year-old slugger will finish the season with 185 RBIs.

**1969**  Steve Carlton of the St. Louis Cardinals sets a modern major league record for most strikeouts in a nine-inning game when he fans 19 in the Cardinals' 4-3 loss to the New York Mets at Busch Stadium.

**1977**  Slugger Dave Kingman is on the move again, this time traded by the California Angels to the New York Yankees. After also suiting up for the New York Mets and the San Diego Padres earlier this year, Kingman becomes the first and only major leaguer to play in all four divisions in the same season.

**2002**  Curt Schilling of the Arizona Diamondbacks strikes out his 300th batter of the season in a 6–5 win over the Milwaukee Brewers. With fellow ace Randy Johnson already at 317 strikeouts, the two become the first pair of teammates to each reach the 300-strikeout plateau in the same season.

# 16

**1924**  Jim Bottomley of the St. Louis Cardinals goes 6-for-6 and collects a major league-record 12 RBIs in a 17–3 rout of the Brooklyn Robins.

(i) Coincidentally, the Robins were managed by Wilbert Robinson, the man who set the previous single-game record of 11 RBIs while playing for the Baltimore Orioles in 1892.

**1960**  Pitching in his 16th big league season, 39-year-old Warren Spahn of the Milwaukee Braves throws the first no-hitter of his career and sets a new Braves record with 15 strikeouts as he shuts out the Philadelphia Phillies 4-0 at County Stadium.

(i) Spahn's masterpiece came just one month after teammate Lew Burdette no-hit the very same Philadelphia Phillies on August 18.

**1975**  Pittsburgh Pirates second baseman Rennie Stennett matches Wilbert Robinson's major league record by collecting seven hits in a nine-inning game as the Pirates pummel the Chicago Cubs 22-0 at Wrigley Field.

**1993**  Dave Winfield of the Minnesota Twins becomes the 19th major leaguer to reach 3,000 career hits when he singles against Oakland Athletics closer Dennis Eckersley in a 5-1 victory at the Metrodome.

**1996**  Minnesota Twins designated hitter Paul Molitor collects the 3,000th hit of his major league career when he triples off Kansas City Royals starter Jose Rosado in the Twins' 6-5 loss at Kauffman Stadium.

# 17

**1916**  George Sisler of the St. Louis Browns throws a six-hit shutout, defeating ace Walter Johnson and the Washington Senators 1-0. The win is Sisler's second victory over the Big Train in as many starts.

(i) This was the last major league pitching victory for Sisler who, despite posting a 1.00 ERA in 1916, soon converted full-time to first base and gained Hall of Fame credentials as one of the era's greatest hitters.

**1941**  After storming through the minors, twenty-year-old Stan Musial makes his big league debut for the St. Louis Cardinals in the midst of a heated pennant race. Musial, batting third and playing right field, goes 2-for-4 and drives in two runs to lead the Cards to a 3-2 home win over the Boston Braves.

(i) Musial batted .426 in 12 games with the Cardinals in 1941.

**1947**  Major League Baseball hands out its first-ever Rookie of the Year Award to Dodgers first baseman Jackie Robinson, who will finish his first season in Brooklyn with a .297 batting average, 125 runs scored and a league-leading 29 stolen bases.

 In 1941, Jackie Robinson became the first UCLA Bruin to letter in four sports in the same year when he starred in baseball, basketball, football and track.

**1979**  Kansas City Royals star George Brett collects his 20th triple of the season in a 16–4 thumping of the California Angels, becoming the first major leaguer since Willie Mays in 1957 to reach 20 home runs, 20 triples and 20 doubles in the same season.

**1984**  Reggie Jackson of the California Angels belts his 500th career home run, a seventh-inning shot off Bud Black in a 10–1 loss to the Kansas City Royals. Jackson becomes the 13th member of the 500 Home Run Club exactly 17 years after hitting his first major league homer, and he accomplishes the feat at the same ballpark — Anaheim Stadium.

**1984**  Five days after striking out 16 in a game with the Pittsburgh Pirates, New York Mets rookie Dwight Gooden does the same to the Philadelphia Phillies in a 2–1 loss. Doc's total of 32 strikeouts over two consecutive starts matches the major league record.

**1993**  In front of more than 60,000 spectators at Anaheim Stadium, Texas Rangers legendary fireballer Nolan Ryan records his major league-record 5,714th and final strikeout when he fans Greg Myers in the Rangers' 2-1 loss to the California Angels.

**1998**  Denny Neagle improves to 15-11 with a 1–0 victory over the Arizona Diamondbacks, distinguishing the Atlanta Braves as the first major league team since the 1930 Washington Senators to boast five 15-game winners. The Braves quintet also includes Tom Glavine, Greg Maddux, Kevin Millwood and John Smoltz.

**2004**  San Francisco Giants slugger Barry Bonds joins Hank Aaron and Babe Ruth in the 700 Home Run Club when he takes Jake Peavy deep in the third inning of the Giants' 4-1 home win over the San Diego Padres.

**2018**  In an 8-0 win over the Cincinnati Reds at Miller Park, Milwaukee Brewers outfielder Christian Yelich becomes just the third player in modern major league history to hit for the cycle twice in one season. Yelich also becomes the first major leaguer to hit for the cycle twice in the same season against the same team, having done so in a 6-for-6 effort against these same Reds on August 29.

> [i] Yelich's scorching second half, in which he slashed .367/.449/.770 with 25 homers and 67 RBIs in 65 games, helped him capture the 2018 National League MVP award.

# 18

**1897** At Cleveland's League Park, Cy Young of the host Spiders throws the first of his three career no-hitters, blanking the Cincinnati Reds 6-0. Four Spiders errors prevent Young from recording a perfect game.

**1922** St. Louis Browns star George Sisler sees his modern major league-record 41-game hitting streak come to an end when he goes 0-for-4 against Bullet Joe Bush and the New York Yankees in the Browns' 3-2 loss.

**1984** The Detroit Tigers clinch the American League East title when they hand the Milwaukee Brewers a 3-0 defeat at Tigers Stadium. After starting the season with records of 9-0 and 35-5, the Tigers join the 1927 New York Yankees as the only teams in American League history to spend every day of the season in first place.

**1986** California Angels 40-year-old slugger Reggie Jackson joins Babe Ruth and Stan Musial as the only players in major league history to homer three times in one game after reaching age 40 when he goes deep off Dennis Leonard, David Cone and Dan Quisenberry in the Angels' 18-3 drubbing of the Kansas City Royals at Kaufmann Stadium.

**1996** Roger Clemens of the Boston Red Sox ties his own major league record by striking out 20 in a 4–0 victory over the Detroit Tigers. The 34-year-old allows only five hits and does not walk a batter.

# 19

**1901** All major league games are cancelled in observance of a national day of mourning for the recently deceased U.S. President William McKinley, who was shot five days earlier while attending the Pan-American Exposition in Buffalo, New York.

**1955** Chicago Cubs 24-year-old shortstop Ernie Banks establishes a new major league record when he belts his fifth grand slam of the season in the Cubs' 6-5 loss to the St. Louis Cardinals at Busch Stadium.

> [i] Banks' mark remained the major league high until Don Mattingly of the New York Yankees surpassed it by one in 1987.

**1984**  Pete Rose of the Cincinnati Reds doubles in the 3rd inning of a 4-2 win over the Atlanta Braves to become the first player in major league history to collect 100 or more hits in 22 straight seasons. The historic hit also allows Rose to match Stan Musial's National League-record total of 725 career doubles.

**2001**  Albert Pujols of the St. Louis Cardinals establishes a new National League rookie record when he drives in his 120th run of the season in an 8–2 win over the Milwaukee Brewers. The 21-year-old slugger breaks the previous mark set in 1930 by Wally Berger of the Boston Braves.

**2011**  New York Yankees star closer Mariano Rivera tosses a perfect ninth inning to earn his record-setting 602nd career save in the Yankees' 6–4 victory over the Minnesota Twins. The 41-year-old Rivera passes Trevor Hoffman on the all-time saves list.

# 20

**1919**  On Babe Ruth Day at Fenway Park, the Bambino ties Ned Williamson's single-season home run mark of 27 when he hits a game-winning solo shot off Lefty Williams in Boston's 5-4 defeat of the Chicago White Sox.

> ⓘ  Ruth took sole possession of the record four days later when he slugged a home run over the roof at the Polo Grounds.

**1924**  Grover Cleveland Alexander earns the 300th win of his major league career as he leads the Chicago Cubs to a 7-3, 12-inning victory over the New York Giants at the Polo Grounds.

**1968**  Mickey Mantle of the New York Yankees hits the 536th and final home run of his stellar career off Boston Red Sox starter Jim Lonborg in the Yankees' 4-3 loss at Yankee Stadium.

**1998**  Cal Ripken Jr.'s major league-record consecutive games played streak ends at 2,632 when he asks to be taken out of the Baltimore Orioles lineup prior to their game with the New York Yankees.

**2013**  Alex Rodriguez of the New York Yankees sets a new major league mark when he blasts his 24th career grand slam in the Yankees' 5–1 win over the San Francisco Giants. The historic clout breaks Rodriguez's tie with Lou Gehrig atop the all-time grand slam list.

# 21

**1892**  John Clarkson becomes the fifth member the 300 Win Club when he pitches his Cleveland Spiders to a 3–2 home victory over the Pittsburgh Pirates.

1934 The Dean brothers are masterful in the St. Louis Cardinals' doubleheader sweep of the Brooklyn Dodgers as Dizzy holds Brooklyn hitless until the eighth inning in the opener, eventually posting a three-hitter in the 13-0 win, while younger brother Paul no-hits the Dodgers in Game 2, winning 3-0.

(i) The Dean dominance on this day was a harbinger of good things to come in the postseason, as each would win two games in the Cardinals' 1934 World Series victory over the Detroit Tigers.

1970 Oakland Athletics 21-year-old pitcher Vida Blue, a late-season call-up from the American Association's Iowa Oaks, no-hits the Minnesota Twins at Oakland-Alameda County Coliseum, allowing just a fourth-inning walk to Harmon Killebrew in the 6-0 win. Blue becomes the youngest major leaguer to throw a no-hitter since Paul Dean of the St. Louis Cardinals, who accomplished the feat exactly 36 years earlier.

(i) Just 10 days earlier Blue one-hit the Kansas City Royals in a 3-0 win.

(i) In 28 starts between his September call-up in 1970 and his All-Star start in 1971, Vida Blue went 19-3 with a 1.53 ERA.

1999 After fanning 12 Toronto Blue Jays in a 3-0 victory to lift his season strikeout total to 300, Pedro Martinez breaks the Red Sox franchise record of 291 strikeouts set by Roger Clemens in 1988 and also joins Randy Johnson as the only pitchers in history to register 300-strikeout campaigns in both major leagues.

2001 In the first New York City sporting event since the 9/11 Terrorist Attacks, a crowd of 41,235 at Shea Stadium sees catcher Mike Piazza hit a dramatic two-run homer in the 8th inning to give the Mets a 3-2 win over the Atlanta Braves.

# 22

1911 At Forbes Field, Boston Rustlers 44-year-old pitching legend Cy Young records the 511th and final victory of his 22-year major league career when he goes the distance in a 1-0 defeat of the Pittsburgh Pirates.

1912 Eddie Collins of the Philadelphia Athletics steals six bases in a game for the second time in 12 days, this time against the St. Louis Browns at Sportsman's Park. Collins will remain the last major leaguer to record six stolen bases in a single game until Otis Nixon matches the feat on June 16, 1991.

1969  San Francisco Giants star Willie Mays joins Babe Ruth as the only players in major league history to reach the 600-home run plateau when he pinch-hits for rookie George Foster and belts a game-winning, two-run homer off Mike Corkins in the Giants' 4-2 win over the Padres at San Diego Stadium.

1993  Nolan Ryan's remarkable 27-year playing career comes to an abrupt end when he tears the ulnar collateral ligament in his right elbow six batters into his start for the Texas Rangers against the Seattle Mariners. The 46-year-old Ryan finishes his career with 5,714 strikeouts and seven no-hitters - both all-time major league records.

2002  Greg Maddux of the Atlanta Braves joins Cy Young as the only pitchers in Major League Baseball history to win 15 or more games in 15 consecutive seasons as he tosses seven strong innings to earn a 4-1 victory over the Florida Marlins.

2006  Washington Nationals outfielder Alfonso Soriano becomes the first major leaguer in history to reach 40 home runs, 40 doubles and 40 stolen bases in the same season when he lines a double in the Nationals' 3-2 win over the New York Mets at Shea Stadium.

2015  Hall of Fame catcher and New York Yankees icon Lawrence Peter "Yogi" Berra dies at age 90 in West Caldwell, New Jersey. Remembered fondly for his many "Yogisms" and his remarkable baseball talent and success, Berra won three MVP awards and garnered 15 straight All-Star selections as a central figure on a Yankees dynasty that won 14 pennants and 10 World Series titles during his 19-year playing career.

2017  Los Angeles Dodgers first baseman Cody Bellinger establishes a new National League rookie mark for home runs when he belts his 39th of the season in the Dodgers' 4-2 home victory over the San Francisco Giants. Bellinger eclipses the previous record set by Wally Berger in 1930 and matched by Frank Robinson in 1956.

> (i) Later that year, the 22-year-old Bellinger was unanimously voted National League Rookie of the Year.

# 23

1908  At the Polo Grounds, a game-ending base running mistake by Giants rookie first baseman Fred Merkle costs New York a critical win over the Chicago Cubs in one of the most controversial games in major league history. The 19-year-old Merkle failed to advance to second base following an apparent game-winning single by teammate Al Bridwell, and when Cubs second baseman Johnny Evers alertly retrieved a ball from the outfield and completed the force out at second, Chicago argued that the run shouldn't count. Umpire Hank O'Day agreed, and officially ended the game as a 1-1 tie due to impending darkness.

> ⓘ The fateful incident, known simply as "Merkle's Boner," proved especially costly for New York when the Cubs caught them in the standings by season's end and won a replay of the game on October 8 to claim the National League pennant.

**1956** Ozzie Virgil becomes the first Dominican to play in a major league game when he starts at third base for the New York Giants in their 6-2 loss to the Philadelphia Phillies.

**1962** Maury Wills of the Los Angeles Dodgers eclipses Ty Cobb's 47-year-old single-season stolen base record when he steals his 97th base in the Dodgers' 12-2 loss to the St. Louis Cardinals at Busch Stadium.

> ⓘ Wills added seven more stolen bases by season's end.

**1978** California Angels 27-year-old outfielder Lyman Bostock, a .311 hitter over four major league seasons, dies one day after being hit by an errant shotgun blast while riding in his uncle's car in Gary, Indiana.

**1983** Philadelphia Phillies 38-year-old lefty Steve Carlton becomes the 16th member of the 300 Win Club when he defeats the St. Louis Cardinals 6-2 at Busch Stadium.

**1984** Sparky Anderson, who previously piloted the Cincinnati Reds to 100-win seasons in 1970, 1975 and 1976, guides the Detroit Tigers to their 100th win of the season, becoming the first manager in major league history to oversee 100-win teams in both leagues.

**1988** Jose Canseco of the Oakland Athletics becomes the first major leaguer to amass 40 home runs and 40 stolen bases in the same season when he swipes two bases in Oakland's 9-8, 14-inning win over the Milwaukee Brewers.

# 24

**1931** Lefty Grove's dominance continues as he improves his season record to 31-3 with a complete game 9-4 victory over the Boston Red Sox. Astonishingly, the Philadelphia Athletics ace has recorded 46 wins and nine saves against only five losses since July 25, 1930.

1940  Boston Red Sox slugger Jimmie Foxx joins Babe Ruth in the 500 Home Run Club when he launches a sixth-inning solo shot in Boston's 16–8 win over the Philadelphia Athletics. Teammates Ted Williams, Joe Cronin and Jim Tabor also homer in the sixth, marking the first time an American League team tallies four home runs in one inning.

1957  Ted Williams' modern major league-record streak of reaching base safely in 16 consecutive plate appearances comes to an end when Washington Senators pitcher Hal Griggs retires the Red Sox star on a ground out. Williams will homer off Griggs in his next at-bat, providing the winning margin in Boston's 2-1 victory.

1974  Detroit Tigers great Al Kaline enters the 3,000 Hit Club in his hometown of Baltimore when he doubles off Orioles starter Dave McNally in a 5-4 Tigers loss.

1979  Pete Rose of the Philadelphia Phillies reaches the 200-hit plateau for a record 10th time when he lines a second-inning single in the Phillies' 7–2 home loss to the St. Louis Cardinals.

1984  The Chicago Cubs are playoff bound for the first time since 1945 when staff ace Rick Sutcliffe fires a two-hitter in the Cubs' division-clinching 4-1 win over the Pittsburgh Pirates at Three Rivers Stadium.

2009  *Sporting News* names St. Louis Cardinals star Albert Pujols the Major League Baseball Athlete of the Decade.

> (i) From 2001-2009, Pujols batted .334 and slugged .628 while averaging 41 home runs, 43 doubles, 124 RBIs and 119 runs scored per season.

2010  Cincinnati Reds reliever Aroldis Chapman throws the fastest pitch ever recorded in a major league game when he reaches 105.1 miles per hour while facing the San Diego Padres at PetCo Park.

# 25

1910  Philadelphia Athletics right-hander Jack Coombs' major league-record string of 53 scoreless innings comes to an end in the seventh inning of his 3-1 win over Ed Walsh and the Chicago White Sox.

> (i) Coombs finished the 1910 regular season with a stingy 1.30 ERA and an American League-record 13 shutouts. His excellence continued in the postseason, where he won three games in the Athletics' World Series triumph over the Chicago Cubs.

1929   Miller Huggins, the former New York Yankees manager who guided the team to its first six pennants and three World Championships, dies at age 51 at New York City's Saint Vincent's Catholic Medical Center.

> (i) In 1932, the Yankees installed a monument in Huggins' honor near the flagpole in centerfield at Yankee Stadium, beginning a tradition that later extended to many other Yankee greats.

1954   The Cleveland Indians eclipse the legendary 1927 New York Yankees' American League record of 110 wins when they thump the Detroit Tigers 11-1 at Cleveland Stadium.

1955   Detroit Tigers 20-year-old outfielder Al Kaline surpasses Ty Cobb to become the youngest batting champion in major league history when he finishes the season with an American League-leading .340 average.

1965   More than 12 years after his last big league appearance, 59-year-old Satchel Paige becomes the oldest pitcher in major league history when he takes the mound for the Kansas City Athletics and tosses three scoreless innings in a 5–2 home loss to the Boston Red Sox. Paige records a strikeout and allows just one hit - a Carl Yastrzemski double.

1965   San Francisco Giants 34-year-old star Willie Mays becomes the oldest major leaguer to date to hit 50 home runs in a season when he goes deep in the Giants' 7-5 win over the Milwaukee Braves at Candlestick Park. Mays was also the youngest to accomplish the feat when he slugged 51 home runs in 1955.

1974   Dr. Frank Jobe performs a revolutionary procedure when he replaces pitcher Tommy John's damaged left ulnar collateral ligament with a tendon from John's right wrist.

> (i) The reconstructive procedure, now commonly known as "Tommy John surgery" allowed its namesake to record 164 additional major league victories.

1986   Houston Astros right-hander Mike Scott caps an outstanding season by firing a 2-0 no-hitter against the San Francisco Giants. The victory seals the National League West title for the Astros.

> (i) Scott claimed the NL Cy Young Award in 1986 after posting an 18-10 record and leading the league in ERA (2.22) and strikeouts (306).

1989   Wade Boggs of the Boston Red Sox becomes the first modern major leaguer to reach 200 hits in seven straight seasons when he goes 4-for-5 in

Boston's 7-4 win over the New York Yankees. Boggs also becomes the first player in major league history to reach 200 hits and 100 walks in four consecutive seasons, topping the streak he shared with Lou Gehrig.

1997 Montreal Expos ace Pedro Martinez exits his last start of 1997 with 305 Ks and a 1.90 ERA, becoming the first major leaguer since Steve Carlton in 1972 to reach 300 strikeouts in a season while maintaining an ERA below 2.00.

2003 At Toronto's SkyDome, first baseman Carlos Delgado becomes the 15th player in major league history to slug four home runs in one game, leading the host Blue Jays to a 10-8 win over the Tampa Bay Devil Rays.

2007 At 23 years of age, Prince Fielder of the Milwaukee Brewers becomes the youngest major leaguer to hit 50 home runs in a season when he connects twice in the Brewers' 9-1 win over the St. Louis Cardinals. The slugging first baseman also makes history as one half of the first father-son duo to each reach the 50-homer plateau, joining his father Cecil who hit 51 round-trippers for the Detroit Tigers in 1990.

2016 Miami Marlins pitcher Jose Fernandez and two others are killed when the boat they are aboard crashes into a rocky jetty on the southern tip of Miami's South Beach. The 24-year-old Fernandez, a two-time All-Star and the 2013 NL Rookie of the Year, was one of baseball's brightest stars at the time of his death.

2017 Hulking outfielder Aaron Judge of the New York Yankees breaks Mark McGwire's 30-year-old major league rookie mark of 49 home runs when he slugs a solo shot in the seventh inning of the Yankees' 11-3 home win over the Kansas City Royals.

ⓘ Judge finished his record-breaking campaign with 52 homers.

2018 Washington Nationals star Max Scherzer becomes just the 17th pitcher in modern major league history to reach 300 strikeouts in a season when he fans 10 in the Nationals' 9-4 win over the Miami Marlins.

# 26

1908 At Brooklyn's Washington Park, Ed Reulbach of the Chicago Cubs becomes the only pitcher in major league history to throw shutouts in both ends of a doubleheader when he defeats the host Superbas by scores of 5-0 and 3-0.

1961 New York Yankees outfielder Roger Maris matches Babe Ruth's single-season record of 60 home runs when he sends a Jack Fisher pitch into the right field bleachers at Yankee Stadium in the third inning of a 3-2 win over the Baltimore Orioles.

**1981**   Houston Astros ace Nolan Ryan throws his major league-record fifth career no-hitter, blanking the Los Angeles Dodgers 5-0 at the Astrodome.

**1993**   At Mile High Stadium, the Colorado Rockies draw 70,069 fans to the final home game of their inaugural season, pushing their major league-record home attendance figure to 4,483,350.

**2012**   Washington Nationals wunderkind Bryce Harper joins Tony Conigliaro as the only teenagers to reach 20 home runs in a major league season when he goes deep against Philadelphia Phillies starter Kyle Kendrick in the Nationals' 8-4 win.

**2013**   New York Yankees great Mariano Rivera, baseball's all-time saves leader, throws his final pitch at Yankee Stadium and is met at the mound by longtime teammates Derek Jeter and Andy Pettitte for a memorable pitching change. Rivera breaks down in tears before exiting the field one last time to a thunderous standing ovation.

# 27

**1914**   Cleveland Indians great Nap Lajoie joins Cap Anson and Honus Wagner in the 3,000 Hit Club when he doubles against the New York Yankees in the Indians' 5-3 home victory.

**1923**   Twenty-year-old Lou Gehrig of the New York Yankees records the first home run of his illustrious career when he goes deep off Boston Red Sox starter Bill Piercy in the Yankees' 8-3 win at Fenway Park.

**1938**   In the Detroit Tigers' 10-2 win over the St. Louis Browns at Briggs Stadium, Tigers slugger Hank Greenberg sets a single-season major league record when he homers twice in a game for the eleventh time. Greenberg's historic power display moves him to within two home runs of Babe Ruth's record total of 60 with five games left to play.

(i)   Greenberg fell short of Ruth's mark after going homerless down the stretch.

**1968**   St. Louis Cardinals star Bob Gibson lowers his ERA to a National League-record 1.12 when he closes out his extraordinary season with a 1–0 win over the Houston Astros.

**1973**  Nolan Ryan of the California Angels breaks Sandy Koufax's modern single-season strikeout record by one when he fans 16 Minnesota Twins in a 5-4, 11-inning victory to finish the year with 383 Ks.

 Ryan's remarkable strikeout total for 1973 could have climbed even higher had he not opted out of his final scheduled start.

**1998**  St. Louis Cardinals slugger Mark McGwire finishes his historic season with a flurry as he homers twice against the Montreal Expos for a second straight game to push his single-season major league record to 70 home runs.

**1998**  In only his second major league start, Toronto Blue Jays right-hander Roy Halladay comes within one out of throwing a no-hitter before Bobby Higginson of the Detroit Tigers breaks it up with a pinch-hit home run. Halladay recovers to complete a 2–1 win.

**2005**  A victory by the New York Mets over the Philadelphia Phillies lifts the Atlanta Braves to their 14th straight division title — the longest such streak in professional sports history.

**2012**  In the Detroit Tigers' key 5-4 win over the Kansas City Royals, right-hander Doug Fister of the Tigers sets a new American League record by striking out nine consecutive batters. Fister's streak ends just one strikeout short of Tom Seaver's major league mark when catcher Salvador Perez grounds out weakly on a 1-2 pitch.

# 28

**1941**  Carrying a .3995 batting average into the final day of the season, 23-year-old Ted Williams of the Boston Red Sox opts to risk his ".400" average by playing in a doubleheader with the Philadelphia Phillies. Williams responds with six hits in eight at-bats to finish the season at .406, distinguishing himself as the last major leaguer to bat .400 in a season.

[i] In addition to his stellar batting average, Ted Williams achieved career bests in on-base percentage (.553) and slugging percentage (.735) while striking out only 27 times.

**1951**  Allie Reynolds of the New York Yankees fires his second no-hitter of the season, blanking the Boston Red Sox 8–0. Ted Williams fouls out to end the game after Yankees catcher Yogi Berra had dropped a foul ball earlier in the at-bat.

**1960**  At Fenway Park, Red Sox slugger Ted Williams homers in the final at-bat of his extraordinary career, sending a Jack Fisher pitch deep into the right-centerfield bleachers in the eighth inning of Boston's 5-4 win over the Baltimore Orioles. True to form, Williams refuses to tip his cap to the New England fans with whom he's had a love-hate relationship throughout his 19-year Red Sox career.

(i)  Famed writer John Updike memorialized the moment in his short story "Hub Fans Bid Kid Adieu," published the following month in *The New Yorker* magazine.

(i)  At the time of his retirement, the Splendid Splinter ranked third behind Babe Ruth and Jimmie Foxx with 521 home runs, second behind only Ruth with a .634 slugging percentage and first with a .483 on-base percentage.

**1974**  Making his final start of the year, Nolan Ryan of the California Angels hurls his third career no-hitter in a 4–0 shutout of the Minnesota Twins at Anaheim Stadium. Ryan fans 15 and pushes his season win total to a career-high 22.

**1988**  Orel Hershiser of the Los Angeles Dodgers throws ten shutout innings against the San Diego Padres to extend his streak of scoreless innings to 59, breaking the major league record set by Don Drysdale in 1968.

**1997**  Upon finishing the season with a National League-best .372 batting average, San Diego Padres 37-year-old star Tony Gwynn ties Honus Wagner's record of eight National League batting titles and becomes the first National Leaguer to win four consecutive batting crowns since Rogers Hornsby claimed six straight from 1920-1925.

**2011**  After trailing the Atlanta Braves by 10 ½ games in the National League Wild Card race five weeks earlier, the St. Louis Cardinals cap a remarkable late-season surge by winning the Wild Card on the season's final day as Cards ace Chris Carpenter blanks the Houston Astros 8-0 while the Braves drop a 4-3, 13-inning decision to the Philadelphia Phillies. The resilient Cardinals' excellent play will carry over into the postseason, where they'll survive their way to a World Series title.

(i)  After August 25 the Braves lost 20 of 31 games, including five straight to end the season, while St. Louis went 23-9.

**2011**  After moving into playoff contention with a late-season surge, the Tampa Bay Rays pull off a stunning 8-7 victory over the New York Yankees on the final day of the regular season to win the American League Wild Card race.

The Rays come all the way back from a late 7-0 deficit, scoring six runs in the eighth inning and adding another in the ninth on pinch-hitter Dan Johnson's clutch two-out solo home run. In the bottom of the 12th inning with the score still tied, star third baseman Evan Longoria sends the Tropicana Field crowd into a frenzy when he launches his second home run of the game, giving Tampa Bay the walk-off win and a spot in the playoffs.

> (i) The Rays, who were nine games behind the Boston Red Sox on August 31, fashioned a 17-10 record in September to finish one game ahead of Boston at season's end.

**2011**   Despite entering the month of September with the American League's best record, the Boston Red Sox fail to make the playoffs when they cough up a ninth-inning lead in Baltimore and fall 4-3 to the Orioles.

> DID YOU KNOW? Prior to this game, the 2011 Red Sox were 77-0 when leading after eight innings.

**2019**   In his final start of the regular season, Justin Verlander of the Houston Astros reaches two significant milestones when he records his 300th strikeout of the year and the 3,000th strikeout of his career in a 6-3 road victory over the Los Angeles Angels. Verlander becomes the 19th pitcher in modern major league history to reach 300 strikeouts in a season and the 18th to amass 3,000 career Ks.

**2019**   Pete Alonso of the New York Mets breaks Aaron Judge's rookie home run record when he slams his 53rd homer of the season in the Mets' 3-0 win over the Atlanta Braves at Citi Field.

> DID YOU KNOW? In 2019, Pete Alonso became the first rookie in modern baseball history to lead the majors in home runs.

# 29

**1954**   In Game 1 of the World Series at the Polo Grounds, one of the most iconic plays in baseball history occurs as New York Giants star Willie Mays makes "The Catch" - a racing, over-the-shoulder grab of Vic Wertz's 440-foot blast to centerfield that preserves an eighth-inning 2-2 tie with the Cleveland Indians. The Giants eventually win in the 10th inning when pinch-hitter Dusty Rhodes loops a three-run, walk-off homer to right off Bob Lemon which, ironically, travels just 270 feet.

**1957**   With John McGraw's widow Blanche and several former New York Giants stars - including pitchers Carl Hubbell and Rube Marquard - among the

11,606 in attendance, the San Francisco-bound Giants play their final home game at the Polo Grounds, losing 9-1 to the Pittsburgh Pirates.

1957   At 39 years of age, Ted Williams becomes the oldest player in history to win a major league batting title when he finishes the season with a stellar .388 average.

(i)   The Boston Red Sox icon broke his own record the following season when he repeated as batting champion.

1962   In the Milwaukee Braves' 7-3 victory over the Pittsburgh Pirates at County Stadium, 41-year-old ace Warren Spahn notches career win No. 327 to surpass Eddie Plank as the winningest left-handed pitcher in major league history.

1968   In the "Year of the Pitcher," Boston Red Sox star Carl Yastrzemski wins the American League batting title with a .301 average - the lowest league-leading batting average in major league history.

(i)   Danny Cater of the Oakland Athletics finished second with a .290 average, while the league collectively batted a record-low .230.

1975   Hall of Famer Charles Dillon "Casey" Stengel, nicknamed "The Old Perfessor," dies at age 85 in Glendale, California. Following a successful 14-year playing career, the colorful Stengel earned great acclaim as the manager of the New York Yankees from 1949-1960, guiding this juggernaut to ten pennants and seven World Series titles during his tenure.

1978   Jim Rice of the Boston Red Sox becomes the first American Leaguer since Joe DiMaggio in 1937 to reach 400 total bases in a season when he singles and doubles in Boston's 11–0 win over the Toronto Blue Jays.

2018   The New York Yankees eclipse the 1997 Seattle Mariners' major league record of 264 home runs when rookie second baseman Gleyber Torres goes deep in the Yankees' 8-5 win over the Boston Red Sox at Fenway Park.

(i)   With Torres hitting his homer from the No. 9 spot in the batting order, the Bronx Bombers also became the first team in major league history to produce 20 or more home runs from every spot in the lineup.

2019   In the Houston Astros' 8-5 close-out win over the Los Angeles Angels, Astros right-hander Gerrit Cole extends his run of spectacular domination when he notches his 16th straight victory and reaches 10 strikeouts in a game for a major league-record ninth consecutive start. Cole finishes the regular season with a franchise-best 326 Ks and MLB-record 13.8 strikeouts per nine innings.

Gerrit Cole's 326 strikeouts in 2019 were the most by a right-handed pitcher since Nolan Ryan fanned 341 for the California Angels in 1977.

**2019**   One hundred years into the Live Ball Era, home run hitting in baseball reaches dizzying new heights as the 2019 regular season comes to a close. A major league-record 6,776 home runs were hit this year as 14 teams established new single-season franchise records. Leading the way are the Minnesota Twins, who set a big league mark with 307 homers.

# 30

**1916**   The New York Giants claim the 26th and final victory of their major league record-setting win streak, defeating the Boston Braves 4-0 at the Polo Grounds.

**1927**   New York Yankees star Babe Ruth breaks his own single-season home run record when he launches his 60th homer of the season off Washington Senators pitcher Tom Zachary in the eighth inning of the Yankees' 4-2 win at Yankee Stadium.

> ⓘ This historic game also marked the final major league appearance for Washington Senators legendary pitcher Walter Johnson, who flied out to Ruth in the ninth inning while pinch-hitting for Zachary.

**1945**   Three-and-a-half months after returning from military service in World War II, slugger Hank Greenberg sends the Detroit Tigers to the World Series when his dramatic, ninth-inning grand slam against the St. Louis Browns at Briggs Stadium gives the Tigers a 6-3 win and the pennant on the final day of the regular season.

**1956**   At 16 years and 10 months of age, Jim Derrington of the Chicago White Sox becomes the youngest pitcher to start a modern major league game. The teenager tosses six innings and strikes out three in Chicago's 7–6 loss to the Philadelphia Athletics. Derrington also makes history as the youngest American League player to collect a base hit when he singles in the fourth inning.

**1972**   Pittsburgh Pirates star Roberto Clemente slashes hit No. 3,000, a fourth-inning double off New York Mets starter Jon Matlack in the Pirates' 5-0 win at Three Rivers Stadium.

> ⓘ Sadly, the historic hit was also Clemente's last as he perished three months later in a New Year's Eve plane crash while attempting to bring relief aid to earthquake victims in Nicaragua.

1980 Oakland Athletics 21-year-old outfielder Rickey Henderson breaks Ty Cobb's 65-year-old American League single-season stolen base record when he swipes his 97th base of the season in the Athletics' 5-1 win over the Chicago White Sox.

1988 For the second time in consecutive starts, Dave Stieb of the Toronto Blue Jays loses a no-hit bid with two outs in the ninth inning. Jim Traber of the Baltimore Orioles spoils Stieb's chance at history on this day, six days after Julio Franco of the Cleveland Indians had done the same.

1992 At Anaheim Stadium, Kansas City Royals legend George Brett enters the 3,000 Hit Club with an infield single off Tim Fortugno as part of a four-hit day in the Royals' 4-0 win over the California Angels.

1999 Randy Johnson of the Arizona Diamondbacks matches Nolan Ryan's major league record of 23 double-digit strikeout games in one season when he fans 11 in the D'backs' 5-3 win over the San Diego Padres.

2007 In the Philadelphia Phillies' 6-1 division-clinching win over the Washington Nationals, Phillies shortstop Jimmy Rollins lines a triple to become just the fourth major leaguer to reach 20 doubles, 20 triples, 20 home runs and 20 stolen bases in the same season. The other members of the 20-20-20-20 Club are Wildfire Schulte (1911), Willie Mays (1957) and Curtis Granderson, who accomplished the feat just three weeks earlier.

(i) Rollins, the eventual 2007 National League MVP, also became the first player in major league history to collect at least 20 doubles (38), 20 triples (20), 20 home runs (30) and 40 steals (41) in a single season.

# OCTOBER

## 1

**1903** In the first modern World Series game, Jimmy Sebring of the Pittsburgh Pirates records the first-ever Series home run when he belts a solo shot off Cy Young in the Pirates' 7–3 victory over the Boston Americans.

**1919** In Game 1 of the infamous 1919 World Series, the Cincinnati Reds drive 29-game winner Eddie Cicotte from the mound with a five-run fourth inning and coast to a 9-1 victory over the Chicago White Sox. Just prior to the game, the heavily favored White Sox oddly became betting underdogs. Despite this, few suspect that the Series is fixed.

**1922** St. Louis Cardinals star Rogers Hornsby becomes the first modern National League player to bat at least .400 in a season when he collects three hits in a 7-1 win over the Chicago Cubs to finish at .401.

> (i) The Rajah also established new National League records with 42 home runs, 152 RBIs and a .722 slugging percentage.

**1932** At Wrigley Field, Babe Ruth's legendary "Called Shot" home run off Chicago Cubs starter Charlie Root helps power the New York Yankees to a 7-5 win in Game 3 of the World Series. The homer, belted deep into the center field bleachers immediately after Ruth allegedly pointed in that direction, remains one of the most disputed and celebrated moments in baseball lore.

**1950** In front of a capacity crowd at Ebbets Field, the Philadelphia Phillies claim the National League pennant on the season's final day as Dick Sisler's clutch 10th inning, three-run homer off Don Newcombe propels the Phillies to a dramatic 4-1 victory over the powerful Brooklyn Dodgers. Ace Robin Roberts earns his 20th win of the season, securing the Phillies' first pennant in 35 years.

> (i) In the bottom of the ninth, Phillies outfielder Richie Ashburn made a game-saving play when he threw out Cal Abrams at the plate.

**1961** On the final day of a memorable season in New York, Yankees outfielder Roger Maris breaks Babe Ruth's hallowed single-season home run record when he belts No. 61 off Boston Red Sox starter Tracy Stallard in the Yankees' 1-0 win.

**1978**  On Fan Appreciation Day at San Diego Stadium, Gaylord Perry of the Padres joins Walter Johnson and Bob Gibson in the 3,000 Strikeout Club when he whiffs Joe Simpson in the eighth inning of a 4-3 win over the Los Angeles Dodgers.

> (i) Ozzie Smith, who was then a 23-year-old Padres rookie, performed the first of his trademark backflips for the fans on this day.

**2004**  Before a capacity crowd at Safeco Field, Seattle Mariners star Ichiro Suzuki surpasses George Sisler's 84-year-old single-season hit record when he collects hit No. 258 in the Mariners' 8-3 win over the Texas Rangers.

> (i) Ichiro finished his extraordinary season two days later with 262 hits, 20 more than any other single-season total since 1930.

**2006**  Minnesota Twins star Joe Mauer becomes the first catcher to win an American League batting championship when he edges out Derek Jeter of the New York Yankees for the title.

> (i) After leading the AL in batting average again in 2008 and 2009, Mauer became the only catcher in major league history to capture three batting titles.

**2007**  In a one-game playoff to determine the National League Wild Card winner, the Colorado Rockies advance to the postseason in dramatic fashion when they defeat the San Diego Padres 9–8 in 13 innings. The victory is the Rockies' 14th in their last 15 games.

> (i) Colorado's extraordinary hot streak continued in the National League playoffs, where they went 7-0 before being swept by the Boston Red Sox in the World Series.

**2018**  Major League Baseball experiences a statistical first when the 2018 regular season produces more strikeouts (41,207) than hits (41,019).

# 2

**1908**  Two future Hall of Famers match up in one of the greatest pitching duels in history as Chicago White Sox ace Ed Walsh strikes out an American League-record 15 batters and surrenders just one unearned run yet takes the loss as Addie Joss of the host Cleveland Naps pitches a perfect game.

**1920**  Following two days of rain, the Pittsburgh Pirates and the Cincinnati Reds square off in the last tripleheader in big league history, with Cincinnati winning the first two games and Pittsburgh claiming the finale.

> (i) Rookie Clyde Barnhart of the Pirates hit safely in each game, distinguishing himself as the only player in modern baseball history to record a hit in three major league games on the same day.

**1949**  A crowd of 68,000 at Yankee Stadium sees the New York Yankees defeat the Boston Red Sox 5-3 in a winner-take-all game for the American League pennant. Rookie Jerry Coleman's eighth-inning bloop three-run double provides the bulk of the scoring for the Yankees while starter Vic Raschi goes the distance for the win. Red Sox slugger Ted Williams goes 0-for-2 and narrowly misses out on his third Triple Crown when his .34275 batting average dips just below that of George Kell (.3429).

> (i) The National League pennant race also went down to the wire as the Brooklyn Dodgers defeated the Philadelphia Phillies 9-7 in 10 innings on this day to finish one game ahead of the St. Louis Cardinals.

**1963**  At Yankee Stadium, Sandy Koufax of the Los Angeles Dodgers sets a World Series record by striking out 15 batters in a 5-2 victory over the New York Yankees in Game 1. Koufax fanned the first five batters he faced and nine of the first 12 before coasting to the mark.

> (i) The Yankees were swept in this World Series for the first time in franchise history, as Dodgers starters Koufax, Don Drysdale and Johnny Podres along with relief ace Ron Perranoski limited the Bombers to a total of just four runs.

**1966**  Superstar pitcher Sandy Koufax helps clinch the National League pennant for his Los Angeles Dodgers when he defeats Jim Bunning and the host Philadelphia Phillies 6-3 on just two days rest.

> (i) This was Koufax's last career win.

**1968**  St. Louis Cardinals ace Bob Gibson overwhelms the Detroit Tigers in Game 1 of the 1968 World Series, striking out a Series-record 17 in a 4-0 complete game victory.

**1978**  In a dramatic one-game playoff for the American League East title between the Boston Red Sox and New York Yankees, light-hitting Bucky Dent's three-run homer off starter Mike Torrez in the seventh inning gives the Yankees a 3-2 lead, and Reggie Jackson's solo shot in the eighth provides the winning margin in the Yankees' 5-4 victory at Fenway Park.

With the Kansas City Royals, Los Angeles Dodgers and Philadelphia Phillies already having advanced to the postseason, the Yankees' win marked the only time in major league history that all four defending division winners repeated.

2012 Seven years after his only major league plate appearance ended in a beaning, Adam Greenberg gets a second chance when he pinch-hits for the Miami Marlins after signing a one-day contract. The 31-year-old strikes out on three pitches against New York Mets knuckleballer R.A. Dickey, but receives loud applause from a crowd that appreciates his courageous effort.

# 3

1904 New York Giants star Christy Mathewson sets a modern major league single-game strikeout record when he fans 16 in a 3-1 complete game victory over the St. Louis Cardinals.

1920 St. Louis Browns star George Sisler's three-hit day against the Chicago White Sox pushes his season hit total to 257, establishing a major league record that will survive into the 21st century.

> (i) In addition to his production at the plate on this day, Sisler also stole three bases and pitched a perfect ninth inning, striking out two.

1947 In Game 4 of the World Series, New York Yankees starter Bill Bevens falls one out short of throwing the first no-hitter in postseason history when Brooklyn Dodgers pinch-hitter Cookie Lavagetto lines a two-run double, giving the Dodgers a 3-2 walk-off win.

> (i) In what would be the only World Series start of his career, Bevens issued a Series-record 10 walks.

1951 In the deciding Game 3 of the first-ever National League playoff series, the New York Giants claim a stunning 5-4 walk-off win over the Brooklyn Dodgers when third baseman Bobby Thomson hits a three-run homer off reliever Ralph Branca in the bottom of the ninth. As Thomson rounds the bases and pandemonium ensues, Giants radio announcer Russ Hodges delivers one of the most iconic calls in sports broadcasting history: "There's a long drive ... it's gonna be, I believe ... The Giants win the pennant! The Giants win the pennant! The Giants win the pennant! The Giants win the pennant! Bobby Thomson hits into the lower deck of the left-field stands! The Giants win the pennant and they're going crazy! They're going crazy!" The dramatic win, dubbed the "Miracle of Coogan's Bluff," completes a remarkable late-season World Series run for the Giants, who trailed the Dodgers by 13 games in mid-August before going 39-8 down the stretch to force the tie-breaker series.

**1962**  In the finale of a three-game playoff to determine the National League pennant winner, the San Francisco Giants stage a dramatic rally, scoring four runs in the ninth inning to defeat the Los Angeles Dodgers 6-4 at Dodger Stadium. Veteran lefty Billy Pierce, who threw a three-hit shutout in the first game of the series, pitches a perfect ninth for the save.

> (i) The Giants trailed Los Angeles by four games on September 22, but forced the playoff series by finishing 5-2 while the Dodgers won just one of their final seven games.

**1974**  Frank Robinson becomes the first African American manager in Major League Baseball history when he agrees to take on that role with the Cleveland Indians.

**1982**  After losing the first three games of a season-ending four-game set in Baltimore to fall into a first place tie with the Orioles, the Milwaukee Brewers come up big in Game 162, winning 10-2 to claim their first American League East title. Shortstop Robin Yount leads the Milwaukee offense with two home runs and a triple while veteran starter Don Sutton earns the win.

> (i) The Brewers also reeled off three straight do-or-die wins one week later to defeat the California Angels in the American League Championship Series.

**1990**  George Brett of the Kansas City Royals goes 1-for-1 in his final game of the season, raising his batting average to a league-leading .329. After previously winning batting crowns in 1976 and 1980, Brett becomes the first player in major league history to claim batting titles in three different decades.

**2012**  Detroit Tigers star Miguel Cabrera finishes the season with an American League-leading .330 average, 44 homers and 139 RBIs, becoming just the 15th player to win the Triple Crown and the first since Boston's Carl Yastrzemski in 1967.

# 4

**1906**  The Chicago Cubs finish the regular season with 116 wins and only 36 losses, good enough for a major league-record .763 winning percentage.

> (i) Frank Chance's juggernaut led all National League clubs in offense, defense and pitching.

1922   The entire World Series is broadcast live over the radio for the first time in history as sportswriter Grantland Rice provides play-by-play reporting of the New York Giants-New York Yankees series at the Polo Grounds for station WJZ in Newark, New Jersey.

1948   The Cleveland Indians capture the American League pennant by defeating the Boston Red Sox 8-3 in a one-game playoff at Fenway Park. Indians player-manager Lou Boudreau goes 4-for-4 with two home runs while his rookie pitcher Gene Bearden gives up just five hits while going the distance.

> (i) Cleveland went on to defeat the Boston Braves in the World Series, with the knuckleballing Bearden earning a shutout victory in Game 3 and a five-out save in the deciding Game 6.

1955   At Yankee Stadium, the Brooklyn Dodgers win a long-awaited World Series title as 23-year-old lefty Johnny Podres blanks the New York Yankees 2-0 in Game 7. The Dodgers, who had fallen to the Yankees in all five of their previous World Series clashes, got a huge lift in the sixth inning when reserve outfielder Sandy Amoros made a tremendous catch and throw, turning Yogi Berra's potential game-tying liner into a rally-killing double play.

1964   After trailing the Philadelphia Phillies by 6 1/2 games just two weeks earlier, the St. Louis Cardinals end one of the most memorable playoff races in baseball history by earning an 11-5 victory over the New York Mets to win the National League pennant, finishing one game ahead of both the Phillies and Cincinnati Reds. While the Cardinals won 10 of their final 13 games, the Phillies, a club which held a comfortable lead throughout most of the season, collapsed down the stretch, losing 10 straight games to surrender first place.

1987   The Detroit Tigers complete a thrilling stretch drive, closing out a three-game sweep of the Toronto Blue Jays to claim the American League East title after having trailed the Blue Jays by 3 1/2 games with just over one week to play. Veteran lefty Frank Tanana twirls a six-hit shutout while outfielder Larry Herndon accounts for the game's only run with a second-inning homer.

2001   Rickey Henderson of the San Diego Padres eclipses Ty Cobb's all-time record of 2,245 runs scored when he hits a third-inning homer in the Padres' 6-3 win over the Los Angeles Dodgers.

# 5

1888   Pud Galvin of the Pittsburgh Alleghenys becomes the first pitcher to amass 300 major league wins when he claims a 5-1 road victory over the Washington Nationals.

1908   Chicago White Sox star pitcher Ed Walsh earns his league-leading 40th win of the year by defeating the Detroit Tigers 6-1. The victory extends the dramatic American League pennant race between the White Sox, Tigers and Cleveland Indians to the season's final day.

1918   Former National League infielder Eddie Grant becomes the first major leaguer killed in action during World War I when he's shot while leading a daring mission in the Meuse-Argonne offensive to rescue the "Lost Battalion" trapped behind German lines.

1929   Lefty O'Doul of the Philadelphia Phillies finishes the season with a National League-record 254 hits after going 6-for-9 in a doubleheader split with the New York Giants.

 Lefty O'Doul spent the first four years of his major league career as a pitcher before a sore arm forced him to the outfield. His historic 1929 campaign was his first as a full-time position player.

1941   With the Brooklyn Dodgers one pitch away from knotting the World Series at two games apiece, Mickey Owens, the normally sure-handed Dodgers catcher, drops a third strike from reliever Hugh Casey, allowing Tommy Henrich of the New York Yankees to safely reach first base. The Yankees quickly seize the opportunity, scoring four runs in the inning to win 7-4 and move one step closer to their ninth World Championship.

1947   At Yankee Stadium, Brooklyn Dodgers reserve outfielder Al Gionfriddo makes one of the most memorable plays in World Series history in the sixth inning of Game 6 when he robs New York Yankees star Joe DiMaggio of a potential three-run home run with a racing, spinning catch against the bullpen gate in deep left field to help preserve the Dodgers' 8-6 win.

ⓘ This was the final major league appearance for the 25-year-old Gionfriddo.

1953   The New York Yankees claim their unprecedented fifth straight World Championship after defeating the Brooklyn Dodgers 4-3 in Game 6. Second baseman Billy Martin led the way for the Yankees, collecting a record-setting 12 hits in the Series, including a walk-off RBI single in the deciding game.

1954   Future Hall of Famer Oscar McKinley Charleston dies at age 57 in Philadelphia, Pennsylvania. Considered by many to be the greatest all-around player in the history of the Negro Leagues, the fiery Charleston excelled at hitting for both average and power, and his great arm and blazing speed allowed him to revolutionize center field play. In addition to his dominance as a player, Charleston also earned acclaim as one of the league's greatest managers.

2001  At San Francisco's Pac Bell Park, Barry Bonds of the host Giants breaks Mark McGwire's single-season home run record when he slugs his 71st homer of the season off Chan Ho Park in the first inning of an 11-10 loss to the Los Angeles Dodgers.

# 6

1926  New York Yankees star Babe Ruth becomes the first player in history to hit three home runs in one World Series game, powering the Yankees to a 10-5 win over the St. Louis Cardinals in Game 4 at Sportsman's Park. With each majestic blast outdistancing the one before it, Ruth's final home run travels an estimated 530 feet to the distant center field bleachers, making it the longest home run in World Series history.

1945  The fabled "Curse of the Billy Goat" has its genesis at Game 4 of the 1945 World Series as Billy Goat's Tavern owner Bill Sianis and his pet billy goat, in attendance at Wrigley Field to see the hometown Chicago Cubs take on the Detroit Tigers, are kicked out of the park because of the goat's foul smell. Angered by the slight, Sianis places a curse on the Cubs. The legend of the curse proliferates when Chicago loses the World Series and repeatedly fails to win another National League pennant.

1966  Baltimore Orioles twenty-year-old right-hander Jim Palmer becomes the youngest pitcher to throw a World Series shutout when he defeats Sandy Koufax and the Los Angeles Dodgers 6-0 in Game 2.

1984  In Game 4 of the National League Championship Series, postseason veteran Steve Garvey hits a dramatic walk-off home run against Chicago Cubs closer Lee Smith, giving the San Diego Padres a 7-5 victory and evening the series at two games apiece.

1985  Phil Niekro of the New York Yankees earns his 300th career win as he goes the distance in the Yankees' 8-0 road victory over the Toronto Blue Jays. The knuckleballer becomes just the 18th major leaguer to amass 300 wins and, at age 46, the oldest pitcher in the 20th century to toss a shutout.

1991  New York Mets pitcher David Cone ties the National League single-game strikeout record when he fans 19 batters in a 7-0 win over the Philadelphia Phillies.

2001 At Seattle's Safeco Field, the host Mariners match the 1906 Chicago Cubs' single-season record of 116 wins when they pick up a 1–0 victory over the Texas Rangers.

2006 John Jordan "Buck" O'Neil, a star player and manager in the Negro Leagues and a trailblazing scout and coach in the majors, dies at age 94 in Kansas City, Missouri. Remembered as one of baseball's greatest ambassadors, the charismatic and ebullient O'Neil became especially cherished in later years for his remarkable contributions to the game.

2010 In Game 1 of the National League Division Series, Roy Halladay of the Philadelphia Phillies throws the first postseason no-hitter since Don Larsen's perfect game in the 1956 World Series as he shuts down the Cincinnati Reds 4-0 at Citizens Bank Park.

> ⓘ A fifth-inning walk to Jay Bruce was the only baserunner allowed by Halladay, who also pitched a perfect game earlier in the year on May 29.

# 7

1925 Former New York Giants star pitcher and future Hall of Famer Christopher "Christy" Mathewson, nicknamed "Big Six" and "Matty," dies at age 45 in Saranac Lake, New York. Mathewson utilized his famous fadeaway pitch and pinpoint control to compile a tremendous 373-188 record during his 17-year big league career. He won 30 or more games four times, including a modern National League-record 37 wins in 1908, and led the Giants to five pennants and one World Championship during his long tenure with the club.

1969 The St. Louis Cardinals trade Curt Flood to the Philadelphia Phillies in a seven-player deal. Rather than report to the Phillies, Flood will instead choose to challenge Major League Baseball's reserve clause.

1984 At a raucous Jack Murphy Stadium, the San Diego Padres claim their first National League pennant with a dramatic come-from-behind 6-3 win over the Chicago Cubs in Game 5 of the NLCS. The Padres, who lost the first two games of the series by a combined score of 17-2, rally late against Cubs ace Rick Sutcliffe, scoring the game's final four runs in the seventh after a key error by Chicago first baseman Leon Durham extends the inning.

> ⓘ Sutcliffe, the eventual 1984 NL Cy Young Award winner, carried a personal 15-game win streak into this game.

2001  Eight-time batting champion Tony Gwynn of the San Diego Padres goes 0-for-1 in the final game of his remarkable career to finish with a lifetime batting average of .338, the highest of any major leaguer since Ted Williams (.344) retired in 1960.

2001  With over 60,000 in attendance at Qualcomm Stadium to celebrate Tony Gwynn's final major league game, San Diego Padres outfielder Rickey Henderson adds to the special day by blooping a double in the first inning to become the 25th member of the 3,000 Hit Club.

2001  Barry Bonds extends his own single-season record when he belts home run No. 73, leading the San Francisco Giants to a 2-1 victory over the Los Angeles Dodgers on the season's final day. The 37-year-old Bonds also finishes with a .863 slugging percentage to eclipse the mark set by Babe Ruth in 1920.

2018  Atlanta Braves 20-year-old outfielder Ronald Acuña Jr. becomes the youngest major leaguer to hit a postseason grand slam, helping the Braves stave off elimination against the Los Angeles Dodgers in Game 3 of the NLDS. Acuña surpasses the mark set by Mickey Mantle, who at age 21 belted a grand slam in the 1953 World Series.

# 8

1908  In a makeup of the controversial "Merkle's Boner" tie game from September 23, the Chicago Cubs claim a 4-2 come-from-behind win over the New York Giants at the Polo Grounds to win the National League pennant. Cubs ace Mordecai "Three Finger" Brown, who entered the game in relief in the first inning, outduels New York's 37-game winner Christy Mathewson to earn the victory.

> (i) The Cubs went on to win their second straight World Championship, defeating the Detroit Tigers four games to one in the World Series.

1929  Philadelphia Athletics manager Connie Mack's peculiar choice of seldom-used Howard Ehmke as his starting pitcher for Game 1 of the World Series pays off when Ehmke strikes out a Series record-setting 13 batters while going the distance in the Athletics' 3-1 win over the Chicago Cubs.

1956  Don Larsen throws the only perfect game in World Series history, leading the New York Yankees to a 2-0 win over the Brooklyn Dodgers in Game 5 at Yankee Stadium.

1957  Brooklyn Dodgers owner Walter O'Malley officially notifies the National League of his intention to move the Dodgers franchise to Los Angeles.

**1995**  In the deciding Game 5 of the American League Division Series at the Kingdome, Edgar Martinez's clutch two-run double in the 11th inning gives the Seattle Mariners a thrilling 6-5 come-from-behind victory over the New York Yankees. The Mariners come all the way back from a two-games-to-none deficit to advance to the ALCS, thanks in large part to Martinez, who batted .571 in the series, and Ken Griffey Jr., who blasted five home runs.

> (i) In the final games of his major league career, Don Mattingly batted .417 in the ALDS and drove in a team-leading six runs for the Yankees.

# 9

**1910**  With the batting title and a new Chalmers 30 automobile on the line, Nap Lajoie of the Cleveland Indians goes 8-for-9 in a season-ending doubleheader with the St. Louis Browns to push his average to .384, threatening Detroit Tigers star Ty Cobb's league lead. Controversy will soon follow when it's revealed that Browns manager Jack O'Connor manipulated his defense on that day, allowing Lajoie six bunt base hits and another easy infield single. The drama will only intensify when American League president Ban Johnson investigates and finds no wrong-doing. The matter will finally be defused when the official statistics are announced and Cobb is declared the batting champion by a point. The Chalmers Automobile Company, no doubt thrilled with all the attention, ultimately awards both Cobb and Lajoie a new car.

**1919**  In Game 8 of the World Series at Comiskey Park, the underdog Cincinnati Reds coast to a 10-5 victory and claim their first-ever World Championship. Chicago White Sox pitcher Lefty Williams takes the loss after giving up four runs and retiring just one batter before being pulled from his start. Immediately afterward, rumors will circulate that the Series had been thrown.

**1928**  The New York Yankees finish off a four-game World Series sweep of the St. Louis Cardinals as Babe Ruth slugs three of the Yankees' five home runs in a 7-3 win at Sportsman's Park. Yankees first baseman Lou Gehrig adds his fourth homer of the series, tying Ruth's two-year-old record for most home runs hit in a single postseason.

> (i) While Ruth and Gehrig flexed their muscles in the World Series, batting a collective .593 with seven home runs, their teammates combined to hit just .196 with two homers.

**1934**  At Detroit's Navin Field, St. Louis' "Gashouse Gang" Cardinals defeat the Tigers 11-0 in Game 7 to win their third World Championship in nine seasons.

Dean brothers Dizzy and Paul, who together won 49 games during the regular season, combine to earn all four Series victories for St. Louis.

 The 1934 World Series was the last in which both teams were led by player-managers (Frankie Frisch for the Cardinals and Mickey Cochrane for Detroit).

**1966** At Memorial Stadium, the Baltimore Orioles capture their first-ever World Series title with a surprising sweep of the Los Angeles Dodgers as lefty Dave McNally earns a four-hit, 1-0 victory in Game 4. Series MVP Frank Robinson's fourth-inning home run off Don Drysdale produces the game's only run.

ⓘ McNally's shutout was the third straight for the Orioles, who set a World Series record with 33 consecutive scoreless innings pitched.

DID YOU KNOW? In Game 1 of the 1966 Fall Classic, Baltimore Orioles slugger Boog Powell became the first former Little League World Series participant (Lakeland, Florida; 1954) to appear in a big league World Series game.

**1996** In Game 1 of the American League Championship Series, the New York Yankees, who trail the Baltimore Orioles 4-3 in the eighth inning, catch a crucial break when Derek Jeter's bases-empty drive to the top of the right field fence at Yankee Stadium is incorrectly ruled a home run despite fan interference by a 12-year-old named Jeffrey Maier. The controversial homer extends the game into extra innings, where Bernie Williams' 11th-inning solo shot gives the Yankees a 5-4 win.

# 10

**1920** In an eventful game filled with World Series firsts, the Cleveland Indians defeat the visiting Brooklyn Robins 8-1 in Game 5 at Dunn Field. Indians outfielder Elmer Smith hits the first grand slam in World Series history in the first inning and teammate Bill Wambsganss executes the first Series triple play in the fifth to support a complete game effort by 31-game winner Jim Bagby, who also went deep in the fourth inning to become the first pitcher to homer in World Series play.

**1924** A capacity crowd at Griffith Stadium sees the hometown Washington Senators capture their first World Championship and beloved 36-year-old ace Walter Johnson win his first World Series game as the Senators come from behind to claim a 4-3, 11-inning victory over the New York Giants in the deciding Game 7. A bad-hop single by Bucky Harris, Washington's 27-year-old "Boy Manager," knots the game at three in the eighth and Earl McNeely's grounder past third baseman Fred Lindstrom three innings later delivers the walk-off win for the Senators. Johnson, the losing pitcher in Game 1 and Game 5, throws a scoreless final four frames to earn the victory.

 In 1924, the New York Giants became the first franchise to make four consecutive World Series appearances.

**1926**  At Yankee Stadium, the St. Louis Cardinals claim their first World Series title with a dramatic 3-2 come-from-behind win over the New York Yankees in Game 7. After posting complete game victories in Game 2 and Game 6, Cardinals 39-year-old pitching legend Grover Cleveland Alexander enters the game with the bases loaded and two outs in the seventh inning and strikes out Tony Lazzeri to preserve St. Louis' one-run lead. Two innings later, with Alexander nearly flawless in relief, the series ends abruptly when Yankees star Babe Ruth is thrown out trying to steal second.

**1957**  In Game 7 of the World Series, Lew Burdette of the Milwaukee Braves earns his third complete-game victory over the New York Yankees, winning 5-0 at Yankee Stadium to give the Braves their first World Championship in Milwaukee.

ⓘ Braves 23-year-old outfielder Hank Aaron batted .393 in the series with three home runs and 7 RBIs while Series MVP Burdette surrendered just two earned runs in 27 innings of work.

 In 1957, Milwaukee Braves righty Lew Burdette became the first pitcher since Christy Mathewson in 1905 to throw two shutouts in one World Series.

**1968**  At Busch Stadium, the Detroit Tigers come back from a three-games-to-one deficit to win the World Series as lefty Mickey Lolich earns his third Series win, defeating superstar pitcher Bob Gibson and the St. Louis Cardinals 4-1 in Game 7. Jim Northrup's two-out, two-run triple in the seventh inning off Gibson keys the victory for Detroit.

ⓘ The Tigers joined the 1925 Pirates and 1958 Yankees as the only teams to win a World Series after trailing three games to one. Series MVP Mickey Lolich recorded three complete-game victories and a 1.67 ERA while star outfielder Al Kaline led the Tigers offense with a .379 average, two home runs and eight RBIs.

St. Louis Cardinals ace Bob Gibson had another dominant Fall Classic in 1968, setting a World Series record with 35 strikeouts, while teammate Lou Brock collected a Series record-tying 13 hits and seven stolen bases.

1980   In Game 3 of the American League Championship Series, the Kansas City Royals complete a sweep of the New York Yankees and advance to their first World Series as Royals star George Brett's long three-run homer off reliever Goose Gossage powers Kansas City to a 4-2 come-from-behind victory.

(i) The Royals had been defeated by the Yankees in the ALCS in 1976, 1977 and 1978, making this series-clinching win at Yankee Stadium especially satisfying.

# 11

1911   Ty Cobb of the Detroit Tigers and the Chicago Cubs' Frank "Wildfire" Schulte are named as the first recipients of the Chalmers Award for their respective leagues. Both winners receive a Chalmers Model 30 automobile.

(i) Cobb led the American League in numerous offensive categories in 1911, including batting average (.420), RBIs (127), runs scored (147) and stolen bases (83), while Schulte's 21 home runs and 107 RBIs led the National League.

1972   With the Pittsburgh Pirates holding a 3-2 ninth-inning lead in the deciding Game 5 of the NLCS, Johnny Bench keys a Cincinnati Reds rally when he launches an opposite field solo home run off Pirates reliever Dave Guisti. The Reds follow with two more singles and win the game two outs later when righty Bob Moose's wild pitch allows George Foster to race home with the pennant-winning run.

 The 1972 Cincinnati Reds were the first team in history to advance to the World Series without owning the best record in their respective league.

1999   In the deciding ALCS Game 5 at Jacobs Field, Boston Red Sox star pitcher Pedro Martinez, who injured his back earlier in the series, makes a surprise entrance in the fourth inning and pitches six no-hit frames to lead the Red Sox to a 12-8 come-from-behind victory over the Cleveland Indians.

2012   The San Francisco Giants defeat the Cincinnati Reds 6–4 in the winner-take-all fifth game of the NLDS. The Giants score all of their runs in a fifth-inning outburst that's highlighted by a Buster Posey grand slam. The win completes a tremendous series comeback that saw the Giants win three straight games in Cincinnati after dropping the first two at home.

# 12

1929   Trailing the Chicago Cubs 8-0 late in Game 4 of the World Series, the Philadelphia Athletics explode for 10 unanswered runs in the bottom of the seventh inning to take a commanding three-games-to-one series lead. The disheartened Cubs will cough up another late lead in Game 5 two days later, giving the Athletics their first World Series title since 1913.

1948   Following a disappointing season, the New York Yankees make one of the best personnel decisions in franchise history when they hire 58-year-old Casey Stengel to replace Bucky Harris as manager despite Stengel's 581-742 career record as field pilot of the Brooklyn Dodgers and Boston Braves. Stengel will guide the Yankees to five World Series titles in his first five seasons in the Bronx and will finish his 12-year tenure with 10 pennants and seven World Championships.

1963   Luis Aparicio, Orlando Cepeda, Roberto Clemente, Juan Marichal, Minnie Miñoso and Tony Oliva are among a group of major leaguers who take part in a Hispanic American All-Star Game at the Polo Grounds. The unique event will be the final baseball game ever played at the Polo Grounds.

1967   In a Game 7 matchup of aces, Bob Gibson strikes out 10 and homers in a 7-2 win over Jim Lonborg and the Boston Red Sox, giving the St. Louis Cardinals their second World Championship in four seasons. Cardinals outfielder Lou Brock batted .414, scored eight runs and set a World Series record with seven stolen bases while Series MVP Gibson gave up just three earned runs and struck out 26 in three dominant wins.

> (i) Red Sox slugger Carl Yastrzemski, the driving force behind Boston's "Impossible Dream" season, did his part in the series, belting three home runs while batting .400.

1980   The Philadelphia Phillies advance to the World Series for the first time in 30 years after defeating the Houston Astros 8-7 in a thrilling winner-take-all National League Championship Series Game 5 at the Astrodome. Facing ace Nolan Ryan and trailing 5-2 in the eighth inning, the Phillies score five times in a rally that's capped off by NLCS MVP Manny Trillo's two-run triple. After the Astros mount a comeback of their own to send the game into extra innings, centerfielder Garry Maddox provides the winning margin for Philadelphia in the 10th when his two-out double plates the deciding run.

(i) The final four games of the 1980 NLCS were decided in extra innings.

1982   At Busch Stadium, Paul Molitor of the Milwaukee Brewers sets a record for most hits in a single World Series game when he goes 5-for-6 against the St. Louis Cardinals in Game 1 to lead the Brewers to a 10-0 victory.

1986   In Game 5 of the ALCS, with the California Angels leading 5-2 and just two outs away from making their first-ever World Series appearance, the Boston Red Sox forge one of the most memorable comebacks in baseball history and defeat the Angels 7-6. Red Sox veteran Don Baylor cuts the 9th-inning deficit to one with a two-run homer, chasing starter Mike Witt, and outfielder Dave Henderson puts Boston ahead one out later with a two-run shot off reliever Donnie Moore. After the Angels respond with a run to send the game into extra innings, Dave Henderson comes through in the clutch again, hitting a sacrifice fly in the 11th inning that plates the winning run.

(i) The Boston Red Sox won the next two games as well to advance to the World Series.

# 13

1903   At Huntington Avenue Baseball Grounds, the Boston Americans win the first modern World Series as pitcher Bill Dinneen gives up just four hits in a 3-0 complete game victory over the Pittsburgh Pirates in Game 8.

1914   Boston's "Miracle Braves" claim the first-ever World Series sweep when they earn a 3-1 victory over Connie Mack's powerful Philadelphia Athletics in Game 4. Pitcher Dick Rudolph goes the distance for his second Series win.

(i) A 61-16 second half fueled by co-aces Rudolph and Bill James, who combined to go 33-3 over that stretch, vaulted the Braves past the three-time defending National League Champion New York Giants after they had trailed New York by as many as 15 games in early July.

1960   One of the most dramatic moments in baseball history takes place at Forbes Field as second baseman Bill Mazeroski hits the first-ever World Series-deciding walk-off home run to give the Pittsburgh Pirates a stunning 10-9 come-from-behind win over the New York Yankees in Game 7. The World Championship is the Pirates' third in club history, and their first since 1925.

(i) The powerhouse Yankees, who finished the regular season with 15 straight wins, came up short in the World Series despite outscoring the Pirates by a combined score of 55-27.

(DID YOU KNOW?) In 1960, Bobby Richardson of the New York Yankees became the first and only player to be named World Series MVP despite playing for the losing team after slugging .667 and driving in a Series-record 12 runs against the Pittsburgh Pirates.

2001 In Game 3 of the ALDS, the New York Yankees avoid elimination with a 1-0 victory over the Oakland Athletics that's highlighted by Yankees shortstop Derek Jeter's memorable "Flip Play." With the Yankees holding a slim 1-0 lead in the seventh inning, Jeter helps keep Oakland off the scoreboard when he chases down an errant throw from right field and shovels the ball to catcher Jorge Posada to nab a surprised Jeremy Giambi at home plate. The heads up defensive gem is viewed as a momentum-shifter for the Yankees, who will come back to defeat the 102-win Athletics in the series.

# 14

1896 Superstar outfielder Oscar Charleston, one of the preeminent figures in the history of the Negro Leagues, is born in Indianapolis, Indiana.

1906 Chicago's "Hitless Wonders" White Sox, a club that won 93 regular season games despite batting a league-low .230, complete one of the greatest upsets in World Series history when they defeat the 116-win Chicago Cubs 8-3 in Game 6 to win the World Championship.

(i) White Sox ace Ed Walsh dominated the Cubs' potent offense in the series, winning two games while posting a 0.60 ERA and striking out 17.

1908 At a special meeting held in Detroit on the morning of Game 6 of the World Series, a group of sportswriters form the Baseball Writers' Association of America to combat their poor treatment at ballparks. The organization will quickly gain the full support of both major leagues and will succeed in improving working conditions for writers throughout baseball.

1965 Superstar pitcher Sandy Koufax, working on just two days rest, leads the Los Angeles Dodgers to their second World Series title in three years as he fires a three-hitter in Game 7 to defeat the Minnesota Twins 2-0 at Metropolitan Stadium.

(i) Koufax made headlines earlier in the series when he sat out Game
1 because it fell on the Jewish holy day Yom Kippur.

1972 Catcher Gene Tenace becomes the first player in baseball history to
homer in his first two World Series at-bats, leading the Oakland Athletics to a
3-2 Game 1 victory over the Cincinnati Reds.

1976 After a 12-year hiatus, the New York Yankees advance to the World
Series in dramatic fashion when first baseman Chris Chambliss homers on
the first pitch he sees in the bottom of the ninth inning to give the Yankees a
7-6 win over the Kansas City Royals in Game 5 of the ALCS. The clutch hit sets
off a mass overflow of fans onto the field, and Chambliss needs a police escort
to reach home plate.

(i) Chambliss batted .524 in the series and drove in eight runs.

1984 In Game 5 of the World Series, Kirk Gibson hits two upper deck home
runs at Tiger Stadium to power the Detroit Tigers to an 8-4 win over the San
Diego Padres, giving Detroit its first World Series title since 1968.

1985 In the ninth inning of a pivotal NLCS Game 5 at Busch Stadium, with
the series and the score tied 2-2, St. Louis Cardinals shortstop Ozzie Smith
jumps on a Tom Niedenfuer fastball and hits the first left-handed home run of
his eight-year career to give the Cardinals a 3-2 victory over the Los Angeles
Dodgers. The stunning blast moves St. Louis broadcaster Jack Buck to famously
exclaim "Go crazy, folks, go crazy!"

(i) The Cardinals went on to win their fourth straight game to finish off
the Dodgers in Game 6 thanks in large part to another memorable
home run - Jack Clark's ninth-inning, three-run blast off Niedenfuer
that gave St. Louis a 7-5 victory.

1992 Pinch-hitter Francisco Cabrera sends the Atlanta Braves to the World
Series when he caps off their three-run, ninth-inning rally by delivering a
two-out, two-run single against Pittsburgh Pirates reliever Stan Belinda to give
the Braves a dramatic 3-2 walk-off win in Game 7 of the NLCS.

2003 In Game 6 of the NLCS at Wrigley Field, with the Chicago Cubs leading
the Florida Marlins 3-0 and just five outs away from advancing to their first
World Series appearance in 58 years, the game takes a dramatic turn when
Cubs fan Steve Bartman deflects a foul ball that is about to be caught by
Chicago left fielder Moises Alou. The Cubs unravel after the incident, allowing
eight runs in the inning on five hits, three walks and an error, and eventually
lose 8-3. Chicago's season will end one day later when the Marlins come from
behind again to win 9-6 in the series finale.

# 15

1923   The New York Yankees capture their first World Series title when they finish off the New York Giants with a 6-4 come-from-behind win in Game 6 at the Polo Grounds. Babe Ruth leads the way for the Yankees, batting .368 with a team-high three home runs, eight walks and eight runs scored in the series.

1946   In Game 7 of the World Series, Enos Slaughter's run-scoring mad dash from first on Harry Walker's double in the eighth inning keys the St. Louis Cardinals' World Series-clinching 4-3 win over the Boston Red Sox at Sportsman's Park. Cardinals lefty Harry Brecheen tosses two scoreless innings of relief to earn his third Series win.

1986   In Game 6 of the NLCS, the New York Mets claim a dramatic 7-6, 16-inning win over the Houston Astros to advance to the World Series. After scoring three runs in the ninth to force extra innings, the Mets score three more in the 16th and secure the victory when lefty Jesse Orosco extinguishes a Houston rally to earn his third relief win of the series.

1988   In Game 1 of the World Series, with the Los Angeles Dodgers trailing the Oakland Athletics by a run with two outs in the bottom of the ninth inning, a badly-hobbled Kirk Gibson pinch-hits a two-run homer off ace reliever Dennis Eckersley to give the Dodgers a stunning 5-4 victory. Legendary broadcaster Vin Scully captures the iconic moment perfectly, exclaiming "In a year that has been so improbable, the impossible has happened."

(i) Buoyed by Gibson's clutch hit, the Dodgers went on to win the World Series over the heavily favored Athletics in five games.

# 16

1912   In a do-or-die game at Fenway Park, the Boston Red Sox end one of the most exciting World Series in history when they claim a 3-2 walk-off win over the New York Giants. With Giants ace Christy Mathewson on the mound and leading by a run in the bottom of the 10th inning, the Red Sox catch a break when New York centerfielder Fred Snodgrass muffs Clyde Engle's lazy fly ball, putting Engle on second to lead off the inning. Following a fly out and a base on balls, the Giants' defense errs again when Tris Speaker's catchable pop fly drops safely in foul territory between first baseman Fred Merkle and catcher Chief Meyers. Given new life, Speaker quickly capitalizes, lining a single to tie the game. After Mathewson walks cleanup hitter Duffy Lewis, Red Sox third baseman Larry Gardner lofts a sacrifice fly to right that delivers the winning run and gives Boston its second World Championship.

1962  With the New York Yankees holding a 1-0 lead over the San Francisco Giants and needing just one more out to seal Game 7, the World Series comes to a dramatic close when Giants slugger Willie McCovey, batting with two runners in scoring position, rockets a low line drive that Yankees second baseman Bobby Richardson snares to end the game. Series MVP Ralph Terry earns the win after throwing a complete game four-hitter.

DID YOU KNOW? From 1923 through 1962, the New York Yankees won a remarkable 20 World Championships.

1969  The New York Mets' miracle season reaches its culmination in Game 5 of the World Series as the underdog club earns a 5-3 come-from-behind victory over the Baltimore Orioles at Shea Stadium to win their first World Series title.

(i) A memorable moment occurred in the sixth inning of this game when home plate umpire Lou DiMuro overturned his call and awarded Mets outfielder Cleon Jones first base after manager Gil Hodges argued that a shoe polish smudge on the baseball proved that his player was hit by a pitch. The call loomed especially large after Series MVP Donn Clendenon followed with a home run.

2003  At Yankee Stadium, a thrilling ALCS between the New York Yankees and the Boston Red Sox comes to an abrupt end when Yankees third baseman Aaron Boone homers on knuckleballer Tim Wakefield's first pitch of the 11th inning to give New York a 6-5 win in Game 7. The Yankees earlier erased a 5-2 deficit in the eighth by scoring three runs off weary ace Pedro Martinez, setting the stage for Boone's dramatic hit.

# 17

1911  One day after hitting a game-winning homer off the New York Giants' Rube Marquard in Game 2 of the World Series, Philadelphia Athletics third baseman Frank "Home Run" Baker adds to his legendary postseason performance by launching a ninth-inning home run against ace Christy Mathewson that ties Game 3 at one. Baker later singles during a two-run rally in the 11th inning that wins the game for the Athletics.

1971  In Game 7 of the World Series, the Pittsburgh Pirates successfully complete their march to a championship as star outfielder Roberto Clemente hits a key home run off Baltimore Orioles starter Mike Cuellar to back Steve Blass' complete game four-hitter in the Pirates' 2-1 win. The 37-year-old

Clemente is named World Series MVP after batting .414 and wowing a national audience with his all-around excellence.

1974   The Oakland Athletics earn a 3-2 Game 5 victory over the Los Angeles Dodgers to three-peat as World Champions, joining the New York Yankees as the only franchises in baseball history to win at least three straight World Series titles.

1979   At Memorial Stadium, Willie "Pops" Stargell powers the "We Are Family" Pittsburgh Pirates to a World Championship when he hits a pivotal two-run homer off Baltimore Orioles starter Scott McGregor in the Pirates' 4-1 come-from-behind victory in Game 7. The 39-year-old Stargell is named World Series MVP after batting .400 with three homers, four doubles and seven RBIs.

1989   Just minutes before Game 3 of the "Battle of the Bay" World Series between the Oakland Athletics and San Francisco Giants is due to begin, the Loma Prieta earthquake rocks the San Francisco Bay area, killing 63 people and causing more than $7 billion in damage. All those gathered at Candlestick Park for the game are kept in relative safety, although much of the surrounding area is devastated by the 6.9 magnitude quake. Game 3 will be rescheduled for October 27, momentarily postponing the Athletics' series sweep.

2004   In Game 4 of the ALCS, the Boston Red Sox claim a dramatic 6-4, 12-inning victory over the New York Yankees to avoid elimination. Boston pinch-runner Dave Roberts' crucial stolen base in the ninth helps send the game into extra innings, where slugger David Ortiz wins it for the Red Sox with a walk-off two-run homer. The comeback victory will prove pivotal in Boston's unlikely march to the World Series.

# 18

1950   Eighty-seven-year-old Connie Mack retires as manager of the Philadelphia Athletics after guiding the club for 50 straight seasons, ending a 53-year managerial career that produced a major league-record 3,731 wins along with five World Series titles and nine pennants.

1960   New York Yankees ownership relieves 70-year-old Casey Stengel of his managerial duties over concern that he is too old for the job, prompting Stengel to famously quip "I'll never make the mistake of being 70 again." In 12 seasons with Stengel at the helm, the Yankees experienced the greatest run of success in major league history, winning 10 pennants and seven World Championships.

**1977**  In Game 6 of the World Series, New York Yankees slugger Reggie Jackson earns the nickname "Mr. October" when he launches three home runs on consecutive pitches from three different Los Angeles Dodgers pitchers to lead New York to an 8-4, series-clinching win at Yankee Stadium.

> (i) Taking into account his home run against Don Sutton in his final at-bat of Game 5 and his four-pitch walk in his first plate appearance of Game 6, Jackson hit four home runs on four consecutive swings over the two World Series games.

# 19

**1946**  In a memorable swap of top-end talent, the New York Yankees acquire hard-throwing right-hander Allie Reynolds from the Cleveland Indians in exchange for perennial All-Star second baseman Joe Gordon. The 29-year-old Reynolds will develop into one of the best pitchers in the American League after the trade, and will help lead the Yankees to six World Series titles by going 131-60 in eight seasons in New York. Gordon will find success in Cleveland as well, contributing heavily to the Indians' 1948 World Championship run and garnering three All-Star selections in four seasons with the club.

>  While attending Oklahoma A&M on a track scholarship, Allie Reynolds got his start in baseball when legendary coach Henry Iba coaxed him into throwing batting practice.

**1949**  The Chicago White Sox make one of the best trades in franchise history when they acquire future Hall of Fame second baseman Nellie Fox from the Philadelphia Athletics in exchange for backup catcher Joe Tipton. Fox will develop into a perennial All-Star in Chicago and will earn MVP honors in 1959 after leading the White Sox to the World Series.

**1972**  The Oakland Athletics stage a dramatic comeback against the Cincinnati Reds in Game 4 of the World Series as catcher Gene Tenace and three pinch-hitters string together four consecutive singles in the ninth inning to turn a 2-1 deficit into a 3-2 walk-off win. The victory gives the Athletics a commanding three-games-to-one lead in a series they will eventually win in seven games.

**1981**  In what will become known as "Blue Monday" in Montreal Expos lore, the Los Angeles Dodgers claim a 2-1 victory over the Expos in the deciding Game 5 of the NLCS as Dodgers outfielder Rick Monday's clutch homer off Steve Rogers with two out in the ninth inning provides the winning margin. The dramatic victory sends the Dodgers to the World Series and brings to an end the Expos' one and only postseason appearance.

> (i) Steve Rogers had three wins and a 0.67 ERA in the 1981 postseason prior to his fateful relief appearance in the NLCS finale.

**2004** While fighting their way back from a three-games-to-none deficit in the ALCS, the Boston Red Sox get a big lift from injured starter Curt Schilling in a 4-2 victory over the New York Yankees in Game 6. Schilling, pitching with blood seeping from his surgically stabilized ankle, goes seven strong innings to earn the win.

# 20

**1906** Future Hall of Famer William "Buck" Ewing, early baseball's greatest catcher and one of its finest all-around players, dies at age 47 in Cincinnati, Ohio.

**1931** Slugging outfielder Mickey Mantle, one of baseball's most celebrated icons, is born in Spavinaw, Oklahoma.

**1988** The Los Angeles Dodgers win the World Series as ace Orel Hershiser completes his dream season with a 5-2, four-hit victory over the powerhouse Oakland Athletics in Game 5. Hershiser, soon to be the unanimous NL Cy Young Award winner after posting a 23-8 record in the regular season, claims both the World Series and NLCS MVP trophies after going 3-0 with a 1.05 ERA in the postseason.

**1990** The Cincinnati Reds complete one of the most stunning sweeps in World Series history, defeating the Oakland Athletics 2-1 in Game 4 as Series MVP Jose Rijo retires the last 20 batters he faces to secure the win. Reds outfielder Billy Hatcher bats .750 and collects four doubles and six runs scored in the series, while the Cincinnati bullpen trio of Norm Charlton, Rob Dibble and Randy Myers, dubbed the "Nasty Boys," combine to pitch 8 2/3 scoreless innings.

> (i) The Oakland Athletics, easily the major's best team during the 1990 regular season, outscored the Boston Red Sox by a combined score of 20-4 in an ALCS four-game sweep prior to their quick World Series exit.

**1996** In the Atlanta Braves' 12-1 win in the World Series opener at Yankee Stadium, Braves 19-year-old outfielder Andruw Jones becomes the youngest player to hit a home run in a World Series game when he launches a two-run shot off New York Yankees starter Andy Pettitte in the 2nd inning. Jones makes more history the following inning when he homers again, this time joining Gene

Tenace as the only players in history to hit home runs in their first two World Series at-bats.

**2004** In the ALCS finale at Yankee Stadium, the Boston Red Sox become the first team in major league history to overcome a three-games-to-none deficit to win a postseason series as they defeat the New York Yankees 10-3 in Game 7. Outfielder Johnny Damon leads Boston's offensive attack with two home runs and six RBIs. Red Sox slugger David Ortiz, who recorded walk-off hits in Game 4 and Game 5 and drove in 11 runs in the series, is named ALCS MVP.

# 21

**1973** At Oakland-Alameda County Coliseum, the Oakland Athletics win their second straight World Championship as Bert Campaneris and Reggie Jackson each hit two-run homers to power Oakland to a 5-2 victory over the New York Mets in Game 7. Jackson, who also had two key run-producing hits against Tom Seaver in Game 6, is named World Series MVP.

**1975** Carlton Fisk's memorable 12th-inning game-ending home run off the left field foul pole at Fenway Park gives the Boston Red Sox a 7-6 come-from-behind win over the Cincinnati Reds in Game 6 of the World Series. Red Sox pinch-hitter Bernie Carbo's clutch three-run homer in the eighth inning tied the game at six, and Boston outfielder Dwight Evans' spectacular catch of Joe Morgan's deep drive to right in the 11th inning preserved the tie, setting the stage for Fisk's iconic blast.

ⓘ This game is widely regarded as one of the greatest in baseball history.

**1976** At Yankee Stadium, the Cincinnati Reds win their second straight World Series title as star catcher Johnny Bench homers twice and drives in five runs to lead the Reds to a 7-2 Game 4 victory over the New York Yankees.

 In 1976, the Cincinnati Reds became the first team in the divisional era to sweep through the postseason after going 3-0 against the Philadelphia Phillies in the NLCS and winning all four games against the New York Yankees in the World Series.

**1980** The Philadelphia Phillies defeat the Kansas City Royals 4-1 in Game 6 at Veterans Stadium to capture the first World Championship in the club's 98-year history. The Phillies get seven strong innings from ace Steve Carlton and an eventful two-inning save from reliever Tug McGraw, who sets off a wild celebration after striking out Willie Wilson to end the game.

**1998**  The New York Yankees complete their historic 1998 season by sweeping the San Diego Padres in the World Series, earning a 3-0 Game 4 win to claim their major league-record 24th World Championship. With 114 wins in the regular season and 11 more in the playoffs, the Yankees' total of 125 victories easily surpasses the previous major league record of 118 set by the Chicago Cubs in 1906.

> (i)  The 1998 New York Yankees' .714 winning percentage (125-50) is the major league's highest since the "Murderer's Row" Yankees of 1927, who finished at .722 (114-44).

# 22

**1845**  The first known baseball box score appears in the *New York Morning News* as a summary report of a match between The New York Ball Club and a team from Brooklyn.

**1920**  A grand jury indicts Chicago White Sox players Shoeless Joe Jackson, Eddie Cicotte, Happy Felsch, Fred McMullen, Swede Risberg, Buck Weaver and Lefty Williams as well as their former teammate Chick Gandil on nine counts of conspiracy to defraud for their alleged throwing of the 1919 World Series.

**1973**  Legendary batsman Ichiro Suzuki is born in Kasugai, Japan.

**1975**  At Fenway Park, one of the most thrilling World Series in history comes to an end as the Cincinnati Reds overcome a 3-0 deficit to claim a dramatic 4-3 Game 7 win. Tony Perez's two-run blast against Bill Lee's blooper pitch gets the Reds on the board in the sixth inning and, after a single from Series MVP Pete Rose ties the game one inning later, Joe Morgan's soft liner to center in the ninth plates Ken Griffey with the winning run. After several recent near misses, the powerhouse Reds get their first World Championship in 35 seasons.

 DID YOU KNOW? In 1975, the Cincinnati Reds came from behind in all four of their World Series wins.

**1992**  Legendary broadcaster Walter Lanier "Red" Barber dies at age 84 in Tallahassee, Florida. Barber began his baseball play-by-play career with the Cincinnati Reds in 1934 and ended it with the New York Yankees in 1966, but it was during his time with the Brooklyn Dodgers from 1939-1953 that "The Ol' Redhead," with his folksy, detailed and colorful reporting style, established himself as the master of his craft. In 1978, he and Mel Allen were honored as the first recipients of the Ford C. Frick Award by the Baseball Hall of Fame.

**2000** In Game 2 of the World Series at Yankee Stadium, the much-anticipated confrontation between New York Mets catcher Mike Piazza and the man who beaned him earlier in the season - pitcher Roger Clemens of the New York Yankees - turns bizarre when Clemens reacts to a Piazza broken bat foul ball by fielding the jagged bat barrel and hurling it in Piazza's direction. The incident empties both benches but does little to rattle Clemens, who is nearly unhittable in eight innings of work. The Yankees withstand a late Mets rally and win 6-5, extending their record World Series winning streak to 14 consecutive games.

**2011** Slugger Albert Pujols' historic day at the plate powers the St. Louis Cardinals to a 16-7 win over the Texas Rangers in Game 3 of the World Series. In six plate appearances, the Cardinals star ties World Series records with five hits, three home runs and six RBIs, and establishes a new Series mark with 14 total bases.

**2012** In Game 7 of the NLCS, the San Francisco Giants win their sixth straight elimination game of the 2012 postseason, blanking the St. Louis Cardinals 9-0 to advance to the World Series.

> (i) After beating the Cincinnati Reds in three straight road games to close out the NLDS, the resilient Giants soundly defeated the Cardinals in the final three games of the NLCS, outscoring them by a combined score of 20-1. San Francisco had a much easier time of it in the 2012 World Series, where they dispatched of the Detroit Tigers in four games.

# 23

**1876** The first known publication of batting averages occurs when the *Chicago Tribune* includes the new statistic in their summary coverage of the 1876 National League season.

**1886** In one of the most significant games of the 19th century, the American Association Champion St. Louis Browns win the World Championship - and the gate receipts from the entire series - by claiming a 4-3, 10-inning victory over the National League Champion Chicago White Stockings at Sportsman's Park. Chicago pitcher John Clarkson holds St. Louis hitless through six innings as the White Stockings build a 3-0 lead, but the Browns tie the game in the eighth inning and win it in the 10th on Curt Welch's famous "$15,000 slide."

**1945** Branch Rickey of the Brooklyn Dodgers announces his monumental signing of former college and Negro League star Jackie Robinson. The

26-year-old Robinson will soon topple Organized Baseball's longstanding color barrier when he joins the International League's Montreal Royals for a year of seasoning.

1993  In Game 6 of the World Series at Toronto's SkyDome, Joe Carter of the host Blue Jays lines a clutch three-run homer off Philadelphia Phillies closer Mitch Williams in the bottom of the ninth inning to give Toronto a thrilling 6-4 walk-off win and their second straight World Championship.

1996  In Game 4 of the World Series, the New York Yankees stage one of the most dramatic comebacks in postseason history to defeat the Atlanta Braves 8-6 in 10 innings and knot the Series at two games apiece. Trailing 6-0 after five innings, the Yankees score six unanswered runs - capped off by backup catcher Jim Leyritz's three-run homer in the eighth inning off Braves reliever Mark Wohlers - to send the game into extra innings, where they win the game with a two-out, two-run rally in the 10th.

ⓘ  Energized by the critical victory, the Yankees closed out the series two games later to claim their first World Championship since 1978.

# 24

1972  Hall of Famer and legendary trailblazer Jack Roosevelt "Jackie" Robinson dies of a heart attack at age 53 in Stamford, Connecticut. Robinson broke Major League Baseball's color barrier when he debuted with the Brooklyn Dodgers in 1947, and his exceptional character, determination and ability was instrumental in bringing an end to racial segregation in professional baseball. In addition to his immeasurable cultural impact, Robinson had an outstanding baseball career, winning an MVP award in 1949 and leading the Dodgers to six pennants and one World Championship during his ten seasons with the club.

2004  At Fenway Park, Boston Red Sox righty Curt Schilling, playing with a suture in his foot to hold a tendon in place, becomes the first pitcher in history to win a World Series game for three different teams when he throws six strong innings to earn the victory in Boston's 6-2 win over the St. Louis Cardinals in Game 2. Schilling had previously earned a World Series win in 1993 while with the Philadelphia Phillies and again in 2001 as a member of the Arizona Diamondbacks.

2007  The National Baseball Hall of Fame announces that it will honor former Negro League player and manager Buck O'Neil by establishing a lifetime achievement award in his name. O'Neil became the first African

American coach in major league history when he joined the Chicago Cubs staff in 1962, and in later years was cherished as one of baseball's greatest ambassadors.

**2012**  At San Francisco's AT&T Park, Pablo Sandoval of the host Giants joins Babe Ruth, Reggie Jackson and Albert Pujols as the only players to homer three times in a World Series game when he goes deep in his first three at-bats in the Giants' 8-3 win over the Detroit Tigers in Game 1.

# 25

**1884**  In the first official postseason interleague championship series, or "the Championship of the United States" as it was originally called, the National League's Providence Grays complete a three-game sweep of the American Association's New York Metropolitans with an 11-2 win at the Polo Grounds. Providence ace Charles "Old Hoss" Radbourn, who remarkably earned 59 victories during the regular season, wins all three series games in three days without allowing an earned run.

 After losing the first two games of the series, Metropolitans star pitcher Tim Keefe served as umpire in Game 3.

**1978**  After posting a stellar 21-6 record with a 2.73 ERA, San Diego Padres 40-year-old ace Gaylord Perry is named the National League Cy Young Award winner, becoming the oldest recipient of the award to date and the first to win it in both leagues.

**1986**  In Game 6 of the World Series, with the Boston Red Sox leading 5-3 in the 10th inning and just one out away from capturing their first World Championship since 1918, the New York Mets rally behind consecutive singles by Gary Carter, Kevin Mitchell and Ray Knight and tie the game when Red Sox reliever Bob Stanley uncorks a wild pitch that allows Mitchell to score. New York famously wins three pitches later when hobbled Boston first baseman Bill Buckner allows Mookie Wilson's slow grounder to trickle through his legs for the game winner.

**2003**  At Yankee Stadium, 23-year-old Josh Beckett of the Florida Marlins fires a 2-0, five-hit gem against the favored New York Yankees in Game 6, giving the 11-year-old Marlins franchise their second World Series title.

ⓘ Beckett was named World Series MVP after going 1-1 with a 1.10 ERA and 19 strikeouts.

# 26

**1934**  The Boston Red Sox acquire 27-year-old star shortstop Joe Cronin from the Washington Senators in exchange for Lyn Lary and $225,000. Over the next 11 seasons as Boston's player-manager, Cronin will garner five All-Star selections at shortstop while winning more games than any other manager in Red Sox history.

 Joe Cronin became the youngest World Series manager in history when he led the 1933 Washington Senators to the Fall Classic at the age of 26.

**1985**  The Kansas City Royals manage to stay alive in the World Series in dramatic fashion, engineering a memorable ninth-inning rally that gives them a 2-1 walk-off win over the St. Louis Cardinals in Game 6. The Royals catch a break in the final frame when a missed called by first base umpire Don Denkinger turns Jorge Orta's groundout into a leadoff single, and capitalize four batters later when pinch-hitter Dane Iorg's bloop single drives in the tying and winning runs.

ⓘ The Kansas City Royals completed a three-games-to-one series comeback with an 11-0 victory the following day to win their first-ever World Series title.

**1991**  In Game 6 of the 1991 World Series, Kirby Puckett's singular performance helps the Minnesota Twins stave off elimination with a thrilling 4-3, 11-inning victory over the Atlanta Braves at the Metrodome. After tripling to drive in a run and later scoring a run himself in the first inning, Puckett snuffs out a potential Braves rally in the third when he makes a sensational catch against the fence in left-center to rob Ron Gant of a run-scoring extra base hit. In the fifth inning, the star centerfielder pushes the Twins ahead with a sacrifice fly. Finally, with the game deadlocked at 3-3 in the bottom of the 11th, Puckett belts a solo shot off lefty Charlie Leibrandt to give Minnesota the walk-off win.

**1997**  The Florida Marlins win the World Series in dramatic fashion as shortstop Edgar Renteria's two-out, based-loaded single in the 11th inning gives the Marlins a 3-2 walk-off victory over the Cleveland Indians in Game 7.

ⓘ The Marlins managed just one hit against Indians starter Jaret Wright through six innings and trailed 2-0 before Bobby Bonilla's seventh-inning solo homer and Craig Counsell's sacrifice fly in the ninth sent the game into extra innings, setting the stage for Renteria's clutch series-ending hit.

2002 On the way to their first-ever World Championship, the Anaheim Angels stage the greatest World Series comeback ever by a team facing elimination, overcoming a late 5-0 deficit to defeat the San Francisco Giants 6-5 in Game 6 at Edison Field. A three-run homer by Scott Spiezio got the Angels on the board in the seventh inning, and Darin Erstad cut the lead to one with a solo shot in the eighth. After Tim Salmon and Garret Anderson followed with singles, Series MVP Troy Glaus drove them both home with a double to provide the winning margin.

# 27

1986 Two days after their stunning come-from-behind victory over the Boston Red Sox in Game 6 of the World Series, the New York Mets rally again in Game 7, overcoming a three-run deficit with eight late runs to claim a series-clinching 8-5 win at Shea Stadium.

1991 In one of the greatest games in World Series history, veteran right-hander Jack Morris tosses a 10-inning shutout in Game 7, leading the Minnesota Twins to a 1-0 win over the Atlanta Braves. Pinch-hitter Gene Larkin ends the thriller with a single over a drawn-in outfield, scoring Dan Gladden with the series-winning run. With the victory, the Twins become the first team in major league history to go from a last place finish to a World Championship in one season.

> DID YOU KNOW? The Minnesota Twins' 10-inning, 1-0 victory in the deciding game of the 1991 Fall Classic was the first World Series Game 7 to go into extra innings since 1924, when this same franchise - then the Washington Senators - claimed a 12-inning, 4-3 win over the New York Giants to earn their first World Series title.

2002 The Anaheim Angels defeat the San Francisco Giants 4-1 in Game 7 to capture the first World Championship in the 42-year history of the franchise. Starter John Lackey pitches five solid innings to earn the win, becoming the first rookie since Babe Adams in 1909 to win the seventh game of a World Series.

2004 With a 3-0 victory in Game 4, the Boston Red Sox complete a convincing sweep of the St. Louis Cardinals to win the World Series for the first time since 1918 and finally conquer the so-called "Curse of the Bambino." Derek Lowe pitches seven strong innings to win the clincher for the Red Sox, who never trail in the series.

In 2004, Derek Lowe became the first pitcher in major league history to win three series-clinching games in a single postseason.

**2011**  In one of the most exciting games in World Series history, third baseman David Freese's clutch 11th-inning home run gives the St. Louis Cardinals a 10-9 walk-off win over the Texas Rangers in Game 6. The thriller, which includes seven lead changes, sees the Cardinals overcome two-run deficits in both the 9th and 10th innings to set the stage for Freese's heroics.

## 28

**1968**  Following his pitching season for the ages, Bob Gibson is unanimously named the National League Cy Young Award winner. The St. Louis Cardinals ace led the league in wins (22), ERA (1.12), strikeouts (268), shutouts (13) and WHIP (.853).

**2011**  After surviving a dramatic Game 6 despite twice being down to their last strike, the St. Louis Cardinals defeat the Texas Rangers 6-2 in Game 7 to win the franchise's 11th World Series title.

## 29

**1920**  The New York Yankees add a critical piece to their budding empire, hiring Ed Barrow, the 52-year-old baseball sage and former Boston Red Sox skipper, to be their business manager. Over the next 25 seasons with Barrow in charge of baseball operations, the Yankees will dominate the game, winning 14 pennants and 10 World Championships.

**1931**  Pitching Triple Crown winner Lefty Grove of the Philadelphia Athletics is named the American League's Most Valuable Player after posting a career-best 31-4 record with a 2.06 ERA and 175 strikeouts. New York Yankees slugger Lou Gehrig, who set a new AL mark with 185 RBIs, finishes second.

## 30

**1963**  One week after unanimously winning his first Cy Young Award, Sandy Koufax of the Los Angeles Dodgers outpolls St. Louis Cardinals shortstop Dick Groat to claim the National League MVP award.

ⓘ Koufax led the National League in wins (25), ERA (1.88), strikeouts (306), shutouts (11) and WHIP (.875) in the regular season, and dominated the postseason with two wins over the New York Yankees in the Dodgers' World Series sweep.

**2018**   The Washington Nationals win the World Series for the first time in the franchise's 51-year history after claiming a 6-2, come-from-behind victory over the heavily favored Houston Astros in Game 7. The World Series title is the first for the nation's capital since the Senators won in 1924.

 The Nationals, who started the year 19-31, survived five postseason elimination games and defeated a 106-win Dodgers club in the NLDS and a 107-win Astros juggernaut in the World Series during their improbable title run.

DID YOU KNOW? In 2019, the Washington Nationals became the first team in World Series history to capture all four of their wins on the road.

# 31

**2011**   Three days after guiding the St. Louis Cardinals to a World Series title, Tony LaRussa announces his retirement after 33 seasons as a major league manager. The 67-year-old future Hall of Famer finishes his career with 2,728 wins, third on the all-time list behind only Connie Mack (3,731) and John McGraw (2,763).

**2018**   Hall of Famer Willie Lee McCovey, one of baseball's greatest sluggers, dies at age 80 in Palo Alto, California. An imposing offensive force during much of his 22-year big league career, McCovey won three home run titles and two RBI crowns and captured the NL MVP award in 1969. At the time of his retirement in 1980, his 521 lifetime homers were more than any other National League left-handed hitter.

# NOVEMBER

## 1

1966  After another remarkable season in which he led all of baseball in wins (27), ERA (1.73) and strikeouts (317), Sandy Koufax of the Los Angeles Dodgers becomes the first three-time winner of the Cy Young Award.

>  Once again, the vote was unanimous, as was the case in 1963 and 1965.

1997  The Negro Leagues Baseball Museum re-opens in its new and expanded location in the historic 18th and Vine district of Kansas City, Missouri, just around the corner from the YMCA building where the Negro National League was formed in 1920.

2001  At 12:04 AM, New York Yankees shortstop Derek Jeter earns the moniker "Mr. November" when he hits a 10th-inning walk-off home run in the Yankees' 4-3 defeat of the Arizona Diamondbacks in Game 4 of the World Series. Jeter's blast came one inning after Yankees first baseman Tino Martinez's dramatic two-out, two-run homer off Arizona closer Byung-Hyun Kim sent the game into extra innings. Hours later in Game 5, history repeats itself in improbable fashion as the Yankees defeat the D'backs once again by tying the game with a Scott Brosius two-out, two-run home run against Kim in the bottom of the ninth and then winning the game in extra innings.

> DID YOU KNOW? With come-from-behind wins in Game 4 and Game 5 of the 2001 World Series, the New York Yankees became the first team in postseason history to win two straight games when trailing after eight innings.

2017  The Houston Astros defeat the Los Angeles Dodgers 5-1 in Game 7 of the World Series to claim the first World Championship in the franchise's 56-year history. Astros outfielder George Springer, who homered a record-tying five times in the Fall Classic and set new marks with eight extra-base hits and 29 total bases, is names Series MVP.

# 2

**1881**   The American Association, a second professional baseball major league, is founded in Cincinnati, Ohio. The charter members are the Baltimore Orioles, Cincinnati Red Stockings, Louisville Eclipse, Philadelphia Athletics, Pittsburgh Alleghenys and St. Louis Browns. The upstart circuit, pejoratively referred to by the rival National League as "The Beer and Whiskey League," will appeal to working class audiences by offering Sunday games, alcohol sales and cheaper ticket prices.

**1938**   Boston Red Sox slugger Jimmie Foxx, who hit 50 home runs and drove in 175 runs this season, is voted Most Valuable Player of the American League for a record third time.

**1964**   CBS Broadcasting, Inc. becomes the first corporate owner of a Major League Baseball team after purchasing eighty percent of the New York Yankees for $11.2 million.

**1974**   The Atlanta Braves send Hank Aaron to the city where his major league career began when they deal him to the Milwaukee Brewers for outfielder Dave May and a minor league pitcher. Aaron learns of the trade while in Tokyo just hours after defeating Japan's Sadaharu Oh, baseball's future International Home Run King, in a globally televised home run derby.

 Hank Aaron hit 733 home runs during his 21 seasons with the Milwaukee/Atlanta Braves, a record total for a major league player with one franchise.

**1995**   The New York Yankees name veteran skipper and former National League MVP Joe Torre as their new manager, replacing the recently departed Buck Showalter. Despite a pedestrian win/loss record and no playoff appearances in 14 seasons with the Mets, Braves and Cardinals, Torre will prove to be a brilliant hire as he will guide the Yankees to four World Series titles in his first five seasons with the team.

**2016**   In an epic matchup of long-suffering franchises, the Chicago Cubs end their 108-year World Series title drought with a thrilling 8-7, 10-inning victory over the Cleveland Indians in Game 7 at Progressive Field. The win completes the Cubs' climb back from a 3-1 Series deficit, and dashes the Indians' hopes for a first World Championship since 1948.

 The 2016 Chicago Cubs became the first team to rally from a three-games-to-one World Series deficit since the Kansas City Royals accomplished the feat in 1985.

# 3

**1942**  Despite winning the Triple Crown, Boston Red Sox slugger Ted Williams falls short in American League MVP voting, finishing 21 votes behind second baseman Joe Gordon of the New York Yankees.

> (i) While Gordon did have an excellent season, batting .322 and driving in 103 runs for the American League Champs, detractors pointed out that he also led the league in three dubious categories: strikeouts (95), most double plays hit into (22) and most errors at his position (28). For his part, Williams was an offensive force, leading all of baseball in the Triple Crown categories of batting average (.356), home runs (36) and RBIs (137), as well as runs scored (141), walks (145), on-base percentage (.499), slugging percentage (.648) and total bases (338).

**1987**  After bashing 49 homers and driving in 118 runs in his first big league campaign, Mark McGwire of the Oakland Athletics becomes the first player since Carlton Fisk in 1972 to be unanimously voted the American League Rookie of the Year Award winner.

> (i) McGwire's 49 home runs shattered the old rookie record of 38 shared by Wally Berger (Braves, 1930) and Frank Robinson (Redlegs, 1956).

# 4

**1889**  A new major league, named the Players' League, is formed by John Montgomery Ward and the Brotherhood of Professional Baseball Players after National League owners fail to make significant labor concessions. The new league will abolish the reserve clause system and incorporate profit sharing for the players.

> (i) Despite the fact that the Players' League attracted many of baseball's best players and often fared well at the gate, the league folded after just one season due to insufficient funding.

**1950**  Former pitching star Grover Cleveland Alexander, nicknamed "Old Pete," dies at age 63 in St. Paul, Nebraska. Alexander thoroughly dominated the National League during his prime and finished his 20-year Hall of Fame career with a remarkable 373-208 record, 90 shutouts and three Pitching Triple Crowns.

**1955**  Hall of Famer Denton True "Cy" Young dies at age 88 in Newcomerstown, Ohio. A true legend and one of baseball's outstanding pitchers, Young's consistent excellence and durability over his 22-year career produced results which are unapproachable by today's standards. He recorded 32 or more wins in a season five times and 20-plus wins in a season 15 times, and his career total of 511 victories is almost 100 more than any other pitcher in baseball history.

**1980**   Taiwanese-Japanese baseball icon Sadaharu Oh, the world record holder for career home runs as a professional, retires from baseball. The Tokyo Yomiuri Giants first baseman ends his astonishing 22-year career with 868 home runs.

> (i)   Oh, the greatest player in the history of Japan's Nippon Professional Baseball, won a record nine league Most Valuable Player awards.

**2001**   In Game 7 of the World Series, the Arizona Diamondbacks conquer Yankee mystique and baseball's greatest closer as they score two runs against Mariano Rivera in the bottom of the ninth to defeat the New York Yankees 3-2 and win the World Series. D'backs outfielder Luis Gonzalez comes through in the clutch with the game-winning single and Series co-MVP Randy Johnson earns the win in relief.

> DID YOU KNOW?   The four-year-old Arizona Diamondbacks of 2001 are the youngest franchise to win a World Series.

# 5

**1968**   Detroit Tigers pitcher Denny McLain, Major League Baseball's first 30-game winner since Dizzy Dean in 1934, is unanimously selected as the American League Most Valuable Player. The 24-year-old McLain posted a 31-6 record with a 1.96 ERA and 280 strikeouts, leading the Tigers to a 103-win season and a World Series title.

**1996**   After batting .314 and scoring 104 runs for the World Champion New York Yankees in his first major league season, 22-year-old shortstop Derek Jeter is named American League Rookie of the Year, becoming just the fifth player to win the award unanimously.

> DID YOU KNOW?   In the spring of 1996, there was enough uncertainty about Derek Jeter's big league readiness that the New York Yankees brass reportedly considered trading future star closer Mariano Rivera to the Seattle Mariners for journeyman shortstop Felix Fermin.

**2002** Randy Johnson of the Arizona Diamondbacks captures a record-tying fourth straight National League Cy Young Award, and his fifth CYA overall.

> (i) After leading the league with 24 wins, 334 strikeouts and a 2.37 ERA, the "Big Unit" became the first player since the New York Mets' Dwight Gooden in 1985 to win the National League Pitching Triple Crown. Johnson was especially dominant in September, posting a 5-0 record with a miniscule 0.66 ERA.

 In 2002, Arizona Diamondbacks stars Randy Johnson and Curt Schilling became the first duo to finish 1-2 in Cy Young Award voting in consecutive seasons.

# 6

**1887** Walter Johnson, arguably the greatest pitcher in baseball history, is born in Humboldt, Kansas.

**1974** Mike Marshall of the Los Angeles Dodgers becomes the first relief pitcher to win the Cy Young Award. After finishing second to Tom Seaver in 1973, Marshall claims the award this season after saving 21 games and winning 15 more while posting major league record-setting totals of 106 appearances and 208 innings pitched in relief.

> (i) In the middle of this historic season, the ironman reliever set another major league record when he pitched in 13 straight games.

**2007** San Diego Padres pitcher Greg Maddux wins his seventeenth Gold Glove Award, breaking the career mark he previously shared with Jim Kaat and Brooks Robinson.

> (i) Maddux ended his remarkable career with eighteen Gold Glove Awards, winning for a final time in 2008.

# 7

**1928** The Chicago Cubs acquire National League batting champion Rogers Hornsby from the financially troubled Boston Braves for $200,000 and five marginal players.

> (i) In his first season in Chicago, the 32-year-old Hornsby captured his second National League MVP award and helped lead the Cubs to the 1929 World Series.

> (i) After player-manager Hornsby's departure, Boston Braves owner Emil Fuchs managed his own team in 1929, becoming the last

manager without professional playing experience until another Braves owner - Atlanta's Ted Turner - piloted the Braves for one game on May 11, 1977.

**1978**  Despite posting a 25-3 record with 248 strikeouts and a miniscule 1.74 ERA for the pennant-winning New York Yankees, Ron Guidry finishes second to Boston Red Sox outfielder Jim Rice in American League MVP voting. Rice had a monster year of his own, leading the league in home runs (46), RBIs (139), hits (213), triples (15), total bases (406), slugging percentage (.600) and OPS (.970).

 In 1978, Jim Rice became the first American League player to reach 400 total bases in a season since Joe DiMaggio in 1937.

**2017**  Two-time Cy Young Award winner and future Hall of Famer Harry Leroy "Roy" Halladay dies at age 40 near Holiday, Florida when the private plane he is piloting crashes into the Gulf of Mexico.

# 8

**1894**  Future Hall of Famer Michael Joseph "King" Kelly dies of pneumonia at age 36 in Boston, Massachusetts. Kelly's expert batting and base running ability, colorful personality and innovative play earned him tremendous popularity during the 1880s. He was especially dominant during his seven years with the Chicago White Stockings, with whom he won two batting titles and five National League pennants.

**1966**  Triple Crown winner Frank Robinson of the Baltimore Orioles becomes the first player in history to earn MVP honors in both leagues when he's unanimously named American League Most Valuable Player. Robinson previously captured the National League MVP award while with the Cincinnati Reds in 1961.

# 9

**1993**  San Francisco Giants outfielder Barry Bonds wins the National League MVP award for the third time in four years. He joins Stan Musial, Roy Campanella and Mike Schmidt as the National League's only three-time recipients of the award.

ⓘ In his first year in San Francisco after signing as a free agent, Bonds reached career highs in nearly every offensive category, including batting average (.336), home runs (46), RBIs (123), runs scored (129) and OPS (1.136) while also winning his fourth straight Gold Glove Award.

2004 Following a season that saw him come out of temporary retirement to pitch for his hometown Houston Astros, Roger Clemens, at age 42, becomes the oldest pitcher to win the Cy Young Award. He also extends his own record by claiming his seventh CYA, and becomes the first to win the award with four different teams, having done so previously with the Boston Red Sox (1986, '87, '91), Toronto Blue Jays ('97, '98) and New York Yankees ('01).

> (i) The runner-up for the National League Cy Young Award this season was another 40-something ace: Arizona Diamondbacks 40-year-old flamethrower Randy Johnson.

# 10

1948 In a move that nets them a future ace, the Chicago White Sox acquire 21-year-old lefty Billy Pierce and $10,000 from the Detroit Tigers in exchange for veteran catcher Aaron Robinson. Robinson will play well for Detroit in 1949 but will be out of baseball within three seasons, while Pierce will soon establish himself as one of the best pitchers in the American League, winning 186 games and garnering seven All-Star selections during his 13 seasons with the White Sox.

1965 San Francisco Giants superstar Willie Mays, who batted .317 with a league-leading 52 home runs this season, is named National League MVP, beating out Los Angeles Dodgers ace Sandy Koufax for the honor. It's Mays' second National League MVP award, and it comes eleven years after he won his first as a 23-year-old in 1954.

> (i) Koufax had a fantastic season in his own right, going 26-8 with a 2.04 ERA while setting a new major league single-season record for strikeouts with 382.

# 11

1981 First-year pitching sensation Fernando Valenzuela of the Los Angeles Dodgers wins the National League Cy Young Award, becoming the first rookie to be so honored in the 26-year history of the award. Valenzuela, who led the league with eight shutouts and 180 strikeouts, edges out the Cincinnati Reds' Tom Seaver by three votes.

In 1981, Fernando Valenzuela became the first rookie to lead the National League in strikeouts.

**1998** The Chicago White Sox acquire 22-year-old first baseman Paul Konerko from the Cincinnati Reds in exchange for outfielder Mike Cameron. Konerko will blossom in Chicago, becoming the face of the franchise and one of the top players in White Sox history.

**2019** After leading the New York Mets with a rookie-record 53 home runs and 120 RBIs, powerhouse first baseman Pete Alonso is named National League Rookie of the Year.

 Alonso's RBI total in 2019 was the most by a rookie since Albert Pujols drove in 130 runs in 2001.

# 12

**1986** Roger Clemens of the Boston Red Sox wins the American League Cy Young Award unanimously, joining the Detroit Tigers' Denny McLain (1968) as the only pitchers to do so. The 23-year-old Clemens went 24-4 this season with 238 strikeouts and a league-leading 2.48 ERA.

> The Rocket got off to a scorching start in 1986, winning his first 14 starts (and starting and winning the All-Star game). One of those victories came against the Seattle Mariners on April 29, a game in which Clemens set a new major league record for strikeouts in a nine-inning game with 20.

**1993** Hall of Famer William Malcolm "Bill" Dickey dies at age 86 in Little Rock, Arkansas. The longtime New York Yankees catcher, known for his defensive skill and adept hitting, garnered 11 All-Star selections during his 17-year big league career and finished with a .313 lifetime batting average and 202 home runs. He was an invaluable contributor on a Yankees team that won eight pennants and seven World Series titles during his tenure.

**2001** St. Louis Cardinals 21-year-old phenom Albert Pujols, who batted .329 with 37 home runs and 130 RBIs this season, wins the National League Rookie of the Year Award by unanimous vote.

> Despite being just one year removed from Class A baseball, Pujols set several National League rookie records, including most RBIs, extra base hits (88) and total bases (360).

**2001** Seattle Mariners outfielder Ichiro Suzuki is named American League Rookie of the Year after leading the league in batting (.350), hits (242) and stolen bases (56).

 Ichiro Suzuki was the first rookie to win a batting title since Tony Oliva of the Minnesota Twins led the American League with a .323 average in 1964.

**2012** Los Angeles Angels 21-year-old center fielder Mike Trout is unanimously voted American League Rookie of the Year, becoming the youngest player in league history to win the award. Trout had one of the greatest rookie seasons in major league history, becoming the first rookie to hit 30 home runs and steal 40 bases in a season after batting .326 with 30 home runs and leading the league in steals (49) and runs scored (129).

 Mike Trout, as a 21-year-old rookie, became the first player in major league history to hit 30 home runs, steal 45 bases and score 125 runs in the same season.

# 13

**1979** Pittsburgh Pirates 39-year-old first baseman Willie Stargell becomes the oldest winner of a Most Valuable Player award to date when he and Keith Hernandez of the St. Louis Cardinals are named National League co-MVPs. Stargell, nicknamed "Pops" in reference to his leadership and father-figure status, batted .281 with 32 home runs and 82 RBIs during the regular season before powering his "We Are Family" Pirates to a World Championship by dominating the postseason.

In 1979, Willie Stargell became the first player to win Most Valuable Player honors in the regular season, League Championship Series and World Series.

**1995** Atlanta Braves ace Greg Maddux wins the National League Cy Young Award for an unprecedented fourth straight time, finishing with a remarkable 19-2 record and a league-leading 1.63 ERA.

ⓘ Maddux also became the first National League pitcher since Sandy Koufax in 1965 and 1966 to win consecutive Cy Young Awards unanimously.

 Greg Maddux's Adjusted ERA+ totals of 271 in 1994 and 260 in 1995 are the two best single-season marks in the National League's modern era.

**2000** After fashioning one of the most dominant seasons in baseball history, Pedro Martinez of the Boston Red Sox is named the unanimous winner of the American League Cy Young Award, in the process becoming the first AL pitcher to win the award unanimously in consecutive seasons.

> ⓘ In a season for the ages, Martinez produced, among other things, the highest ERA+ figure (291) in the modern era and the lowest WHIP (.7373) in the history of baseball.

> **DID YOU KNOW?** In 2000, Pedro Martinez became the only starting pitcher in major league history to have more than twice as many strikeouts in a season (284) than hits allowed (128).

**2017** Following a season in which he belted 52 homers to topple Mark McGwire's 30-year-old rookie home run record, New York Yankees outfielder Aaron Judge is unanimously named American League Rookie of the Year.

**2019** Houston Astros star Justin Verlander caps off a season filled with highlights by winning his second Cy Young Award, edging out teammate Gerrit Cole. The 36-year-old Verlander posted a stellar 21-6 record with 300 strikeouts and led the majors in wins, WHIP (.803) and innings pitched (223).

> ⓘ Gerrit Cole was spectacular in his own right, going 20-5 with a 2.50 ERA and a major league-best 326 strikeouts.

> **DID YOU KNOW?** In 2019, Justin Verlander and Gerrit Cole became the first pair of teammates to each win 20-plus games in the same season since Randy Johnson and Curt Schilling accomplished the feat for the 2002 Arizona Diamondbacks and Pedro Martinez and Derek Lowe did the same for the 2002 Boston Red Sox. The Verlander-Cole duo was also the first since Johnson and Schilling in 2002 to each record 300 or more strikeouts in the same season.

# 14

**1946** Ted Williams of the pennant-winning Boston Red Sox, who hit .342 with 38 home runs and 123 RBIs in his first season back following three years of military service, wins the American League Most Valuable Player award for the first time. Two-time reigning AL MVP Hal Newhouser finishes second in the voting.

**1957**  Hank Aaron of the World Champion Milwaukee Braves captures the National League Most Valuable Player award, outpolling Stan Musial of the St. Louis Cardinals and Braves teammate Red Schoendienst. The 23-year-old Aaron batted .322 and led the league with 44 home runs, 132 RBIs and 118 runs scored.

(i)  Aaron would finish in the top three in MVP voting seven times during his illustrious career, but this would remain his only MVP award.

**1973**  Reggie Jackson of the Oakland Athletics is named the unanimous winner of the American League Most Valuable Player award. Despite playing his home games in the pitcher-friendly Coliseum, Jackson led the league in several offensive categories, including home runs (32), RBIs (117), runs scored (99) and slugging percentage (.531).

(i)  Jackson also earned World Series MVP honors in 1973 after slugging .586 and driving in six runs against the New York Mets.

**2018**  New York Mets ace right-hander Jacob deGrom captures the National League Cy Young Award with the lowest win total ever for a starting CYA winner. Despite a pedestrian 10-9 record, deGrom wowed the voters with a miniscule 1.70 ERA and .912 WHIP to go along with 269 strikeouts in 217 innings pitched. Two-time reigning NL Cy Young Award winner Max Scherzer, who went 18-7 with 300 strikeouts, finishes a distant second.

DID YOU KNOW?  In 2018, Jacob deGrom set an all-time record when he allowed three runs or less in 29 straight starts.

# 15

**1961**  New York Yankees outfielder Roger Maris, the new single-season home run record holder, wins his second consecutive American League MVP award after edging out teammate Mickey Mantle by four votes.

(i)  In 1960, Maris topped Mantle by just three MVP votes.

**1983**  Cal Ripken Jr. of the World Champion Baltimore Orioles is named the Most Valuable Player in the American League, outdistancing teammate Eddie Murray in the voting. The 23-year-old Ripken, who led the league in hits (211), doubles (47) and runs scored (121), becomes the first player to win the Rookie of the Year and MVP awards in consecutive seasons.

**2004**  San Francisco Giants outfielder Barry Bonds extends his own major league record when he wins his seventh National League MVP award. The slugging star is coming off a season in which he led the NL in batting (.362) and slugging (.812) and set new all-time single-season records with 232 walks and a .609 on-base percentage.

 In 2004, 40-year-old Barry Bonds surpassed Willie Stargell as the oldest player to win a Most Valuable Player award.

**2012** In a much-anticipated vote, Detroit Tigers third baseman Miguel Cabrera, the first Triple Crown winner in 45 years, wins the American League Most Valuable Player award over Rookie of the Year Mike Trout of the Los Angeles Angels. The MVP race sparked debate between defenders of traditional baseball stats, who pointed to Cabrera's Triple Crown numbers, and supporters of more advanced metrics, who touted Trout's overall value.

# 16

**1977** Rod Carew of the Minnesota Twins caps off a career year by capturing the American League MVP award. The future Hall of Famer led the league in batting average (.388), hits (239), runs scored (128), triples (16) and OPS (1.019).

 Rod Carew's total of 239 hits in 1977 was the most by any major league player since 1930.

**1998** Following a season in which he won his second straight Pitching Triple Crown after notching 20 wins, a 2.65 ERA and 271 strikeouts, Roger Clemens of the Toronto Blue Jays sets a new all-time major league record when he claims his fifth Cy Young Award.

ⓘ The Rocket was the first American League pitcher to claim consecutive Pitching Triple Crowns since Lefty Grove accomplished the feat in 1930 and 1931.

**1999** Pitching Triple Crown winner Pedro Martinez of the Boston Red Sox is unanimously voted the American League Cy Young Award winner after going 23-4 with a 2.07 ERA and 313 strikeouts. Having won the National League Cy Young Award in 1997 while with the Montreal Expos, Martinez becomes only the third pitcher to win the award in both leagues, joining Gaylord Perry and Randy Johnson.

 In 1999, Pedro Martinez bested his own all-time mark when he recorded at least one strikeout in 40 consecutive innings.

# 17

1959   One year after Orlando Cepeda of the San Francisco Giants won the National League Rookie of the Year Award by unanimous vote, Cepeda's teammate and fellow future Hall of Famer Willie McCovey duplicates the feat after batting .354 and slugging .656 with 13 home runs and 38 RBIs in just 52 games.

1971   Oakland Athletics 22-year-old lefty Vida Blue becomes the youngest major leaguer to date to capture a Most Valuable Player award. Blue led the American League with a 1.82 ERA and eight shutouts to go along with a 24-8 record and 301 strikeouts, and helped propel the Athletics to their first postseason berth in 40 years.

1979   Rotisserie League Baseball, the best-known form of early fantasy baseball, begins to take shape when Daniel Okrent sketches out the first draft of rules for this statistics-based game on a flight to Texas. Within two weeks, Okrent and a group of literary friends and colleagues will meet in New York and establish the Rotisserie League Baseball Association, named after the eatery (La Rotisserie Francaise) where the meeting takes place.

# 18

1949   Brooklyn Dodgers infielder Jackie Robinson, who led the National League with a .342 batting average and 37 stolen bases, becomes the first African American player to win the Most Valuable Player award.

1966   Less than three weeks after winning his third Cy Young Award, 30-year-old Los Angeles Dodgers ace Sandy Koufax shocks the baseball world by announcing his retirement from baseball due to heightened concern about his arthritic left elbow. Koufax finishes his sensational 12-year big league career with a 165-87 record and a 2.76 ERA.

1981   Mike Schmidt of the Philadelphia Phillies captures his second straight National League MVP award, joining Ernie Banks (1958, 1959) and Joe Morgan (1975, 1976) as the only National League players to win the award in consecutive seasons. The Gold Glove third baseman batted .316 during the strike-shortened season and led the league in home runs (31), RBIs (91), runs scored (78), walks (73), on-base percentage (.435) and slugging percentage (.644).

1987   Chicago Cubs outfielder Andre Dawson becomes the first player in major league history to win a Most Valuable Player award while playing for a last place team. "The Hawk" paced the National League with 49 home runs and 137 RBIs and won his seventh Gold Glove Award while his Cubs scuffled to a 76-85 record.

1991   President George H. W. Bush presents Baseball Hall of Famer and former Marine fighter pilot Ted Williams with the Presidential Medal of Freedom.

2000   Outfielder Ichiro Suzuki, soon to become the first Japanese position player in major league history, signs a three-year contract with the Seattle Mariners.

> (i) Prior to joining the Mariners, Ichiro won three MVP awards and seven batting titles in seven full Nippon Professional Baseball seasons.

# 19

1979   Former California Angels ace Nolan Ryan becomes the first Major League Baseball player to top $1 million in annual salary when he signs a four-year, $4.5 million deal with the Houston Astros.

1986   Mike Schmidt of the Philadelphia Phillies is named the National League's Most Valuable Player for a third time, joining the select company of Stan Musial and Roy Campanella as the NL's only three-time winners of the award. After moving back to his natural position of third base this past season, the future Hall of Famer responded by winning his tenth Gold Glove Award and leading the league in home runs (37), RBIs (119) and slugging percentage (.547).

> (i) The home run crown was Schmidt's National League-record eighth, surpassing the mark he shared with former Pittsburgh Pirates slugger Ralph Kiner.

# 20

1984   Just four days after his 20th birthday, pitcher Dwight Gooden of the New York Mets becomes the youngest player to date to win the National League Rookie of the Year Award. Gooden went 17-9 with a 2.60 ERA during his historic campaign, and set a new major league rookie record with 276 strikeouts.

> (i) In the final nine starts of his rookie season, Gooden was especially dominant, going 8-1 with a 1.07 ERA and 105 strikeouts in 76 innings.

 In 1984, 19-year-old Dwight Gooden established a new major league record for strikeouts per 9 innings with 11.39, eclipsing the mark of 10.71 set by Sam McDowell in 1965.

2001  American League Rookie of the Year Ichiro Suzuki of the Seattle Mariners edges out the Oakland Athletics' Jason Giambi and Mariners teammate Bret Boone to win the AL Most Valuable Player award, joining Fred Lynn (1975) as the only major leaguers to capture MVP and Rookie of the Year honors in the same season.

# 21

1920  Stan Musial, one of baseball's greatest and most beloved stars, is born in Donora, Pennsylvania.

1934  The New York Yankees take a chance on injured Pacific Coast League star Joe DiMaggio, acquiring him from the San Francisco Seals for cash and five players. The 19-year-old DiMaggio, who had a record 61-game hitting streak while with the Seals in 1933, will fully recover from a knee injury and become one of the greatest and most celebrated players in major league history.

> ⓘ  While playing one final season for San Francisco in 1935, DiMaggio won league MVP honors after batting .398 and driving in 154 runs for the league champion Seals.

1958  Former New York Giants star outfielder Melvin Thomas "Mel" Ott, nicknamed "Master Melvin," dies at age 49 in New Orleans, Louisiana. Despite his small stature, Ott slugged his way to six home run titles during his 22-year Hall of Fame career. The fan favorite and perennial All-Star was the first player in National League history to reach 500 career home runs, finishing with 511.

1969  Exactly 49 years after Stan Musial was born in the same town, Ken Griffey Jr., the supremely talented Hall of Fame center fielder, is born in Donora, Pennsylvania.

1988  Hall of Famer Carl Owen Hubbell, nicknamed "King Carl" and the "Meal Ticket," dies at age 85 in Scottsdale, Arizona. Master of the screwball, the longtime New York Giants ace compiled a 253-154 career record while winning two MVP awards and leading the National League in wins and ERA three times each.

2011  Detroit Tigers ace Justin Verlander is named American League Most Valuable Player, becoming the first starting pitcher since Roger Clemens in 1986 to claim the award. The powerful right-hander won the Pitching

Triple Crown this season after pacing the AL with 24 wins, a 2.40 ERA and 250 strikeouts.

# 22

**1954**  The Pittsburgh Pirates select 19-year-old outfielder Roberto Clemente with the first pick in the Rule 5 Draft after he's left unprotected by the Brooklyn Dodgers. The selection will prove to be a brilliant one for the Pirates as Clemente will develop into a transcendent star in Pittsburgh.

**1957**  New York Yankees centerfielder Mickey Mantle wins his second straight American League MVP award, this time in a narrow victory over Boston Red Sox slugger Ted Williams. The results are controversial to some, as Williams bested Mantle in batting average (.388 to .365), home runs (38 to 34), and slugging percentage (.731 to .665).

> ⓘ  Although the 38-year-old Williams had a truly spectacular year at the plate, Mantle nearly matched him offensively and provided far more value in the field, all while leading the Yankees to the pennant.

**1989**  Free agent outfielder Kirby Puckett becomes the first major leaguer to earn at least $3 million per season when he re-signs with the Minnesota Twins for $9 million over three years.

# 23

**1962**  Los Angeles Dodgers shortstop Maury Wills, whose 104 stolen bases this season set a modern major league record, wins the National League MVP award in a controversial vote. Wills outpolls San Francisco Giants star Willie Mays (.304 average, 49 home runs, 141 RBIs) and Dodgers teammate Tommy Davis (.346, 27, 153) despite having a league-average .720 OPS.

> ⓘ  Wills was credited with reintroducing the value of the stolen base to the National League. In 1962, when he topped Ty Cobb's 47-year-old single-season record of 96 stolen bases, Wills had more steals than any other team in the league.

**2010**  Texas Rangers outfielder Josh Hamilton wins the American League MVP award, continuing his ascension from the much-publicized drug and alcohol addiction that marred his early career. Despite missing most of September after breaking two ribs, Hamilton finished with 32 homers and 100 RBIs to go along with his league-leading .359 average.

# 24

1953   The Brooklyn Dodgers hire little-known minor league skipper Walter Alston to replace Chuck Dressen as their manager. Alston will retain that role for the next 23 seasons, leading the Dodgers to 2,040 regular season wins, seven National League pennants and four World Championships during his tenure.

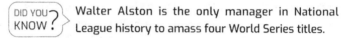 Walter Alston is the only manager in National League history to amass four World Series titles.

1982   Cal Ripken Jr. is named American League Rookie of the Year after batting .264 with 28 home runs and 93 RBIs for the Baltimore Orioles.

2003   Hall of Famer Warren Edward Spahn, the winningest left-hander in major league history, dies at age 82 in Broken Arrow, Oklahoma. During his stellar 21-year career, Spahn reached 20 wins in 13 different seasons, threw two no-hitters and finished with a 363-245 lifetime record. The 14-time All-Star also earned the prestigious Purple Heart and Bronze Star for his service in World War II.

# 25

1914   Iconic center fielder Joe DiMaggio, the esteemed "Yankee Clipper," is born in Martinez, California.

1941   All-Star shortstop Lou Boudreau becomes the youngest full-time manager in modern major league history when the Cleveland Indians hire the 24-year-old "Boy Wonder" to replace Roger Peckinpaugh.

ⓘ Coincidentally, Peckinpaugh holds the distinction of being Major League Baseball's youngest-ever interim manager, having guided the New York Yankees for three weeks in 1914 at the age of 23.

1944   Kenesaw Mountain Landis, baseball's autocratic first commissioner, dies at age 78 in Chicago, Illinois.

2002   The Boston Red Sox hire 28-year-old Theo Epstein as their new general manager, making him the youngest GM in major league history. Epstein, a lifelong Red Sox fan who grew up near Fenway Park, had previously served as Director of Baseball Operations for the San Diego Padres.

ⓘ Under Epstein's guidance, the Red Sox finally broke the "Curse of the Bambino" by winning the 2004 World Series, its first championship in 86 years. Epstein later helped the Chicago Cubs end an even longer World Championship drought in 2016.

Theo Epstein's grandfather, Philip G. Epstein, and great-uncle, Julius J. Epstein, won Academy Awards for the screenplay of *Casablanca* in 1942.

# 26

**1975**  Boston Red Sox center fielder Fred Lynn easily outdistances John Mayberry of the Kansas City Royals and Red Sox teammate Jim Rice to win the American League Most Valuable Player award, becoming the first rookie to capture MVP honors. Lynn batted .331 and led the league in runs scored (103), doubles (47) and slugging percentage (.566) while helping Boston capture the American League pennant.

 While playing collegiately at the University of Southern California, Fred Lynn won three College World Series titles in three years. His USC teammates included future major league All-Stars Steve Busby, Steve Kemp and Roy Smalley.

**2009**  Longtime New York Yankees public address announcer Bob Sheppard officially retires at the age of 99. Nicknamed "The Voice of God" by Reggie Jackson, Sheppard had been the Yankees' full-time announcer from 1951 to 2007 before his declining health forced him to step down.

# 27

**1941**  New York Yankees centerfielder Joe DiMaggio, who reached celebrity status this season after his record 56-game hitting streak captivated the baseball world, is named American League Most Valuable Player for the second time in his career. Ted Williams of the Boston Red Sox finishes second in the voting, failing to win the award despite batting .406 and leading the league in home runs, runs scored, on-base percentage and slugging percentage.

**1947**  Joe DiMaggio of the World Champion New York Yankees wins his third American League Most Valuable Player award, edging out Triple Crown winner and reigning MVP Ted Williams of the Boston Red Sox by one vote (202-201). The voting results spark controversy as Williams (.343 average, 32 home runs, 162 RBIs, 125 runs scored), who far outperformed DiMaggio (.315, 20, 97, 97) offensively, was left completely off one writer's 10-man ballot.

1956 Brooklyn Dodgers pitcher Don Newcombe wins the inaugural Cy Young Award, beating out Dodgers teammate Sal Maglie, New York Yankees lefty Whitey Ford and Warren Spahn of the Milwaukee Braves. Newcombe topped the majors in wins (27, against only 7 losses), winning percentage (.794) and WHIP (.989), and helped lead the Dodgers to a National League pennant.

1972 The New York Yankees acquire power-hitting third baseman Graig Nettles and catcher Jerry Moses from the Cleveland Indians in exchange for prospect Charlie Spikes and backups John Ellis, Jerry Kenney and Rusty Torres. Nettles will flourish in New York, winning a home run title in 1976 and helping the Yankees to World Championships in 1977 and 1978.

> (i) Eyebrows were raised when Indians general manager Gabe Paul resigned shortly after the Nettles trade to join the new Yankees ownership syndicate.

1997 Hall of Famer and Negro League legend Walter Fenner "Buck" Leonard dies at age 90 in Rocky Mount, North Carolina. A smooth fielder and excellent pure hitter, Leonard teamed with Josh Gibson to form the most feared batting duo in Negro League history and helped propel the Homestead Grays to nine consecutive Negro National League championships from 1937 to 1945.

2012 Marvin Miller, former union chief and one of the most influential figures in the history of professional baseball, dies at 95 in his home in New York City. During his tenure as executive director of the Major League Baseball Players Association from 1966 to 1982, Miller oversaw sweeping changes in the sport that advanced players' rights, including the dismantling of the reserve clause and the advent of salary arbitration and free agency.

>  During Marvin Miller's 17-year directorship of the MLB Players Association, the average salary of a major league player rose from $19,000 to $241,000 and the MLBPA became the strongest labor union in the country.

# 28

1958 Baseball wunderkind Carl Yastrzemski signs with the Boston Red Sox for a reported $108,000 bonus plus the cost of his continuing college education. The future Hall of Famer will make his Red Sox debut in 1961, replacing Boston icon Ted Williams as the everyday left fielder.

As a two-sport star at New York's Bridgehampton High School, Carl Yastrzemski broke the Long Island high school basketball scoring record previously held by NFL legend Jim Brown.

2003 The Boston Red Sox acquire ace right-hander Curt Schilling from the Arizona Diamondbacks for pitchers Casey Fossum, Brandon Lyon and Jorge de la Rosa and prospect Michael Goss. The deal will pay immediate dividends for Boston as Schilling will go 21-6 in 2004, helping the Red Sox win their first World Series title in 86 years.

# 29

1916 In an exhibition game held in Kansas City, Missouri, future Hall of Fame pitchers Grover Cleveland Alexander and Walter Johnson face each other for the first time, with Johnson's team winning 3-2. Other major leaguers present that day are Max Carey, Hal Chase, Casey Stengel and Zach Wheat.

1971 The Big Red Machine adds several key cogs when the Houston Astros agree to trade future Hall of Fame second baseman Joe Morgan, César Gerónimo and Jack Billingham to the Cincinnati Reds in exchange for Lee May, Tommy Helms and Jimmy Stewart. The deal, initially criticized in Cincinnati, will turn out to be one of the best in Reds history.

1976 Free agent outfielder Reggie Jackson signs a five-year, $2.96 million contract with the New York Yankees, becoming the highest paid player in baseball history to date.

ⓘ During Jackson's tumultuous tenure, the Yankees won four division titles, three pennants and World Series crowns in 1977 and 1978.

# 30

1948 Lou Boudreau of the World Champion Cleveland Indians captures the American League MVP award, beating out superstars Joe DiMaggio and Ted Williams for the honor. Boudreau batted .355 with 18 home runs and 106 RBIs this past season, all while excelling at shortstop and as manager.

ⓘ Indians owner Bill Veeck almost traded Boudreau to the St. Louis Browns after the 1947 season, but protests by Indians fans kept him in Cleveland.

 Lou Boudreau remains the only manager to win a World Series and Most Valuable Player award in the same season.

1948 With integration underway in Major League Baseball, the Negro National League officially disbands. Four remaining NNL franchises join the Negro American League, which becomes the only "major" Negro League circuit still in operation.

1998 The Arizona Diamondbacks win the Randy Johnson sweepstakes, signing the coveted free agent pitcher to a 4-year, $52.4 million contract. The "Big Unit" will make the D'backs' investment in him look brilliant when he claims four straight Cy Young Awards.

# DECEMBER

## 1

1954   The New York Yankees and Baltimore Orioles complete the largest trade in major league history to date as the Yankees send 10 players, including veteran outfielder Gene Woodling and top prospects Gus Triandos and Hal Smith, to the Orioles in exchange for a seven-player package that includes young righties Don Larsen and "Bullet" Bob Turley.

> [i]   Turley, the most coveted player in the deal, became the first Yankee to win a Cy Young Award when he netted the honor in 1958.

1956   Following a season in which he scored 122 runs and tied Wally Berger's rookie record of 38 home runs, Cincinnati Redlegs outfielder Frank Robinson is unanimously voted the National League Rookie of the Year.

> [i]   With Robinson leading the way, the 1956 Redlegs matched the 1947 New York Giants' then-record total of 221 home runs.

## 2

1914   After being released by the Philadelphia Athletics in October, future Hall of Fame left-hander Eddie Plank signs with the Federal League's St. Louis Terriers. Plank's departure will be just the first of Philadelphia's many cost-cutting moves this offseason. Stalwart pitchers Chief Bender and Jack Coombs will sign elsewhere after being waived, star second baseman Eddie Collins will be jettisoned to the Chicago White Sox and slugger Home Run Baker will sit out over a salary dispute. Following the historic player purge, Connie Mack's once-great baseball machine, World Champs in 1910, 1911 and 1913, will become the majors' worst team, finishing 1915 with an abysmal 43-109 record.

1944   Yomiuri Giants superstar pitcher Eiji Sawamura, who at age 17 became a national hero in his native Japan after striking out Charlie Gehringer, Babe Ruth, Lou Gehrig and Jimmie Foxx in succession in an exhibition game, dies in military combat at the age of 27 when the transport ship he's aboard is sunk by an American submarine in the Pacific Ocean. In five seasons with the Giants,

Sawamura fashioned a 63-22 record with a 1.74 ERA. His accomplishments included three no-hitters and a league MVP award in 1937.

> (i) In 1947, Sawamura's illustrious Japanese Baseball League career was commemorated with the establishment of the Eiji Sawamura Award, an honor annually bestowed upon the top starting pitcher in Japanese professional baseball. Twelve years later he became one of the nine charter members of the Japanese Baseball Hall of Fame.

**1948**  Stan Musial of the St. Louis Cardinals caps off the greatest statistical season of his career by winning his third National League MVP award. His virtuoso performance included league-leading totals in batting average (.376), hits (230), RBIs (131), runs scored (135), doubles (46), triples (18), total bases (429), on-base percentage (.450) and slugging percentage (.702).

> (i) Musial narrowly missed out on capturing the Triple Crown when his home run total fell one short of the 40 posted by the Pirates' Ralph Kiner and the Giants' Johnny Mize.

**1981**  Fernando Valenzuela of the World Champion Los Angeles Dodgers is named National League Rookie of the Year after going 13-7 with a 2.48 ERA and 180 strikeouts. Having already been chosen as the National League's Cy Young Award recipient, Valenzuela becomes the first pitcher to win both major awards in the same season.

# 3

**1968**  The MLB Rules Committee responds to "The Year of the Pitcher" by adopting rule changes designed to increase run production. The most significant alterations include shrinking the strike zone and lowering the pitcher's mound from 15 inches to 10 inches.

> (i) The revised rules had an immediate impact as run scoring increased by nearly 20% in 1969.

**1969**  The Kansas City Royals make arguably their greatest trade ever when they acquire 22-year-old outfielder Amos Otis from the New York Mets in exchange for third baseman Joe Foy and pitcher Bob Johnson. Otis, who batted just .151 in limited action with the Mets, will flourish in Kansas City, finishing his 14-year Royals tenure with 193 home runs, 341 stolen bases and five All-Star Game selections.

**1974**  The Philadelphia Phillies acquire ace reliever Tug McGraw and two others from the New York Mets in exchange for coveted young catcher John

Stearns, outfielder Del Unser and pitcher Mac Scarce. McGraw will play a pivotal role in the bullpen for a Philadelphia club that will claim three straight division titles from 1976-1978, and his exceptional pitching in 1980 will help propel the Phillies to their first World Championship in franchise history.

# 4

1914   Walter Johnson, baseball's preeminent pitcher, signs a lucrative three-year deal with the Federal League's Chicago Whales. The outlaw league's excitement over the monumental signing will be short-lived, however, as Johnson will soon re-sign with the Washington Senators after Senators owner Clark Griffith threatens legal action.

1963   The Philadelphia Phillies get the better of a one-sided deal with the Detroit Tigers when they acquire future Hall of Fame pitcher Jim Bunning and veteran catcher Gus Triandos in exchange for outfielder Don Demeter and pitcher Jack Hamilton. The trade will yield little for Detroit, while the 32-year-old Bunning will prove he has plenty left in the tank, winning 19 games in each of the next three seasons for the Phillies.

2007   The Detroit Tigers make one of the greatest trades in major league history, acquiring 24-year-old slugger Miguel Cabrera along with starter Dontrelle Willis from the Florida Marlins in exchange for a group of six prospects that includes former first round picks Cameron Maybin and Andrew Miller. While the Marlins' haul will provide little value in Florida, Cabrera will soon blossom into a superstar in Detroit and lead the Tigers to four straight division titles from 2011-2014 while winning the Triple Crown in 2012 and back-to-back MVP awards in 2012 and 2013.

# 5

1951   Joseph Jefferson Jackson, nicknamed "Shoeless Joe," dies at age 64 in Greenville, South Carolina. One of baseball's greatest pure hitters, Jackson batted a rookie-record .408 in 1911, led the American League in triples three times and compiled a .356 batting average over 13 big league seasons. The star outfielder's career came to an abrupt end in 1920 after he was banished from baseball due to his alleged involvement in the infamous 1919 Black Sox scandal.

1973   The Los Angeles Dodgers acquire reliever Mike Marshall from the Montreal Expos in exchange for veteran outfielder Willie Davis. In 1974, Marshall's Cy Young Award-winning season will help propel the Dodgers to the National League pennant.

1978   Pete Rose becomes the highest-paid athlete in team sports when he leaves his hometown Cincinnati Reds and signs a four-year, $3.2 million deal with the Philadelphia Phillies.

1990   In a blockbuster trade, the Toronto Blue Jays acquire future Hall of Fame second baseman Roberto Alomar and outfielder Joe Carter from the San Diego Padres in exchange for first baseman Fred McGriff and shortstop Tony Fernandez.

# 6

1942   Future Hall of Famer Amos Wilson Rusie dies at age 71 in Seattle, Washington. Nicknamed "The Hoosier Thunderbolt" in reference to his tremendous pitching speed, Rusie led the National League in strikeouts five times and won 30 or more games four times during his nine full big league seasons, finishing his career with a 246-174 record.

1955   Hall of Famer Johannes Peter "Honus" Wagner, nicknamed "The Flying Dutchman," dies at age 81 in Carnegie, Pennsylvania. Considered by many to be the greatest shortstop in baseball history, Wagner was one of the true superstars of the Deadball Era, combining excellence in the field and on the basepaths with a potent bat. He won a National League-record eight batting titles and finished his spectacular 21-year career with a .328 batting average, 3,420 hits, 643 doubles and 723 stolen bases.

1990   At an auction in New York City, a Shoeless Joe Jackson autograph sells for $23,100, the most money ever paid to date for a 19th- or 20th-century signature.

# 7

1937   The Boston Red Sox acquire 19-year-old Ted Williams from the San Diego Padres of the Pacific Coast League. Red Sox GM Eddie Collins trades a package of marginal players and $35,000 for the future Hall of Famer.

1939   Lou Gehrig, who retired from the New York Yankees earlier in the year after being diagnosed with amyotrophic lateral sclerosis, is elected to the Baseball Hall of Fame by special vote after the BBWAA agrees to waive the waiting period.

1947   Johnny Bench, the preeminent catcher in Major League Baseball history, is born in Oklahoma City, Oklahoma.

**1995**  The New York Yankees find a replacement for retiring star Don Mattingly when they acquire first baseman Tino Martinez, along with relievers Jeff Nelson and Jim Mecir, from the Seattle Mariners in exchange for left-hander Sterling Hitchcock and third baseman Russ Davis. Martinez will average 29 home runs and 115 RBIs during the next six seasons in New York, contributing greatly to a Yankees club that will win four of the next five World Championships.

**2006**  Cherished baseball ambassador Buck O'Neil is posthumously awarded the Presidential Medal of Freedom by President George W. Bush. O'Neil, a former Negro League player and manager and Major League Baseball scout and coach, was selected for the honor because of his "excellence and determination both on and off the baseball field," according to the White House news release.

# 8

**1914**  Philadelphia Athletics owner Connie Mack, dubious of his ability to retain his top talent, sells star second baseman and 1914 Chalmers Award winner Eddie Collins to the Chicago White Sox for $50,000. Chicago's hefty investment will prove to be a wise one, as Collins will bat .331 during his 12-year tenure with the White Sox and help lead the club to a World Championship in 1917.

**1958**  Hall of Famer Tristram E. "Tris" Speaker, nicknamed "The Grey Eagle," dies at age 70 in Lake Whitney, Texas. Considered to be one of the greatest all-around outfielders in baseball history, Speaker nearly matched his rival Ty Cobb at the plate and on the basepaths, and his revolutionary play in centerfield was without equal. He set career records with 792 doubles and 449 outfield assists, and his 3,514 hits and .345 lifetime batting average each rank fifth all-time.

**1992**  Coveted free agent Barry Bonds becomes baseball's highest-paid player when he signs a 6-year, $43.75 million contract with the San Francisco Giants.

**2011**  The Los Angeles Angels of Anaheim sign free agent Albert Pujols to baseball's second-largest contract to date. Pujols, who previously won three MVP awards in 11 seasons with the St. Louis Cardinals, agrees to a 10-year, $254 million deal, smaller only than the 10-year, $275 million contract Alex Rodriguez signed with the New York Yankees in 2007.

# 9

**1923**  While traveling to Chicago aboard the Twentieth Century Limited for baseball's winter meetings, 47-year-old Wild Bill Donovan, former major league pitcher and manager and current skipper of the Eastern League's New Haven club, dies along with eight other passengers when the train crashes outside of Forsyth, New York. Future Yankees Hall of Fame executive George Weiss, who was in the berth above Donovan at the time of the crash, escapes with a non-life threatening injury while National League President John Heydler and Philadelphia Phillies owner William F. Baker, also aboard, are unhurt.

1930   Andrew "Rube" Foster, known as the "Father of Black Baseball," dies at age 51 in Kankakee, Illinois. After a highly successful career as a pitcher and then manager in early black baseball, Foster garnered special acclaim as the architect of the Negro National League – the first successful professional league for African American baseball players.

> (i) Foster's invaluable work as a pioneering executive and one of baseball's great visionaries earned him induction into the Baseball Hall of Fame in 1981.

1965   In one of the most memorable trades in major league history, the Cincinnati Reds ship future Hall of Fame outfielder Frank Robinson, deemed "an old 30" by Reds GM Bill DeWitt, to the Baltimore Orioles in exchange for pitchers Milt Pappas and Jack Baldschun and outfielder Dick Simpson. In 1966, Robinson will win the American League MVP award after capturing the Triple Crown and leading the Orioles to a World Series title.

1992   Reigning Cy Young Award winner Greg Maddux signs a five-year, $28 million free agent deal with the Atlanta Braves. The 26-year-old Maddux will win Cy Young Award honors in each of the next three seasons and go 89-33 with a sensational 2.13 ERA over the course of his new contract.

> (i) In signing with Atlanta, Maddux spurned the New York Yankees' five-year, $34 million offer.

# 10

1935   Connie Mack of the Philadelphia Athletics sells his last great asset, sending 28-year-old star slugger Jimmie Foxx along with pitcher Johnny Marcum to the Boston Red Sox for pitcher Gordon Rhodes, minor leaguer George Savino and $150,000.

1946   Walter Johnson dies at age 59 in Washington, DC. In 21 seasons with the Washington Senators, "The Big Train" recorded 417 career wins, a record 110 shutouts and 3,509 strikeouts while winning two MVP awards, five ERA crowns and an all-time best 12 strikeout titles. Arguably the greatest pitcher in baseball history as well as one of the game's most humble and respected superstars, Johnson took his rightful place in Cooperstown in 1936 as a charter member of the Baseball Hall of Fame.

**1971**   The California Angels pull off one of the most lopsided trades in baseball history, acquiring 24-year-old pitcher Nolan Ryan and three prospects from the New York Mets in exchange for veteran shortstop Jim Fregosi. While Fregosi, a six-time All-Star in nine full seasons with the Angels, will provide little help in New York, the fireballing Ryan will come into his own after the deal, winning 138 games and throwing four no-hitters during his eight-year tenure in California while averaging a remarkable 300 strikeouts per season.

**1984**   The New York Mets land seven-time All-Star catcher Gary Carter, acquiring him from the Montreal Expos in exchange for infielder Hubie Brooks, catcher Mike Fitzgerald, outfielder Herm Winningham and pitcher Floyd Youmans. Carter will quickly prove his worth in New York, belting a career-best 32 home runs in 1985 and playing a vital role in the Mets' 1986 World Championship run.

# 11

**1917**   The Philadelphia Phillies agree to send superstar pitcher Grover Cleveland Alexander along with his battery mate Bill Killefer to the Chicago Cubs in exchange for two marginal players and $55,000. The 30-year-old Alexander had just completed one of the most dominant runs in baseball history, having led the National League in wins and strikeouts in each of the three previous seasons.

**1959**   After a disappointing third place finish in 1959, the New York Yankees revive their fortunes by acquiring All-Star outfielder Roger Maris in a seven-player deal that sends Hank Bauer, Don Larsen, Norm Siebern and Marv Throneberry to the Kansas City Athletics. The 25-year-old Maris will quickly rocket to stardom in New York, winning MVP honors in 1960 and again in 1961, the magical season in which he broke Babe Ruth's vaunted single-season home run record.

> (i)   With Maris and slugger Mickey Mantle powering their reenergized offense, the Yankees returned to the top of the league, winning the next five American League pennants.

**2000**   Free agent shortstop Alex Rodriguez signs a landmark 10-year, $252 million contract with the Texas Rangers. The deal agreed upon by Rangers owner Tom Hicks, which mortified many rival baseball executives, is easily the most lucrative contract in sports history, eclipsing NBA great Kevin Garnett's six-year, $126 million pact.

**2013**  Major League Baseball's rules committee votes to ban home plate collisions in response to growing concern for player safety.

> ⓘ The sentiment to limit or ban home plate collisions greatly intensified after San Francisco Giants star catcher Buster Posey was seriously injured while blocking the plate on May 25, 2011.

**2017**  The rich get richer as the New York Yankees, Major League Baseball's top home run hitting team in 2017, acquire National League MVP and Home Run Champ Giancarlo Stanton from the Miami Marlins for infielder Starlin Castro and two minor leaguers.

# 12

**1903**  Chicago Cubs president Jim Hart, suspicious of pitcher Jack Taylor's work in a postseason City Series with the White Sox, deals his 21-game winner to the St. Louis Cardinals for rookie pitcher Mordecai "Three Finger" Brown in a four-player swap. The trade proves to be one of the best in Cubs history when Taylor lasts just four more years in the majors while Brown develops into a Hall of Famer with Chicago, going 186-83 with a 1.75 ERA over the next nine seasons while leading the Cubs to four National League pennants and two World Championships.

**1933**  In a fire sale of historic proportions, Philadelphia Athletics owner-manager Connie Mack, in search of cash to stay solvent, trades several of his top players at baseball's winter meetings. Mack sends ace pitcher Lefty Grove along with Max Bishop and Rube Walberg to the Boston Red Sox for Bob Kline, Rabbit Warstler and $125,000, and deals star catcher Mickey Cochrane to the Detroit Tigers for Johnny Pasek and $100,000. He then packages Pasek with former 20-game winner George Earnshaw in a trade to the Chicago White Sox for Charlie Berry and $20,000. The systematic dismantling is a death blow for Mack's final dynasty in Philadelphia.

**1980**  The Milwaukee Brewers make one of the most pivotal trades in franchise history, acquiring future Hall of Famers Rollie Fingers and Ted Simmons along with starter Pete Vuckovich from the St. Louis Cardinals in exchange for pitchers Lary Sorensen and Dave LaPoint and outfielders David Green and Sixto Lezcano. Fingers will win MVP and Cy Young Award honors in 1981 after leading the majors with 28 saves and a 1.04 ERA, and Vuckovich will claim the Cy Young Award the following year after winning 18 games. The pair's brilliant pitching, along with Simmons' run production and steady leadership, will help propel the Brewers to their first two postseason births in 1981 and 1982.

1998  Pitcher Kevin Brown becomes the first player in major league history to receive a nine-figure contract when the Los Angeles Dodgers sign him to a seven-year, $105 million deal.

# 13

1956  After being traded by the Brooklyn Dodgers to the New York Giants, Jackie Robinson chooses to retire from baseball rather than report to the Dodgers' crosstown rival.

2000  Two days after Alex Rodriguez signed a major league record-setting deal with the Texas Rangers, 28-year-old slugger Manny Ramirez agrees to an eight-year, $160 million contract with the Boston Red Sox, making him the second highest paid player in baseball history.

2007  Former United States Senator George Mitchell releases his much-anticipated investigative report on the use of illegal performance-enhancing substances in Major League Baseball. The 409-page document details the pervasive use of anabolic steroids and human growth hormone in baseball, linking 89 current and former major league players, including such stars as Roger Clemens, Barry Bonds, Gary Sheffield, Andy Pettitte, Miguel Tejada and Jason Giambi, to PEDs and calls for tighter regulation within the sport.

# 14

1949  The New York Giants acquire shortstop Alvin Dark and second baseman Eddie Stanky from the Boston Braves in exchange for shortstop Buddy Kerr, pitcher Red Webb and outfielders Sid Gordon and Willard Marshall. The deal works out well for New York, especially in 1951 when the double play combination plays a pivotal role in the Giants' thrilling pennant-winning season.

1985  Roger Maris dies at age 51 in Houston, Texas after a two-year battle with lymphatic cancer. As a 27-year-old with the New York Yankees in 1961, the powerful outfielder was thrust into the national spotlight when he broke Babe Ruth's hallowed single-season home run record. Maris earned American League MVP honors in 1960 and 1961 and was part of seven pennant-winning teams during his memorable 12-year career.

# 15

1900  After missing the previous two seasons with arm problems, legendary fireballer Amos Rusie is traded by the New York Giants to the Cincinnati Reds for 20-year-old pitcher Christy Mathewson. Rusie, who claimed five strikeout titles and won nearly 30 games per year in eight seasons with the Giants, will last just three starts with the Reds before retiring from baseball while Mathewson will become a baseball icon in New York, winning 372 games during his extraordinary 17-year tenure with the Giants.

1980   All-Star outfielder Dave Winfield becomes the highest-paid player in the history of sports to date when he signs a 10-year, $23 million contract with the New York Yankees.

2010   Former Cleveland Indians star Robert William Andrew "Bob" Feller, nicknamed "Rapid Robert," dies at age 92 in Cleveland, Ohio. Renowned for his blazing fastball, Feller was one of the best right-handed pitchers in baseball history, leading the American League in wins six times and in strikeouts seven times. The eight-time All-Star also fashioned three no-hitters and 12 one-hitters, both records at the time of his retirement in 1956. Feller, who also earned distinction as a decorated soldier in World War II, was inducted into the Baseball Hall of Fame in 1962.

# 16

1974   Jim "Catfish" Hunter becomes the first free agent in modern baseball history when arbitrator Peter Seitz rules that Oakland A's owner Charles Finley's failure to pay an insurance premium constitutes a breach of Hunter's contract. After a two-week bidding war, Hunter will sign a landmark five-year, $3.2 million deal with the New York Yankees.

2009   The Philadelphia Phillies bolster their rotation, acquiring veteran starter Roy Halladay from the Toronto Blue Jays in exchange for three highly touted prospects - pitcher Kyle Drabek, catcher Travis d'Arnaud and outfielder Michael Taylor. Halladay will prove to be every bit the ace the Phillies had hoped for as the big right-hander will win the Cy Young Award in his first year in Philadelphia and finish second the next after going a combined 40-16 with a 2.40 ERA while leading the Phillies to the postseason in both seasons.

2011   A new five-year collective bargaining agreement between Major League Baseball owners and the Players' Association provides for human growth hormone testing, limits on draft pick signing bonuses and the inclusion of a second Wild Card team for each league beginning in 2013.

# 17

1924   The New York Yankees acquire four-time 20-game winner Urban Shocker from the St. Louis Browns in exchange for pitchers "Bullet Joe" Bush,

Milt Gaston and Joe Giard. Shocker will go 49-29 over the next three seasons in New York, helping the Bronx Bombers to two pennants and the 1927 World Championship.

# 18

1886  Legendary outfielder Ty Cobb, one of baseball's most extraordinary players and fiercest competitors, is born in Narrows, Georgia.

# 19

1914  Rather than face legal action by Washington Senators owner Clark Griffith over reserve clause rights, star pitcher Walter Johnson renounces the lucrative contract he signed with the Federal League's Chicago Whales two weeks earlier and agrees to stay with the Washington Senators at a lesser rate.

2002  Japanese slugging star Hideki Matsui, nicknamed "Godzilla," agrees to a three-year, $21 million contract with the New York Yankees. Matsui will spend the next seven seasons in the Bronx, posting four 100-RBI campaigns and garnering a pair of All-Star selections while attracting a legion of fans. In 2009, he'll earn a special place in Yankees lore when he powers New York to a World Championship and is named World Series MVP.

2011  The Texas Rangers post a record $51.7 million bid for Japanese pitching sensation Yu Darvish. The 25-year-old Darvish will soon agree to leave the Hokkaido Nippon Ham Fighters and join Major League Baseball, signing a six-year, $60 million contract with the Rangers.

> (i) Darvish made a smooth transition to the majors in 2012, finishing the season with an impressive 16-9 record and 221 strikeouts.

# 20

1926  In a move that the *New York Times* dubs "the biggest deal of modern baseball history," the World Champion St. Louis Cardinals send six-time batting champ Rogers Hornsby to the New York Giants for star second baseman Frankie Frisch in a three-player swap. The Giants will get one big year out of Hornsby before trading him to the Boston Braves, while Frisch will spend the next 11 seasons in St. Louis, winning two World Series titles with the Cardinals.

1933  The Detroit Tigers and Washington Senators swap outfielders, with Detroit receiving future Hall of Famer Goose Goslin in exchange for John Stone.

The 33-year-old Goslin will drive in at least 100 runs in each of the next three seasons and help power the Tigers to an American League pennant in 1934 and a World Championship in 1935.

> ⓘ In Game 6 of the 1935 World Series, Goslin lined a two-out single in the bottom of the ninth to drive home the Series-winning run.

1972  Hall of Famer Charles Leo "Gabby" Hartnett dies on his 72nd birthday in Park Ridge, Illinois. The long-time Chicago Cubs catcher, known for his rifle arm, exceptional defensive skills and dangerous bat, garnered six All-Star selections and the 1935 National League MVP award during his outstanding 20-year major league career.

# 21

1911  Negro League superstar catcher and legendary slugger Josh Gibson is born in Buena Vista, Georgia.

1960  Chicago Cubs owner P.K. Wrigley announces that his club will be led this coming season by a "college of coaches" rather than one central manager. The Cubs will utilize the unorthodox approach for the next two seasons, but poor oversight, infighting and a disastrous 123-193 record will put an end to the experiment.

2007  The Texas Rangers wisely take a chance on 26-year-old outfielder Josh Hamilton, acquiring him from the Cincinnati Reds in exchange for pitchers Edinson Volquez and Danny Herrera. Hamilton, a former elite prospect who enjoyed a breakout rookie season in 2007 after years of drug and alcohol abuse earlier derailed his career, will become a perennial All-Star in Texas and will lead the Rangers to World Series appearances in 2010 and 2011.

# 22

1862  Major League Baseball's winningest manager Cornelius Alexander McGillicuddy, better known as Connie Mack, is born in East Brookfield, Massachusetts.

1980  One of the most notorious clerical blunders in baseball history occurs when Boston Red Sox GM Haywood Sullivan mails new contracts to outfielder Fred Lynn and catcher Carlton Fisk two days after the Basic Agreement deadline, making the All-Star duo eligible for free agency. The Red Sox will soon lose both players when Lynn is preemptively traded to the California Angels and Fisk signs a free agent deal with the Chicago White Sox.

# 23

1967   While skiing at Lake Tahoe, 1967 Cy Young Award winner Jim Lonborg of the Boston Red Sox severely tears ligaments in his left knee. The 25-year-old Lonborg, who helped lead the Red Sox to the World Series this past season after going 22-9 with 246 strikeouts, will pitch 12 more seasons in the big leagues but will never again regain his top pitching form.

DID YOU KNOW?   After retiring from the majors, Jim Lonborg completed dental school in 1983 and began his own practice in Hanover, Massachusetts, 30 miles southeast of Fenway Park.

1975   Arbitrator Peter Seitz declares Andy Messersmith and Dave McNally free agents after the two pitchers sat out the option year of their respective contracts. The watershed decision effectively ends Major League Baseball's ancient reserve clause, as all players will soon gain the right to opt for free agency after six years of major league service.

# 24

1969   In a letter to Commissioner Bowie Kuhn, recently traded veteran outfielder Curt Flood states his refusal to report to the Philadelphia Phillies, noting that he is not a "piece of property to be bought and sold." Flood, with the backing of the MLB Players Association, will soon file a $1 million lawsuit against Major League Baseball, alleging violation of federal antitrust laws. The U.S. Supreme Court will ultimately side with Baseball, but Flood's legal action will be viewed historically as a vital first step in the fight for player free agency.

# 25

1958   Hall of Fame outfielder Rickey Henderson, baseball's electrifying "Man of Steal," is born in Chicago, Illinois.

# 26

1919   Cash-strapped Boston Red Sox owner Harry Frazee agrees to sell 24-year-old Babe Ruth to the New York Yankees for $100,000 and a

$300,000 loan with Fenway Park as collateral. The landmark deal will be announced publicly on January 6, 1920.

1934   The Tokyo-based Yomiuri Giants become Japan's first professional baseball team. Matsutaro Shoriki, head of Yomiuri Shimbun, forms the team primarily from a group of players that recently faced a touring American All-Star team. The Giants will become part of a six-team professional league that will begin play in 1936.

# 27

1874   Cuba's first documented baseball game takes place at a field known as Palmar de Junco, located in the province of Matanzas. A team from Havana defeats the host Matanzas club 51–9.

# 28

1998   The Arizona Diamondbacks make one of the best trades in franchise history when they swap outfielders with Detroit, sending Karim Garcia to the Tigers in exchange for Luis Gonzalez. While Garcia will bat just .236 in 104 games with Detroit before being dealt away, Gonzalez, in eight seasons with the Diamondbacks, will hit 224 home runs (including a career-high 57 in 2001), make five All-Star teams and help lead the club to a World Championship in 2001.

# 29

1878   The Professional Baseball League of Cuba plays its inaugural game as Esteban Bellan, the first Cuban to play pro baseball in the United States, leads the host Habana club to a 21-20 win over Almendares.

# 30

1907   The Mills Commission, appointed by Albert Goodwill Spalding to study the origins of baseball, announces that the game was invented by Abner Doubleday in Cooperstown, New York in 1839. The commission bases its conclusion on the testimony of a man named Abner Graves, who claimed to have witnessed Doubleday scrawl out the game's first ground rules in a Cooperstown cow pasture. Graves "verified" his account by presenting a tattered ball from his childhood. The group's findings will remain the final say on the origins of baseball for over half a century until historians disprove Graves' tale.

1935 Revered pitching icon Sandy Koufax is born Sanford Braun in Brooklyn, New York.

# 31

1972 Pittsburgh Pirates star Roberto Clemente dies in a plane crash just off the coast of San Juan in his native Puerto Rico. The 38-year-old Clemente was overseeing the delivery of relief supplies to earthquake victims in Managua, Nicaragua when the rickety cargo plane he was aboard careened into the ocean shortly after takeoff. The tragedy will send Baseball and Latin America into mourning.

> ⓘ In 18 seasons with the Pittsburgh Pirates, Roberto Clemente collected 3,000 hits and won four batting titles, finishing with a stellar .317 lifetime average. The 12-time All-Star and 12-time Gold Glove Award winner helped lead the Pirates to World Championships in 1960 and 1971, and won an MVP award in 1966.

1974 After becoming modern baseball's first free agent two weeks earlier, reigning American League Cy Young Award winner Jim "Catfish" Hunter ends an unprecedented bidding war when he signs a five-year, $3.2 million deal with the New York Yankees. The new contract, which is easily the most lucrative in major league history, gives Hunter an annual salary that is three times greater than any other player in baseball.

Made in the USA
Coppell, TX
24 August 2021